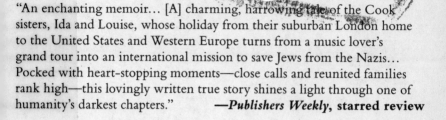

Praise for *The Bra...*

"An enchanting memoir... [A] charming, harrowing tale of the Cook sisters, Ida and Louise, whose holiday from their suburban London home to the United States and Western Europe turns from a music lover's grand tour into an international mission to save Jews from the Nazis... Pocked with heart-stopping moments—close calls and reunited families rank high—this lovingly written true story shines a light through one of humanity's darkest chapters." **—Publishers Weekly, starred review**

"The extraordinary story of two British sisters who became unlikely heroines in helping Jews to flee Nazi persecution." **—The Guardian**

"A breathtaking story." **—Daily Mail**

"The Cook sisters defy the generalisation of social history: they were extraordinary." **—The Telegraph**

"To the outside world, Mary Burchell was a prolific Mills & Boon author who entranced her fans with tales of intrigue, passion and danger. But in private, Burchell—known to her family as Ida Cook—had lived an equally daring life, undertaking risky missions alongside her sister Louise to help rescue Jewish families trapped in pre-war Austria and Germany... Their incredible story is retold in Cook's memoirs." **—Jewish News**

"A unique story, simply told." **—Kirkus Reviews**

THE
BRAVEST
VOICES

A Memoir of Two Sisters'
Heroism During the Nazi Era

IDA COOK

PARK
ROW
BOOKS

PARK
ROW ™
BOOKS ™

Recycling programs
for this product may
not exist in your area.

ISBN-13: 978-0-7783-8809-8

The Bravest Voices: A Memoir of Two Sisters' Heroism During the Nazi Era

First published as We Followed Our Stars in 1950. Reissued as Safe Passage in 2008.

This edition published in 2021.

This edition published by arrangement with Harlequin Books S.A.

Park Row Books
22 Adelaide St. West, 40th Floor
Toronto, Ontario M5H 4E3, Canada
ParkRowBooks.com
BookClubbish.com

Printed in U.S.A.

To my incomparable parents, without whose loving and commonsense upbringing we should never have been capable of doing the things described in this book.

THE
BRAVEST
VOICES

DISCLAIMER

Ida Cook's memoir *The Bravest Voices* was originally published in 1950 under the title *We Followed Our Stars*. The publisher has preserved the original language of the author to accurately represent those times and modes of expression, and to stay true to her story. In addition to being a work of autobiographical nonfiction, it is also a primary source for an account of the Holocaust, and thus the memoir has been kept as it was written for the sake of historical record.

FOREWORD

_____

Romance is not just about love. It's about an attitude to life, and there is little more romantic than a profound faith in the possibility of all things.

It could be a belief that when you kiss the ugly toad he will turn into a handsome prince just as much as a conviction that if you do the right thing you can, against all the odds, save a life. What could be more romantic than helping people, strangers, otherwise condemned to likely death, escape their own country and survive in a new one? For Ida and Louise Cook the spirit of hope, the conviction that everything would come all right in the end, was the essence of life. It pervades the romantic novels written by Ida, but it also guided the daily existence of both sisters. No matter what evils they encountered in the world, what remained constant for them was hope.

When I first discovered this remarkable book it was the unshakable faith of Ida and Louise Cook that they could make a difference that hooked me immediately. It was the artless innocence of two young women flying to another country—at a time when flying itself was dangerously new— defying that country's laws to help desperate people they did not know, that made such a profound impression. I was moved by the sisters' certainty, so rare today in a world where moral equivalence holds sway, that they knew without any ambiguity a clear difference between right and wrong.

Ida and Louise Cook were born at the beginning of the last century; Louise, quieter and more intellectual in Dorking, Surrey, in 1901; Ida, naturally garrulous, three years later in 1904 in Sunderland, Northeast England, where their father, a Customs and Excise officer, was posted. Both came to maturity during the harrowing years of World War One, a war that wiped out almost a generation of young men in England. Two ordinary women who lived in extraordinary times.

In the pages that follow there are innumerable examples of their pluck, to use an almost forgotten contemporary word. How Louise would leave her drab civil service office on a Friday evening, dash to Croydon airport for the last plane to Cologne, then the night train to Munich, where they would, with luck (Ida often credits things going right to good luck, too modest to recognize it is hard work instead) arrive for breakfast on Saturday morning. Minor inconveniences such as toothache and overdrafts were ignored. They spent so much of their own money on these rescue missions that Ida admits toward the end of the book that she was in significant debt.

Money was never one of their gods. They made their own clothes, traveled third class and, even when Ida—known as Mary Burchell—became one of Mills & Boon's bestselling authors earning almost £1,000 a year from her novels, they still sat in the gallery rather than the stalls of their beloved Covent Garden. "We spent thousands in our imagination," she wrote when her advance for two books was a mere thirty pounds. By the time she was earning thousands, she had other ideas.

The problem they were confronting was that the British government, since the Nazi seizure of power in 1933 when Jews had been gradually stripped of all rights, had allowed very few Jewish refugees to flee to Britain, and then only if financial guarantees for their future stability were in place. The situation deteriorated dramatically in November 1938, following the outburst of violence at *Kristallnacht* when thousands of Jewish homes and businesses were destroyed and looted. This night of carnage shocked many British people who until then had ignored the plight of the Jews in Germany and Austria. The British government now agreed to ease immigration restrictions for Jewish children, but were still not prepared to allow unlimited entry for adults, many of whom found it impossible to leave. In this crisis private citizens or organizations had to come up with guarantees to pay for each child's care and education or to provide for an adult, which for a woman, usually meant domestic service. Adult men were accepted only if they had documentary proof that they were in transit and therefore faced the direst problems.

Ida and Louise, partly in order to make financial guarantees easier and because they recognized that those they were rescuing hated the idea of living off charity, offered to smuggle out valuables—mostly jewelry and furs. The refugees could sell these and have something to live on once they arrived in England. But in late 1930s Nazi Germany, smuggling currency or valuables was a serious crime. By helping opponents of the regime, as they did on at least one occasion, they risked their own lives. Yet the only precaution they took was varying their return journey—perhaps coming home through Holland, catching the night boat and arriving at Harwich early on Monday morning so that Louise could walk into her office just in time. Their only weapon was faith in their British passports.

Ida describes their journeys straightforwardly, not enhancing her or her sister's role with the narrative storyteller's skills at her disposal. There is no need for added drama. It soon became, she says, a regular and serious pattern of work. Yet who can forget the image of the nervous and eccentric opera-loving sisters, an image they themselves encouraged as a "cover story," wearing cheap and cheerful clothes, embellished with fine pearls, expensive wristwatches and other jewels. Once, Ida's jumper was adorned with a particularly huge oblong of blazing diamonds—"someone's entire capital"—which she had to pass off as fake paste from Woolworth's.

The smuggling was, she says, "a simple procedure." But Nazi guards often boarded the train at the frontier for currency inspections. "This made things a bit awkward," she writes blithely of an experience that for most young women (or men) would be heart-stoppingly fearful. "We both had rather ingenuous faces!" she says by way of explanation. And yet she admits that they started to be known at Cologne airport "and some awkward and unfriendly questions were asked."

Soon they were doing more—organizing forged documents, traveling the country to raise money and even buying a small London flat for the refugees to live in while they, women in their thirties, continued to live at home with their parents.

But if fear was a forbidden emotion, sympathy and pain certainly were not. Neither sister was ashamed to shed tears, mostly at the agonizing knowledge of the many they could not save and the likely suicides that would result.

In order to demonstrate their lack of fear, they chose deliberately to stay in the big luxury hotels—the Adlon or the Vier Jahreszeiten, where the Nazi chiefs stayed—wearing the borrowed furs with English labels freshly sewn in that they were taking back to England. "Then, if you stood and gazed at them admiringly as they went through the lobby, no one thought you were anything but another couple of admiring fools. That was why we knew them all by sight, Louise and I… Goering, Goebbels, Himmler, Streicher, Ribbentrop. We even knew Hitler from the back." Not only does Ida make light of their courage, she also self-deprecatingly describes her behavior as "ignorant."

"We didn't know—imagine!—in those days we didn't *know* that to be Jewish and to come from Frankfurt-am-Main in Germany…had the seeds of tragedy in it." This was when their first case, Frau Mitia Meyer-Lissman, the official Salzburg lecturer, was entrusted to their care. Thanks to her they soon "saw things more clearly and understood the full horror of what was happening in Germany."

The sisters were in Salzburg in 1934 when Dollfuss, the Austrian chancellor, was assassinated in a bungled Nazi coup attempt. "I blush now to think how ignorant we were of the significance of this event…we were concerned with only one aspect of the murder: would it put a stop to our holiday?" Ida wrote in 1950. But in fact no music lover that summer could have avoided the sense of menace, the atmosphere of doomed enchantment that hung over the festival. And right in the centre of this maelstrom was the charismatic and controversial Austrian conductor, Clemens Krauss.

Krauss is the enormous and looming shadow that stalks the book. An elegant, sometimes dictatorial conductor, Krauss was by virtue of his friendship with Richard Strauss a direct link to the source of musical creation. Director of the

Vienna State Opera and later the Berlin State Opera, Krauss was ambitious to revive the musical life of Salzburg, and he set audiences alight with fervor. He and his glamorous wife, the Romanian soprano Viorica Ursuleac, had what today would be called A-list celebrity status, and Ida and Louise were, unquestionably, star struck.

It was only because of Clemens Krauss and his wife that Ida and Louise started their rescue work, which they could, or would, never have maintained without the constant encouragement and help of those two. His offer to stage favorite operas chosen by Ida and Louise gave added authenticity to their story if questioned by Nazi guards on their travels. But it also took them right to the heart of their earthly pleasures and dreams. Ida is honest enough to recognize that, although it was the pursuit of opera that initially brought them to the refugee work, it was now the pursuit of the refugee work that was made possible only by the support of the great operatic performances. She insists that it was the same naïve technique by which they first learned to save up enough money to visit the United States and meet famous opera singers in the 1920s that helped them now as they "stumbled" into Europe and began to save lives. "You never know what you can do until you refuse to take no for an answer," Ida wrote.

But naïve, with its connotations of foolish ignorance, is not a word that fits Ida or Louise. Ida was too intelligent not to realize, when she came to write her account of those years, that Krauss, who had had to defend himself to a de-Nazification tribunal after the war, was tainted by default. She writes of him: "I know that to speak in praise of any artist who occupied a high position in Hitler's Germany is to tread on very delicate ground. At the first word, even now, tempers rise, private and professional axes are taken out and reground and friendships tremble in the balance. But, in that homeliest of phrases, one must speak as one finds."

Hindsight is easily acquired, and if Ida and Louise had been ignorant in 1934 they were unusually farsighted two or three years later. In the appeasement debate that raged around Britain in the thirties, many of those who thought that the only way to prevent Hitler was to fight him, were accused, like Winston Churchill, of warmongering. Others, such as Prime Minister Neville Chamberlain, believed Hitler was a man who could offer Britons "peace with honor."

A number of so called intellectuals in Britain in the 1930s—not just those who were openly anti-Semitic or pro-Hitler such as Unity Mitford, but those who worshipped German art and culture—refused to believe ill of Hitler or a country that had produced Beethoven, Goethe and Wagner. The popular historian Arthur Bryant, for example, could write in 1937 of German fascists as "peaceable and ordinary folk" fighting for decency, tradition and civilization and, even after *Kristallnacht*, said of Jews that they had "seldom been welcome guests and scarcely ever for long." He argued that they should not be welcome in Britain because they were likely to take "an unfair and disproportionate amount of wealth and power."

Yet Ida and Louise, with no university degrees, were not fooled. They were able to distinguish between high art and fine music and bestiality. They understood that Anglo-German friendship did not require conniving with Hitler to kill Jews. They were born with an innate moral gauge, a spirit level in the brain that tilted as soon as they smelled evil. Courage they learned along the way.

Ida credits her parents, James and Mary Cook, as the source of this courage. "Both parents set a standard of personal integrity that gave us children a never-questioned scale of values and made life so much easier later on," she wrote. One of the most appealing scenes of domestic tranquillity has Ida describing how they had returned from a particularly harrowing time. "I went straight through into the kitchen where Mother was making pastry—which is after all one of the basic things of life.... If she had stopped and made a sentimental fuss of me I would have cried for hours. She just simply went on making pastry...she told me 'you're doing the best you can. Now tell me all about it.'" Such simple pleasures are hard to grasp in this postfeminist world. But from them derived the strength that allowed Ida and Louise not only to accept so unquestioningly the single life that was their lot, but also their duty (another old-fashioned word) toward others.

And through it all is the music. Opera shored up their belief "that there was another world to which we would be able to return one day. Beyond the fog of horror and misery there were lovely bright things that they had once taken for granted." Ida recognized the absurdity of sublime music existing in the midst of a hellhole. But she saw it rather differently. She saw the music as something that counterbalanced their unhappiness at the cruelty they were forced to witness. She refers at one point to the power they had to decide the fate of an individual, power she loathed because of the "terrible, moving and overwhelming thought—I could save life with it." But the real power in the book is the transformative nature of music and especially the high drama of operatic music. These two spinster sisters knew that in the presence of their prima donna heroines, or angels according to Ida, they could pull on their homemade cloaks and assume different personae themselves.

Now, *that's* romance.

After the war Ida and Louise settled back into the family home in south London where they had lived for the past sixty years and into the safe and familiar routines of work and opera, continuing quietly with their refugee and displaced persons work. But in 1950, after Ida published this autobiography (under the title *We Followed Our Stars*), the pair were soon bathed in a halo of publicity and embarked on a round of parties and awards. Several of the refugees fought to have Ida and Louise's work recognized by Yad Vashem, the Israeli authority that honors those who helped save lives during the Nazi period. In 1965 they were declared "Righteous among the Nations" in recognition of their work in rescuing Jews from Germany and from Austria during the dark days of the Nazi regime and in helping them to rebuild their lives in freedom. The citation mentioned twenty-nine families, but the total number of those they helped must be triple this, not all of whom were Jewish.

They never went to Israel, receiving the certificate instead from the Israeli ambassador in London. In 1965 they were two among only four Britons to be so honored.

Ida, the talkative one, was the sister to whom journalists addressed questions and whose fame as a novelist attracted attention. But she was always insistent that whatever honor was granted, it must be for both of them. As she never tired of pointing out, it was Louise who embarked on learning German in order to conduct the interviews. But there was something much deeper. They were dependent on each other. Feted though they now were, especially in America, which had become home for some of those they rescued, their lives remained essentially unvaried until the end. Ida continued to produce romance fiction for Mills & Boon and one work of nonfiction (1979), a ghosted autobiography of the singer Tito Gobbi, her close friend. But her heroines belonged to an earlier world. Her publisher, Alan Boon, commented,

"Mary Burchell [Ida's pen name] wasn't sexy, but she showed an awareness of it…it was a pretended form of sex, not suggestive in any way at all. It was instinct, not participating."

Neither sister married, but that does not mean they didn't have romantic lives. They lived vicariously through their music, through their work or through their refugees. Ida was never ashamed of believing in romance or of writing romantic novels. When she took over as president of the Romantic Novelists' Association in 1966 she declared, "Romance is the quality which gives an air of probability to our dearest wishes….people often say life isn't like that, but life is often exactly like that. Illusions and dreams often do come true."

Ida died on December 24, 1986, at the age of eighty-two. Louise outlived her beloved sister by another five years. After Ida's death she moved to live in the London flat which had been bought for the refugees before the war. Obituaries talked of the sisters' "Scarlet Pimpernel" operation. One of those refugees who wrote to Yad Vashem in Jerusalem in support of their cause described them as "human pillars." Ida said simply, "We called ourselves Christian and we tried to do our best."

Anne Sebba
London
March 2008

Anne Sebba is a biographer, journalist and former Reuters foreign correspondent. She is the author, most recently, of Jennie Churchill: Winston's American Mother.

CHAPTER ONE

To every writer who has ever published a book, there comes eventually that amusing though irritating moment when someone says pensively, "I have always thought that I could write a book—if only I had time."

I have never been able to decide whether the subtle implication is that only those with an unfair amount of time at their disposal ever reach the point of seeing themselves in print, or whether it is a delicate way of saying that in order to write a book one must have neglected more pressing duties.

In my own experience, I can only say that I have never sat down to write a book with the feeling that I had any time in hand. And, apart from the fact that I write, happily and unashamedly, for the wicked old profit motive, any urge I may have has nothing whatever to do with the question of whether I have time or not.

But for some while now, I have had a sneaking sympathy for the "if I had time" school of thought, for this is the book that I have thought *I* should like to write—if only I had time.

I really have not time now. But something, I am not quite

sure what, has pushed me a little further than the "if" stage, and so I have begun the book, which will at least amuse me and some of my friends. And perhaps in the process, I may shed some light on the theory that writing is all a question of time.

To write your recollections or memoirs is to make a claim that, in your estimation at any rate, you have lived some interesting years. It is difficult not to associate a degree of egotism with this claim. But I am hoping a thin line draws a decent distinction between thinking myself an interesting person and being interested in what has happened to me. I am tremendously interested in what has happened to me—and incidentally my sister Louise, whose story this is, as much as my own. That is my sole excuse for supposing that a book about us should fascinate anyone but ourselves.

An autobiography should, I suppose, begin at the beginning of one's life. So—I was born in Sunderland, Durham, the second daughter in a middle-class family of two girls and two boys. My father was an officer and later a surveyor of Customs and Excise. As this work entailed a good deal of moving, we four children were all born in different parts of England. In spite of this, there was always a tremendous sense of stability in our family life.

Although he was born in the country, my father always preferred town life. And my mother, though born within sound of Bow Bells—the now rare distinction that marks the true Cockney—always retained many of the characteristics of her farming ancestors. Without being in the least senti-mental, I can state that both were enormously successful as parents. I should know: my father lived to be ninety-three and my mother eighty-nine, so I knew them a long while.

One of the most revealing conversations I ever had with

my mother occurred just a few weeks before she died. I said to her reflectively, "Mother, I've never seen you cry."

She replied, "What do you mean? I never had anything to cry about. I had it all. I didn't ask very much, but I had everything that mattered. I had a good husband"—I'm glad to say she added—"and good children. A good home and good health. No one must ask for anything else. Anything else is a bonus."

And she meant it. No wonder she—and we—were happy.

Even as children, Louise and I always felt sorry for those children whose mothers had easily hurt feelings or whose fathers either could not assert their authority in their own homes or—the other awful extreme—became domestic tyrants.

Mother was never "hurt." She could be cross with us, of course, which is quite a different thing. But half an hour later, she would be frying potatoes for us in the kitchen. Although we never thought of our father as anything but the head of the household, he would no more have played the domestic tyrant than been found drunk and disorderly in the street.

Both parents set a standard of personal integrity that gave us children a never-questioned scale of values and made life so much easier later on. Once, when we were very young, Dad did present his daughters with a painful problem: He thought it wrong to accept a reward if one found something valuable and could return it to the owner. This, he maintained, was one's duty anyway, and no one should expect to be rewarded, merely for doing what was right.

Louise and I had a tremendous discussion on what to do if ever we found a diamond necklace. Finally, we asked Mother, who was kind and practical enough to suggest that anyone careless enough to lose a diamond necklace really ought to pay something for its recovery. This solution satisfied us completely, and we were able to go on looking for lost diamond necklaces with untroubled minds.

Mother had a great deal of common sense and was a most reassuring person. There is a pleasant story about Louise who, when she was about two, woke up crying in the night. When asked what was the matter, she said there was a dream in her pillow. Mother didn't argue or seek deep reasons for her child's extraordinary assertion. She simply said, "Then we'll change the pillow"—which she did, and Louise slept peacefully after that.

Louise was the eldest child in our family, a blonde, beautiful and angelic baby. My poor parents thought all babies were like that until I arrived to disillusion them.

I am assured on excellent authority that I was the ugliest baby it is possible to imagine. Mother always declared that on his first seeing me, Dad could not help exclaiming, "Good lord! Isn't she ugly!" But later, he was annoyed if anyone told that story, so perhaps it was just a family legend, hardened into fact by repetition.

However, Louise was enchanted with me. So much so that when the nurse took me out for my first airing, Louise was discovered in floods of tears at the bottom of the stairs, as she assumed I was only on loan and was not being brought back.

When I was two, we moved to Barnes, on the outskirts of London, and it is here that I recall the almost fabulous security and radiance of the last of the Edwardian era. I am glad that my memory does at least encompass a general impression of those days, because life before the First World War is impossible to imagine if one never experienced it.

Not that we were the kind of family who took any part in the social life of that—or indeed, any other—period. But I have a composite recollection of security, sunshine—though this could not have been as constant as it seems to me in retrospect—and the magnificence of Ranelagh, as gauged by the motorcars lined up in our road, waiting for the large-hatted and feather-boa-ed owners.

I remember a tremendous balloon race that took place in a thunderstorm, and I remember when a passing airplane was something so amazing that we rushed into the garden, gazed upwards and said confidently, "That's probably Grahame-White." Those days held the joys of choosing oddments for one's Christmas shopping at the penny bazaars and the horrors of a newspaper announcement saying, "Titanic Sinks."

To me, the limit of world wandering was the Albert Memorial. How I loved it. I still love it, come to that. Possibly, if I must be quite truthful about an old friend, I would prefer one fewer gaggle of angels at the summit. Otherwise, it is a dear landmark in more senses than one, and I have wandered around it many times while my father identified and explained those famous figures on it.

I remember my first day at school, when the story of Adam and Eve really impinged on my consciousness for the first time. I wept loudly and embarrassingly for the offenders. There was a very realistic illustration of a smug angel booting an ill clad Adam and Eve out of Paradise, and I think it was the fact that they had little but a goatskin apiece round their middles that especially harrowed me. Years afterwards, someone who knew me well declared there was something symbolic in my howling over the first refugees the world had ever known.

When I was six, and while we were still in Barnes, our brother Bill was born. I don't think I was quite so nice about being the displaced baby as Louise had been. I distinctly remember wondering gloomily if my special saucepan-scraping privileges were threatened. There weren't many child psychologists to put ideas into our heads in those days. I imagine my parents coped with this as sensibly as with all other family problems. Anyway, Bill was such a model baby that even his elder sisters had to be pleased with him.

In the summer of 1912, we moved to Alnwick, the county town of Northumberland, where we stayed through the First World War and until I was fifteen. Jim was born there, a month after war broke out. He disliked the idea that there had ever been a time when the family had not had him, and he frequently prefaced entirely imaginary recollections with the words, "When I were in Barnes."

For Louise and me, these years in Alnwick were extremely happy ones. We genuinely enjoyed our school days at the Duchess' School, originally endowed and initiated with the then Duchess of Northumberland more than a hundred years earlier. The building was across the road from Alnwick Castle and had once been the Dower House. From the windows of our classrooms, we could look out on the castle battlements with their stone figures of fighting men, once used to deceive the invading Scots into thinking the place was better defended than it was.

We lived and played and studied on ground where the history of England and Scotland had been written, and if this fact had not left its mark upon us, we should have been insensitive indeed. We made our own amusements in those lucky, happy days, of course.

Above all, we read—everything, from Beaumont and Fletcher to Captain Desmond, VC. Sometimes Dad would apostrophize what we were reading as "rubbish"—which, no doubt, it was—and I'm sure he would have stopped us at filth for filth's sake. Nor did anyone feel a burning necessity to dot emotional I's or cross sexual T's for us as we ambled happily through four hundred years of varied literature. It amuses me now to realize how much must have gone over my unworried head, but I doubt that I was stunted either emotionally or intellectually as a consequence.

When the family returned to London in the immediate post-war years, it was time for Louise to start earning her living. She entered the civil service, characteristically scoring top marks in Latin in the entrance examination. I followed her a year or two later in the humbler capacity of copying typist. My salary was a modest £2. 6. 0 a week—now £2.30—and very pleased with it I was.

It is always fascinating to look back on any life—particularly one's own—pick out a seemingly unimportant incident, and be able to say, "That was when it all started."

For Louise and me, that point came on an afternoon in 1923, when the late Sir Walford Davies, accompanied by a gramophone, came to the Board of Education to give a lecture on music. Although it was probably not intended for office workers at all, but the school inspectors or some such, Louise somehow wandered into the lecture.

She arrived home slightly dazed and announced to an astonished family, "I must have a gramophone."

That same month, she received one of those unexplained bonuses that used to crop up with the cost-of-living alterations. Her share was sufficient to pay a fairly large deposit on an H.M.V. gramophone, and Mother and I went with her to buy it. This machine cost the fabulously extravagant price of £23.

As well, Louise bought ten records. These single-sided discs were 7/6d in those days—about 38p). She had planned to purchase instrumental music only, notably the "Air on the G String." But the assistant was extremely sympathetic and anxious that ten records should really give us pleasure and suggested a vocal record or two, pointing out that there was a very fine Amelita Galli-Curci record out that month.

We had never heard of Galli-Curci, but after listening to her record of "Un bel dì vedremo," we immediately bought it. To this we cautiously added Alma Gluck's record of "O, Sleep, Why Dost Thou Leave Me?" and felt we had done our duty by vocal records.

It was, I immediately confess, many years before we ever bought another instrumental record. Between them, Galli-Curci and Alma Gluck opened the world of vocal music to us, and we became what can only be described as "voice lovers."

Oh, happy days, when first one becomes a record collector, however modest! Could any collector, amateur or professional, cast his mind back to the days when he painfully accumulated his first two or three records, and say that was not one of the happiest times of his life?

The ravishing moment when, for the first time, the rich beauty of De Luca's incomparable tone melted upon the ear; the very first time Caruso's radiant tenor uttered the opening phrases of the Rigoletto Quartet in matchless style and tones of liquid gold; the very first time Farrar, Gluck, Alda, Martinelli, Destinn, Eames, Chaliapin—oh, all that immortal company—broke upon one's intoxicating sense of awareness. These were never to be forgotten glories.

I recall even now the terrific excitement when double-sided records came in. It was a milestone on the path to the operatic Milky Way. There were Louise and I slowly sampling the early joys of record collecting. And "slowly" was the word. The buying of one new record meant much consultation, much planning and, frequently, going without a few lunches—which is, I still think, the way one *should* come to one's pleasures. That sense of glorious achievement is with me still, fifty years later.

Then, early in 1924, came the announcement that Galli-Curci was to make her English debut in the autumn and give a series of concerts, beginning on October 12, at the Albert Hall. By now, she was very much our favourite gramophone star, and her appearance—in London, in the flesh—was of monumental importance to us. I make no secret of the fact, and no apology for it, that our early years were filled with a considerable amount of naïve hero worship. Even now, I have every sympathy with the sincere, often raw, enthusiasm that lifts some youngster right out of the ordinary world, up to the golden heights of loving admiration for something that is, or appears in youthful estimation to be, perfection.

We scraped a little money together—more cancelled lunches—and bought tickets for her four Albert Hall concerts, as well as the one she was to give at the Alexandra Place—at that time still a concert hall, though one of proportions more suggestive of a railway terminus—. Then we settled down to wait.

But before that autumn came round, another discovery of vital importance struck us. While I was away from home on a short visit, Louise—not used to being on her own, but filled with a vague curiosity—wandered into the gallery of Covent Garden to hear *Madama Butterfly*.

By the time I returned home, Louise had discovered opera and assured me that we must take advantage of the short Grand Season then in progress. Like many timid beginners before me, I doubted that I should enjoy anything in a foreign language, but I agreed to accompany her.

By careful management of our finances, we sampled three operas that season. We heard *Tosca, La Traviata,* and *Rigoletto.*

With this operatic experience behind us, we felt we were making tremendous progress. I thought myself able and willing to discuss the whole range of opera with anyone. When Galli-Curci finally arrived, I remember seeing the evening paper placards on the Saturday before her first concert. They simply stated, "Galli-Curci at any price!"

It would be useless to try to describe the excitement preceding the first concert. Those who have also waited long to hear some musical favourite in person will know exactly what I mean.

Of course, initially it was disappointing to discover that, in the cruel acres of the Albert Hall, the voice sounded much smaller than on the gramophone. But, inexperienced though we were, it did not take us long to separate the natural nervousness of the first half hour and the unsuitability of the hall from the matchless vocal accomplishment.

It is always difficult to describe a voice in words. Since the singer is his or her own instrument, inevitably there must be something intensely personal about a singing voice. Hence few records really capture more than a compromise representation of most singers, though they will remind you powerfully of one you have heard in real life.

Galli-Curci's voice projection was remarkable, and she had a floating quality that was as ravishing as her ornamentation was dazzling. But to me, the most beautiful thing about the sound was the faint touch of melancholy—often found in the very best voices—which gave to certain phrases and notes a quality of nostalgia that went straight to one's heart.

This quality was one reason for her fantastic appeal as a concert singer. Nowadays, I suppose, we would call it communication or audience-identification. But, expressed in its simplest terms, I can only say that when she sang the sentimental old ballad "Long, long ago" as an encore, it was *everyone's* "long, long ago." Since she stirred the roots of everyone's memory, it was difficult to say whether it was the tenderness of her voice or the tenderness of one's recollections that meant more.

By the end of the first concert, Louise and I were already aware that we would never be satisfied until we heard Galli-Curci in opera as well as on the concert platform. But, alas, we found that she sang opera only in New York.

With the simplicity of all truly great ideas, it came to me. If Galli-Curci sang opera only in New York, to New York we must go.

It is at this time, difficult to convey the immensity of this decision for girls like us. Neither of us had any money. In fact, I think we owed Mother five pounds. I was earning my £2. 6. 0 a week; Louise, a little more. We had never spent a night away from home except with friends. There was, of course, no airline across the Atlantic then—the first regular passenger flights were still twenty years in the future—and a trip to the States was something that few seasoned travellers expected to include in their experiences.

But Galli-Curci sang opera only in New York.

To Louise, I simply stated: "I intend to go to New York some time in the next five years to hear Galli-Curci sing in opera. Are you coming, too?"

With profound faith in the possibility of all things, Louise replied. "Rather! How are we going to do it?"

How, indeed?

And here let me say, in tribute to our parents, in that moment the whole of our future—and, if I may stretch prophetic fancy further, the lives of twenty-nine people—depended on the fact that Mother and Dad had always brought us up to believe that if we wanted a thing, it was up to us to work and save for it.

It never occurred to Louise and me to suppose we might get someone else to provide us with what we wanted, or to waste time envying those who, through force of circumstances, could do with ease what we must accomplish with difficulty and sacrifice. All our thoughts were concentrated on how we *could* do it.

That same evening, we worked out our expenses. Roughly at first, then in ruthless detail, we checked almost to a penny. We finally decided that we could do the trip, have an outfit and stay a week or two in New York for £100 each. For those were the happy days when you could go to New York and back, "third tourist" on a Cunarder, for something like £38 return. We also decided we did not want to wait longer than two years. Could we both save £50 a year for two years running? If not, we did not deserve to hear Galli-Curci sing in opera.

Even we realized that our scheme would sound a little mad unless we had already saved at least part of our expenses, so we decided to say nothing to anyone until the end of the first year. We were at the age when one loves to have a secret. But alas, one also longs to tell it. So we decided to make one exception. We would tell Galli-Curci herself.

I wrote of our plans to her in what I realize now was a very artless sort of letter and ended, "We shall come, if we have to arrive in the afternoon, hear you in the evening, and leave the next morning." This was not quite what we meant to do, of course, but it looked lovely written down.

We were lucky indeed with our first prima donna. She replied by return of post: "If you ever succeed in coming to America, you shall have tickets for everything I sing. Come and see me at the Albert Hall on Sunday to say goodbye."

Never in our wildest dreams had we aspired to addressing a musical celebrity in person. It was like being asked to tea at Buckingham Palace. I remember exactly what we wore. Louise had a little black hat we called "the curate," which had to be skewered on with a couple of pins. The glory of my outfit was a blouse I made myself. I had put a lot of work into the revers, and I always wore them outside my coat, so no one could miss their charm.

Galli-Curci received us like old friends. Louise always declares she said only one word at this tremendous interview, and that was, "Goodbye." She was too frightened to say anything else. But I managed to say a bit more. I was always the chatty one.

When Galli-Curci said, "I shall remember you. Just drop me a line, and I'll keep you the seats," I hastily emphasized it would take two years.

She repeated, "I understand. But I shall remember you."

In our simplicity, we thought prima donnas always behaved in this manner. We took her sympathetic interest for granted, implicitly believing her promise to remember us and provide us with the seats. And the wonderful thing was: we were right!

CHAPTER TWO

We went home in a dream that winter afternoon—and the real work began.

It is all very well to *have* these ideas; the great thing is to carry them out. We soon found, like many before us, that if you save what is left at the end of the week—there's nothing left. So we put away our pound at the *start* of the week. After we had paid our very modest contribution at home, our season tickets to town and our insurance, we usually had about ten shillings a week each. From this pittance came our daily lunches—no luncheon vouchers then, of course—our clothes, our amusements and our "extras." We soon found we could not have what was called a "proper lunch" and discovered that a brown roll fills you much better than a white one. We seriously balanced the rival merits of a penny plain-ish bun against those of a three-halfpenny bun with lots of lovely currants. But we also bought a Rand McNally guide to New York, and when we felt hungry, we used to study this and feel better.

But let no one suppose we were not happy. Going without things is neither enjoyable nor necessarily uplifting in itself.

But the things you achieve by your own effort and your own sacrifice do have a special flavour.

By the end of the first year, we each had fifty pounds and thus felt justified in disclosing our plans to our parents. They were a trifle taken aback, I must admit. Our two aunts, who had never been farther than Cornwall in their lives, were simply horrified and exclaimed to Mother, "Mary! You'll never let those girls go. It's hell with the lid off."

Mother was a bit shaken at that thought, but she talked it over with Dad. With characteristic fairness and logic, they concluded that since it was our own money, which we had earned and saved ourselves, we were entitled to spend it in our own way. They added that they thought it a queer way to want to spend the savings of two years, but that that was our business.

Thus encouraged, we tackled the second year. Now the question of clothes for the great undertaking arose; quite a problem it was, too, for it was hard work squeezing a modest outfit *and* a trip to New York all out of a hundred pounds.

As Louise's talents do not run in the dressmaking direction, I made all our clothes myself. She knew just what she wanted, enjoyed the consultations beforehand, and was gratifyingly amazed when the finished product bore a reasonable resemblance to the illustration. But, as she freely confessed, what happened between my picking up the scissors and her groping her way into the finished model was as much a mystery to her as irregular verbs in her beloved foreign languages were to me.

My great support at this period was *Mabs Fashions,* a periodical known to all office girls of my era. *Mabs Fashions* clothed us both.

As the second year neared its end, our savings rose to the required mark. A quiet "family" hotel of engaging respectability in Washington Square had even been recommended to us. There, we were to have everything—full board, private bathroom and all—for the princely sum of four dollars each per day.

At last our *Mabs Fashions'* outfits were ready—and very distinguished we thought them, too. With the greatest of difficulty, we had obtained six weeks' vacation from our offices, half of it unpaid leave; and our passages were booked on the *Berengaria,* then possibly the biggest liner afloat. All that remained was to write to Galli-Curci and tell her we were coming.

Her reply, preserved gratefully and affectionately for all these years, lies before me now!

My dear girls,
I am so happy at last the great moment has come! and I imagine your joy, anticipating your trip to New York. I will be more than happy to have the tickets for you for all my operas and certainly I will sing *Traviata*—we had specially requested this—and will think of the perseverant girls who will be listening. Will you give me right away your address as soon as you arrive and your telephone number too? I want you to have dinner with me some night, when rehearsals are not so heavy. My address from December to February is 1022 Fifth Avenue, N.Y., in my new apartment there. I don't know yet my telephone number but you will be able to get it by calling the office of Evans & Salter, 527 Fifth Avenue. God bless you in your trip; Merry Christmas and au revoir soon.

Sincerely yours,
A Galli-Curci

It was a final crown on all our efforts. We were ready to go. The goodbyes were said and, on one of the last days of

1926, Louise and I set sail for the New World. We had never been to Brighton for the day alone, but we were off to New York.

We had to be on board overnight before sailing in the morning; overwhelmed and with sudden panic, I very nearly came off the boat and went home that night. All the excitement and anticipation, the two years' struggle and the determination dissipated into dreadful homesickness: I could not imagine now why I had ever said I would go nearly three thousand miles away. However, Louise's resolution held firmly and she bolstered up my failing courage.

Everyone's first long voyage is much like everyone else's, of course, and yet individually one's own. We were very cautious and kept ourselves much to ourselves. Well-armed with knowledge about "white slavers"—a great issue in our youth—we knew we were not to talk to any strange men. So we hardly talked to anyone.—I can't think how I managed *that* for a week.—Finally, on the last night on board, we thought the danger was over and told everyone at the table why we had come to America.

This caused a terrific sensation. It is just the kind of mad thing the dear Americans love.

Had we friends in New York? No. Relatives? No. Business? No. Any reason at all for coming other than to hear Galli-Curci sing in opera? No other reason at all.

Fresh sensation! Then someone remarked that Galli-Curci ought to be *told*. It was such a wonderful story.

"But she knows," we explained. "She waited while we saved up the money. She is giving us tickets for everything she sings. And she has promised to sing *Traviata,* because it's our favourite opera."

This really was a bombshell from the two quiet, inconspicuous Britishers in their homemade dresses. Amid the

laughter and congratulations of the people around us, we
became starlets in our own right for a few hours.

The next morning we arrived in New York.

I suppose the first view of Manhattan from the water is still
one of the most fantastic and incredible sights to European
eyes. But in those days, it was especially fantasy-laden. We
had never seen a skyscraper before. At that time, I think no
London building was allowed to rise above twelve storeys.
And some of those early skyscrapers were truly beautiful,
so unlike the faceless horrors of today. Indeed, it is impossible to describe the sheer beauty of New York during the
nineteen-twenties.

We lost our hearts to New York the first day. In spite of
its many changes, it still holds a special unchallenged place
in our affections.

The very respectable friend of a friend collected us from
the boat—Mother, also with white slavers in mind, having
stipulated that this precaution at least must be observed. Having satisfied ourselves that he was who he said he was and
not a super-subtle white slaver, we allowed him to escort us
off the ship and deposit us at our Washington Square hotel.

It was the afternoon by then, and we decided to go out
immediately and find Galli-Curci's agents. We walked—not
daring to get on anything for fear of what it might cost—all
the way up Fifth Avenue to Thirty-Ninth Street, along to
Broadway—according to the instructions we had memorized
from our guide book nearly two years ago—and stood gazing
at the outside of the Metropolitan Opera House. The Old
Met, of course. Now, alas, no longer in existence.

The magic Met—which has resounded to the voices of
every great singer known to us through gramophone records—was, in those days, under the inspired management
of Gatti-Casazza, probably the last of the great impresarios.

Those were the days when you could hear *Traviata* on a Saturday afternoon with Galli-Curci, Beniamino Gigli, and Giuseppe De Luca; go home to eat; and come back for *La Forza del Destino* with Rosa Ponselle, Pinza—just becoming a famous name in America—and Giovanni Martinelli; and find the young Lawrence Tibbett—in the part of Melitone—thrown in for good measure.

No wonder we gazed at the unimpressive exterior in silent awe. Later, we sought out the offices of Evans & Salter and, feeling once more rather shy and far from home, timidly asked, "Please could we have Madame Galli-Curci's telephone number? We have just arrived from England and…"

Before we could get any further, a pleasant American voice called out from an inner office, "Hello! Is that Miss Cook?" And out came Homer Samuels, Galli-Curci's husband, with Lawrence Evans.

Dear Homer! How well he chose the words necessary to make us feel neither oddities nor hysterical fans, but friends and valued admirers. He gave us our tickets for the following evening when Galli-Curci was to sing *Traviata,* asked us about our journey, satisfied himself that we were comfortably established in New York, and finally, reaffirmed that, as soon as there were fewer rehearsals, they would get in touch with us and have us to dinner with them in their new Fifth Avenue apartment.

By the time we staggered out of the office, we already knew that our two years' saving had been worth it. What mattered now the skimpy lunches, the cheese-paring and saving, the day-to-day sacrifices? And we had achieved it ourselves: the happiest state human nature can attain.

In a glow of contentment, we returned to our hotel, admiring the traffic of Fifth Avenue, the skyscrapers of Lower Manhattan, and every American face and form that passed us.

The telephone rang as soon as we reached our room, and Louise lifted the receiver gingerly.

"Who is it?" I hissed anxiously.

"The New York Times," replied Louise succinctly, "wants to know what we look like."

This was right up my street! I seized the telephone and described us—as I saw us. Other questions followed. What did we think of the Prince of Wales? Of the skyline of New York? Of bobbed hair—a great issue at that time?

No one before had ever wanted to know what we thought of anything. It was marvellous, but only the beginning. The next day, several other newspapers wanted to interview and photograph us, as "the two girls who saved their money to cross the Atlantic," etcetera.

That evening we donned our *Mabs Fashions'* evening dresses—the first we had ever had. Mine had a thick cotton georgette background, and superimposed upon it in *plush*— rather like drawing-room chairs—was a design. I had a diamante bow on my stomach, and I thought I was what was then called the cat's whiskers. With Louise equally fetchingly attired, off we went to sit in the stalls at the opera for the first time in our lives. Girls of our type generally *never* sat anywhere but in the gallery, in those days.

Which of us who saw the Met in the great days of the prosperity boom can ever forget the fantastic sight of its glorious, sweeping Diamond Horseshoe, or the display of dresses, furs and jewellery?

The Metropolitan and Covent Garden also looked then as opera houses should look. How I hate the drab austerity of an "undressed" Covent Garden today! Opera is a festive art, and in my view, the audience should pay it the compliment of looking a little festive too. Pushing your way into the stalls of a great opera house in scruffy jeans and a pull-over brands you as either tiresomely common and insensitive, or rather pathetically exhibitionist.

But from our seats in the fourth row of the stalls on that wonderful night, we looked around, enthralled, at the dazzling scene. It remains with me to this day—and during the darkest days of the war, when everything that was gracious, colourful and beautiful had to go—as one of those shining memories to be cherished and treasured.

Galli-Curci, Gigli, and De Luca formed the cast for *La Traviata* that night. Our particular star played a Violetta that fulfilled our most eager hopes and anticipations—worth the two years' wait.

That great first night at the Met we heard the young Gigli for the first time, and although we both preferred him in other roles later, we did know we were hearing a phenomenon. Perhaps for us, the real discovery was De Luca—no longer young, but still at the height of his glory. And the finest baritone we ever heard. His voice, one of the most beautiful possible, had the quality and colour of dark honey in the sunshine; with it went a knowledge of the art of singing, which no one who heard him could ever forget. Even at that time, we knew he was supreme. We have never since had reason to revise this opinion.

Twenty years later, when he was over seventy, we heard him give a recital in New York, and even then he could teach something of the art of singing to almost anyone else I ever heard. Grand old De Luca was one of the glorious company indeed.

At the end of the performance, something wonderful happened. When Galli-Curci came on to take her applause, she picked us out from where we sat clapping in the stalls, and waved to us. I remember thinking, "This is the nearest thing to royalty I shall ever be! I'm being waved at by Galli-Curci across the footlights of the Metropolitan!"

The next day, Galli-Curci asked us to dinner in her apartment. She lived just opposite the Metropolitan Museum on that part of Upper Fifth Avenue then known as Millionaires' Row. She added that she would send a car for us.

Again we donned our *Mabs Fashions'* evening dresses and swept out, we believed, as to the manner born. Our waiting car possessed a chauffeur and a fur rug.—We had hardly ever been in even a taxi before in our lives.—And away we went up Fifth Avenue, to be deposited at an apartment that looked rather like the Wallace Collection to us. At this point there was a slight social hitch: Louise was wearing an evening cloak made by me, with a near-fur collar, and if this collar were roughly handled, it would crackle. As the manservant took the cloak, *the collar crackled.* Louise was mortified, but no one seemed to notice. And then Galli-Curci came running downstairs and into the room.

Oh, Lita! How the years roll back when I recall that evening. I suppose it was later that she became "Lita" to us, for those were not the days when every important fan presumed to address stars by their Christian names. But from that first evening, she was a dear, kind, affectionate friend for life.

She apparently needed no more than a few minutes in our company to realize what kind of girls we were, and she asked almost immediately, "Did your mother mind your coming?"

We admitted that she did rather.

"I know exactly what she thought," Galli-Curci said. "I'll tell you what we will do. We'll all write a card to Momma tonight to tell her that you are in a good house and she needn't worry."

And she did. In the middle of a busy season, she wrote to Mother, assuring her of our safety and happiness. A typical

Galli-Curci gesture, we were to find later, for she combined an extraordinary sensitivity about the feelings of others with the sort of cool common sense one does not always associate with prima donnas.

Years later, one of her great colleagues—who liked her, as a matter of fact—told us many people considered Galli-Curci rather cold and proud. Although a small woman, she had immense dignity and presence, and her Spanish side gave her a rather aristocratic bearing that marked her out in any company. She would have been a fool if she had not known her exact position in the musical world of that day. And Galli-Curci was no fool.

But to us, she was an angel. And she changed our lives.

That first magical evening was like the sort of thing you invent to please yourself, but which never really happens. Plans were made for our enjoyment; we were advised on what to hear at the opera. And, final delight, Homer told us that Arturo Toscanini was returning to New York for the first time, after fifteen years' absence—following his famous quarrel with Gatti-Casazza—and if we wished to go, he would take us.

In those days, we had only a vague idea of Toscanini's position in the musical world, but we accepted with alacrity. Thanks to Homer, we witnessed that wonderful scene of excitement and rejoicing when Toscanini returned to New York.

In this connection, Lita told us an amusing story. Once, during Toscanini's long absence and before the reconciliation between him and Gatti, she said to the famous manager of the Met, "Gatti, why don't you have Toscanini back?"

Gatti regarded her with somewhat sardonic gloom and replied, "When you have had typhoid fever and have had the good fortune to recover, do you ask to have it again?"

That evening was the prelude to an unbelievable four weeks of musical festivity. In addition to hearing Lita once more in *Traviata,* we heard her as Rosina in *Il Barbiere di Siviglia,* and as Gilda in *Rigoletto,* which I still think her greatest part. I never heard another Gilda who even remotely approached her. She was an absolute mistress of the art of recitative, and her coloratura was as effortless, as natural as the spoken word. Also, she was a very good actress. Not a very great one—that is something different—but a very good one. She even *looked* a Gilda—quite a tough assignment for some who have essayed the role. With her oval, Renaissance type of face, her magnificent dark eyes, and that essential touch of melancholy, which could sometimes transform her face as well as her voice, she was the living embodiment of Rigoletto's daughter.

As well as our Galli-Curci performance, we heard *Turandot, Falstaff, Tosca, Romeo and Juliet,* and *La Forza del Destino.* We also heard *La Bohème* and I think that it was on this first visit that we heard Martinelli in *Pagliacci.*

It will be seen from this list that we leaned very much to the Italian side of the operatic repertoire. Later, at our own Covent Garden, we discovered the great German artists of this rich period. But meanwhile, did we have fun among the Italians!

I cannot complete an account of these magical weeks without mentioning the amazing American hospitality we received. I mean the heart-warming welcome Americans extend to anyone they recognize as an eager and interested visitor. Because of the particular events in our later lives, we thought that the golden, happy things of life lay largely on the other side of the Atlantic. Because of those lovely, carefree, happy days of our youth, we found a particular touching significance in the words, "Westward, look, the land is bright."

Like all good things, our American visit could not last forever, and finally we had to go to say goodbye to Lita and Homer. It was a melancholy occasion, but Lita said something that changed everything.

"If you come back one year in the fall, we will give you a really lovely holiday at our home in the Catskill Mountains."

"If you'll wait while we save up the money," we cried, "we'll come. But it takes two years."

Lita promised to wait. And then she added thoughtfully, "Time and distance don't matter, if you are really fond of someone."

A profound and simple assertion, put to the test again and again in the years that followed, but always to prove true.

CHAPTER THREE

We went home on the Aquitania. Third class this time, which was the nearest thing to steerage that existed in our day. In working out our expenses, we had realized that we must travel one way in lowly state; we reasoned that, on the return journey, there would be no emigrants. This was true, but there were deportees—twenty-two of them, if I remember rightly. But it was an experience and we could hardly expect roses all the way.

As we stepped off the *Aquitania* at Southampton, a man approached us: "Are you the Misses Cook?"

When we replied in chorus that we were, he went on, "Well, I'm from the *Daily Mail.*" And a milder version of our *New Yorker* publicity experience began all over again. We returned to the bosom of our amused family as minor celebrities of a moment; to this day, there exists an incredible photograph of Louise and me smirking falsely at each other in an attempt to "look sisterly," as requested by the press.

We were spent out, down to our last shilling. Since we intended to return to New York, I thought it was time I tried to make some extra money and decided—like many a deluded creature before me—that the easiest thing might be to write something. Since they seemed interested, I sent a breezy little article about us and our trip to the *Daily Mail*.

Luckily for me, we *were* news in a very limited way; the article was accepted, and I saw myself in print for the first time. Intoxicated by success, we thought we were famous for life. Needless to say, in two or three days everyone had forgotten all about us, and in rather chastened mood, I pondered on possible topics that would interest *anyone*.

I hit upon a brilliant idea—or so it seemed to me. *Mabs Fashions* might like to have an article on how we made our clothes to go and hear Galli-Curci.

I wrote the article, typed it out carefully on my office machine, and sent it in. It too was accepted. But for a while, this was the full extent of my journalistic career. To become a shorthand-typist, instead of a mere copying typist, I had to take an exam, and this took up all my time and energy.

I passed my exam—top marks in English and bottom marks in shorthand, which is rather thought provoking when one reflects that I was offering myself as a shorthand-typist— and found myself in the Official Solicitor's Department of the Law Courts.

There were four of us in that particular section, and very soon I turned the other three into operatic enthusiasts, with a gramophone apiece. We all earned approximately three pounds a week, made our own clothes, saw life in simple terms, envied no one, often worked shockingly hard, but saved systematically for whatever we wanted and enjoyed it extravagantly when we got it.

The height of social glamour in those days was to sit for two hours over a pot of tea and a roll and butter at a Lyons Corner House, talking endlessly about ourselves, our hopes and the deliciously distant glitter of our favourite stars. The short International Season of Opera at Covent Garden was the most expensive time of the year.

For those unfortunately born too late to know Covent Garden in those days, and for the nostalgic enjoyment of those who shared those joys with us, let me recall the life of a Covent Garden gallery-ite.

I think it was the German conductor, Heger, who was reputed to have said of the Covent Garden audience that our enthusiasm was kindled to red heat by the simple expedient of starvation for ten months, and stuffing for two. Whether he really said it or not, the analogy was, largely speaking, correct. For nearly ten months of the year, Covent Garden was a dance hall, covered with yellow posters bidding anyone who wished to spend one shilling or half a crown to come and dance there.

But in the spring, those notices would be torn down and replaced by the preliminary lists of works and artists for the coming season. On the Sunday afternoon before the opening Monday—could it always have been as sunny as it now seems in retrospect?—the "regulars" gathered—some having seen little of each other since the previous year. Those Floral Street reunions stand out in my memory as among the happiest days of my life.

In those days, the gallery seats could not be reserved. Instead, under the masterly direction of Gough and Hailey, our two "stool men," we hired camp stools, which marked our places whenever we had to leave for such unimportant matters as earning our living. Rumour had it that both Gough and Hailey did a substantial amount of betting on the side. Certainly their financial situation fluctuated in the most extraordinary way, and it was always difficult to know if Gough were employing Hailey or Hailey employing Gough.

But from our point of view, they were splendid. I can see Gough now, pontificating gravely when called on to settle any question of queue-jumping. Not that there was much of this; anyone caught cheating was regarded with boundless contempt and handled with something less than kid gloves.

Apart from the first night of the season—marked by the Sunday gathering—and big "star" nights—when most of the real enthusiasts would gather overnight—we put down our camp stools at six or seven in the morning. Those of us fortunate enough to work near Covent Garden rushed over at lunchtime and sat on our stools, munching sandwiches—or a mere roll and butter if hard up—while watching the stars go to and from rehearsal.

The one disadvantage was that, for those of us who went almost every night, life became a series of late retirings and early risings. But either we were tougher then or youth cares little for that sort of thing. Louise and I regularly caught our last train from Victoria at twenty-to-one in the morning and rose to catch the first train to town next day before six. I was dreadfully weary sometimes. But I remember that my heart was high those early summer mornings, because we lived in a wonderland of opera, of interminable conversations with fellow enthusiasts in the queue, of glimpses at and sometimes even snatches of conversation with the stars, and of a dozen other delights.

Oh, the friendships and enmities of that queue! What book of this kind could be complete without mentioning some of the familiar figures?

Francis had attended every performance of every single opera at Covent Garden since the early nineteen-twenties, usually accompanied by Jenny. Francis had some wonderful turns of phrase from time to time and once uttered the pearl of succinct criticism when we were all recalling a singer we had deplored. "She had an enormous voice," he agreed thoughtfully, "and all of it came from her nose."

George was three when he first queued with his mother, though he didn't actually come into performances until later. He adored Pinza and was the first person the amused basso used to ask for when he passed the queue.

Arthur was attending a finishing school in Switzerland when he received word that Ponselle was to make her Covent Garden debut. Unable to contemplate missing such an event, he wrote immediately to his father. He said he had been seriously considering the future and felt strongly that, instead of wasting money abroad, the time had come for him to assist his father in business. So admirably did he state the case to his unsuspecting parent that, somewhat touched, his father brought him home—just in time for Ponselle's debut. "But, by God, it was a near thing!" was Arthur's invariable comment when he told the tale later.

Dennis cycled up every morning from Forest Gate and once fell asleep on his bicycle, worn out by a series of late operatic nights. He always declared that he remembered seeing the Law Courts, and that the next thing he knew, he was lying on the pavement, fifty yards farther on.

Colin was afterwards to found perhaps the most famous record collectors' centre in England. I have always thought he owed the phenomenal success of his venture partly to his uncompromising statement of views. They carried such shattering conviction.

There was the famous occasion when a customer dared to speak disparagingly of Dame Nellie Melba. "Sir," said Colin, rising in his wrath from behind the counter, "Sir, I would have you know that here we worship at the shrine of Melba. Kindly go out of my shop and never come in again." And if anyone can say "sir" more insultingly than Colin can, I have yet to meet him.

There was Mrs. Price who, with her family, headed the queue for many a long day. She always lingers in my memory as one of the few women who had the gift of dignity and repose. It was she who once consoled me when I was seething with rage over what I considered an unjust musical criticism and encouraged me to judge a performance for myself. "No critic is infallible," she said. "He may be wrong and you may be right."

Then there were Douglas, Jenny, Ray, Noel and Freda—who did most of their courting in the queue and subsequently chose a foreign opera festival as the scene of their honeymoon—Anne, Norwood, Phyllis, Harold—who had written a fan letter to Geraldine Farrar in 1919 and started a regular and entertaining correspondence with that great woman, that lasted until her death forty-seven years later—Mollie—one of my friends and colleagues from the Law Courts days—Reg—whom Mollie afterwards married. There were dozens of them! Chance acquaintances, old friends, part of one's life. Bobby, who was later shot down over the Mediterranean, Peter who died in the North African campaign. Impossible to name them all, but every one represented part of the scene that belongs to those golden days before 1934, when we were young and the world was ours.

And what was the operatic fare offered to us when we handed in our camp stools and scrambled up the stairs to our wooden seats in the gallery?

Well, of course, there is a great deal of nonsense talked about those days, mostly by people who never experienced them. The times I have had people say naïvely, "They didn't *act* much in those days, did they?" or "Of course it was the *star* system then, wasn't it?" or "There were no real *productions,* I imagine."

No one, least of all myself, is going to pretend that there were no poor, dull or even uninspired performances at Covent Garden during the Grand Season of the "old days." There were occasionally perfectly frightful performances, often very good ones, and sometimes truly great and memorable performances, which stand out still as milestones in our memories.

It was, I freely admit, a considerable disadvantage that the opera house inevitably lacked a permanent orchestra and chorus. But this deficiency was usually surmounted with amazing success, first by the wholesale importation of one of the standing London orchestras—as is done today, in the case of Glyndebourne, for instance—and secondly by the natural British genius for choral singing. It was easier than it would have been in most other countries to assemble a chorus of high standard, because the chorus members probably were accustomed to singing together, either in oratorio or as members of some choral society.

Against this background appeared artists—and in some cases whole casts—who were perfectly used to performing together in other parts of the world.

And now for my favourite comment, "They didn't *act* much then, did they?"

Act! Why a man like Chaliapin could act everyone off the stage today with the exception of Callas and Gobbi. It must be forty years or more since I last heard Chaliapin's Boris, but my spine still chills enjoyably as I recall his Clock Scene, where the Czar, who has murdered his way to the throne, sees the ghost of the child he has murdered. And he did the whole thing with a chair and a handkerchief: a monumental and solitary figure in a splendid costume of brocade and fur, he scarcely made a movement at first, only the agitation of

the red handkerchief in his hand showing his growing uneasiness and his incredulous horror. Then, at the moment
when he actually saw the child, he would take the chair on
which he had been sitting and try to hold off the figure, un-
seen to all but him. And we, sweating with heat and terror
in the gallery, could have sworn in the end that we saw the
child too. That was acting!

Of course, in a singer, the first essential is the voice. But it
is useful to put the record straight for those who imagine that
the stars of those days stood stolidly at the footlights and sang.

When people ask, "Are there not just as many great vocal
artists today?" I am afraid the simple, if unpopular, answer
is: No. This is not because God has stopped giving out good
voices. It is because the full development of a great singing
talent is a near-impossibility in a world where everything
from coffee to soup to philosophy and art must be "instant."
Presently someone is going to discover how to grow an instant tree. It won't be much like the tree that has taken years
and years to mature, but it will satisfy quite a number of people who will, incidentally, be rather huffy if you talk about
the superiority of the real thing.

The development of a complete musical artist differed a
little from country to country, but in every case it took time.
In Austria, for instance, anyone lucky enough to be accepted
into one of the famous musical conservatoria faced six years
of study. No agent or talent scout was allowed to approach
the singer during the first five years.—Nor, of course, was
there any chance of preening and twittering on television
to a chorus of uninformed praise.—At the end of the fifth
year, the conservatory would organize a students' concert,
to which agents and talent scouts would be invited. An interested agent or scout would approach the teacher, not the
student, with the request that, in a year's time, he or she

might hear the singer again. An engagement—probably in a provincial opera house, where immensely varied professional experience would be available—might result.

The greatly gifted artist might find a few short cuts, and there was always the occasional phenomenon who conformed to few of these rules. But, generally speaking, any artist who succeeded in the international scene—in parts great or small—had this wealth of understanding and experience behind him or her. What we, the audience, enjoyed was the tip of the iceberg. Underneath was the firm base of knowledge and hard work that supported the performance.

The luckiest—and usually the most gifted—were those who came under the direct influence of one of the great musical directors. Directors like Serafin, Marinuzzi and probably Panizza, or Clemens Krauss, Bruno Walter and, a little later, Kleiber. These were men who knew exactly how to develop a voice rather than exploit it. Not all the greatest conductors had this special flair, though this is no criticism of them. They probably expected to handle the finished article rather than perfect it. This expectation is legitimate if the conductor is truly great and can recognize whether or not the singer is really capable of taking on the projected role. The operatic highways and byways nowadays are strewn with the wrecks of voices called in to support the prestige of a conductor rather than the cause of true singing.

This lack of basic development is combined with over-exposure and over-performing. Everyone wants to hear everything today. By way of the airplane, which is no friend to a singer, artists rush to and fro doing their admired and over-recorded performance of this role and that.

Also, modern recording tends to inflate the size and quality of many voices. A "souped up" recording results in some attractive smallish artist being pressed to sing in large opera

houses. The role is, in life, totally beyond his or her safe capacity. Very soon the individual colour and charm of the
voice disappear, and another good singer fails to reach the
legitimate goal.

In the space of a few paragraphs, one can mention only
a few points, and the whole issue becomes oversimplified.
But in those days, both abroad and here among our British
singers, there was a great deal more of what Eva Turner has
so aptly called the mixture of "inspiration, dedication and
perspiration."

We probably did not know how supremely fortunate we
were. I suppose one never does until the light begins to
fade. But in those happy days, there was a great deal of glory
around us. Naturally, there were always older fans to assure
us that we, who had not heard Destinn, Caruso, Plancon and
other safely dead, could not possibly know what real singing
was. One tactless old boy once asked Louise superiorly if she
had heard "Ternina in '02."

Early in 1929, when the preliminary list of artists and
works were issued, the name of Rosa Ponselle appeared for
the first time. She was to sing three performances of *Norma,*
in which she had recently made a sensation in New York,
and two performance of *La Gioconda.*

This was news indeed! Louise and I had tremendously admired Ponselle when we had heard her in New York, and
we felt in our bones—which were pretty reliable bones in
matters operatic—that she was just what the Italian contingent at Covent Garden would rejoice in.

May 28, 1929. How often have those of us who loved her
recalled that first night Ponselle sang at Covent Garden?
We were at a fever pitch of excitement when, just before the
queue moved in, a tall, striking—indeed, almost melodra-
matic-looking—figure sauntered up Floral Street and stood

for a few moments at the corner. The whisper went round that *this* was Ponselle, though we found it hard to believe that the star of the evening would just stroll up like any of us. I was commissioned to walk past and take a good—though surreptitious—look at her as the *Forza* Leonora we had last seen on the stage of the Metropolitan. This I did. But we were still in some doubt until she walked along the street and in the stage door. That settled all disputes.

I am sure that no one who was there on that extraordinary evening will ever think of Norma as just a nineteenth-century coloratura role. It was written for a great singing actress. And by a great singing actress it must be played or, quite simply, be humbly left alone.

Years and years afterwards, Callas once said to me, "I think you know, Eeda, that to me, Ponselle was probably the greatest singer to us all. But can you tell me how we differed on the stage?"

A very interesting point. And, broadly speaking, the answer is that Ponselle played Norma almost as a goddess. One understood exactly why the tribe worshipped her; and when she proved so much a woman, the shock to the audience was almost a reflection of the shock to the tribe. Callas played Norma as a woman from the beginning, again employing her unrivalled gift of absolute pathos, combined, in this case, with a sort of passionate majesty.

Ponselle was a splendid actress and the greatest singer I ever heard. Callas was an uneven but splendid singer and, without question, the greatest actress I ever saw. How blessed indeed I have been to be alive in the same age as both of them!

At that first Ponselle *Norma,* I think what stunned us all was the almost unbelievable vocal control, displayed immediately in a "Casta Diva" of rocklike security but shimmering tone. She went on to give us an evening of drama and vocal splendour never matched in my experience.

Her voice was warm, as smooth as velvet, and of a dark, exciting colour. From top to bottom, she had a perfectly even scale. Basically this was a natural gift, but *how* she worked to perfect it! Indeed, it is interesting to read the old New York newspapers of November 1918 just after she made her sensational debut opposite Caruso. To every interviewer, she said the same thing: "Don't tell me I'm a great singer. I'm going to be one." And from then until she retired nineteen years later, at the criminally early age of thirty-nine, she never ceased to work like a slave.

Looking back over our years as opera-goers in many countries, Louise and I both consider Ponselle to be the greatest operatic artist we've ever heard. We are not alone. Farrar used to say, "When you are considering singers you must put aside Caruso and Ponselle, and then you may begin." And Fred Gaisberg, in his book on the outstanding stars of recording, opines that "Rosa Ponselle was probably the greatest lirico-spinta that ever lived." I would question that classification of her as a spinta; personally, I would call her a full dramatic soprano, as she was usually regarded. But we certainly agree that her voice was of unrivalled beauty.

Perhaps the most interesting opinion passed upon her voice was expressed by no less a person than Puccini. She met him only once, in the summer of 1924, a few months before he died, when she was staying at a villa near his home. One afternoon, Romano Romani, her teacher, took her to meet the composer, and he asked her to sing for him. She sang him his own "Vissi d'Arte" from *Tosca*—a role she never sang on the stage. And at the end he said, *"Finalmente sento la mia Tosca—ma, ahime, troppo tardi."*—"At last I hear my *Tosca*—but, alas, too late."

"What did he mean, Rosa?" we asked, when she told us the story years later.

"I don't know," she replied simply. "I suppose he already knew he was dying. I didn't like to question him. I just treasured the words."

Matchless Rosa! I am thankful that I heard every performance she ever gave in Europe. There were five in the first year at Covent Garden, seven in the second, nine—I think—in the third, and two performances of *Vestale* in Florence in 1933. I eternally regret not having heard her Donna Anna, her *L'Africaine,* her Luisa Miller, her *Il Trovatore,* her Santuzza and a dozen others. But, as will be seen later, we had claims on our time that could not be denied and we were unable to return to America during the years that mattered.

At the end of the memorable evening of Ponselle's Covent Garden debut, it was no wonder that even the orchestra stood and joined in the storm of applause that broke in wave after wave through Covent Garden. As we stood there, in the front row of the gallery, clapping madly, a complete stranger in the back row of the amphitheatre stalls just below us turned and simply asked, "Well, was it worth it?"

"Worth what?" we said, hardly pausing in our applause.

"The twenty-four hours' queuing you must have done to be where you are," was the reply.

We laughed and said in chorus, "You bet!"

"Well," was his reply, "I'm glad I didn't have to do it, but I think she's worth it, if anyone is."

And this started one of our longest and firmest operatic friendships—with Douglas and his wife, Luigia.

CHAPTER FOUR

When the 1929 season came to an end, Louise and I had a great compensation coming: we were due to sail for the States once more in September. Lita and Homer were waiting to welcome us at Sul Monte, their famous country house built at the top of Bellair Mountain, overlooking the most beautiful part of the Catskill country.

In a sense, the departure and even the journey were something of a repetition of the earlier trip, though perhaps we were a little more experienced—if not worldly, at least more self-possessed than before.

We arrived in New York in the middle of a heat wave, but nothing could dim our enthusiasm for the city, which would always represent excitement and high romance for us. Nevertheless, we were very glad to be going into the cooler, hilly country and very excited that, this time, we were travelling farther afield than New York City.

On a bright Sunday morning, we left Grand Central for our fascinating journey along the banks of the Hudson. We went by train as far as Rhinecliff; there, Homer met us with a car. Perhaps the best impression of our feelings that first day can be gleaned from my rapturous letter written home after our arrival.

Homer drove the car on to the ferry boat, and we were ferried across the Hudson—feeling like a million dollars. There were gorgeous wooded hills rising on every side, so I thought we should just begin to drive up one of them, when Homer smiled and said, "Now, you've a fifty mile drive in front of you." We have found since that they have a station ten minutes from the house, but the darlings thought we should like to be met and driven through the wonderful Catskill country—so it was nothing to Homer to give up most of his day to doing it.

It was heavenly! We stopped halfway, to eat corn soup and fried chicken and Boston cream pie. We dawdled and talked politics. We dawdled a bit more and talked music. And at last, late-ish in the afternoon, we turned up a rough woodland path leading to the top of Bellair Mountain. They own 132 acres right at the top, and Sul Monte—which is just the loveliest place you can possibly imagine—is built on a wonderful plateau with thickly wooded slopes rolling away on either side. You can see sixty miles or more back and front of the house and, on a clear day, right away to the faint purple outline of the Adirondacks.

Homer tooted the horn as we drove up and Lita came running out, crying, "*Here* are the girls!" and there was such a kissing and greeting and talking as you never saw.

It was the beginning of another holiday. Homer and Lita had their own swimming pool, dance hall and cinema on the estate. There was darling Fagin, a shaggy sheepdog, who was very sentimental and friendly, but who hated Lita to play her castanets, which she sometime did, like a true Spaniard, for her amusement and ours. There was the farm to visit and the endlessly beautiful grounds.

Above all, there was the wonderful studio, where Lita practised and sometimes allowed us to come and hear her. She explained how she used to allow the famous top range of her voice to rest almost completely during her holiday.

"Take care of the middle of your voice," she used to say, "and the top will take care of itself. Or, if you prefer—look after the cake! You can always put on the icing afterwards."

She gave another sound piece of advice one evening when we had been discussing *La Gioconda*. She immediately fetched the score and sang quite a chunk of this heavy, dramatic work.

Astounded, I exclaimed, "Why, Lita, I had no idea you could sing like that!"

"Oh, I *can*," she replied, laughing, "but if I *did* I wouldn't have much voice left in six months."

Sometimes later, as I have listened to ill-judged young sopranos happily tearing their way through the fabric of a bright upper register, I have thought of Lita's words about the difference between what one *can* do and what one *should* do.

On another occasion, she decided to sing some excerpts from *Romeo and Juliet,* which Homer said was his favourite role for her. Lita insisted on a certain amount of stage action for the death scene, so Homer was pressed into service. He finally agreed to pose on the studio steps in a dying attitude, with a resigned, "All right, all right. I'm Romeo—in black velvet," while Lita swarmed over him, singing heart-rendingly.

It was great fun being "Galli-Curci's English girls." We were invited out to the surrounding estates, and everyone seemed to vie with each other in an effort to give us the time of our lives. The wife of one millionaire newspaper owner gave an "old style" dance. She took over the whole of a picturesque Dutch inn, and we all drove out thirty miles through the moonlit Catskills to dine by candlelight in old world surroundings and dance until the early hours.

I was still, be it remembered, a three-pound-a-week short-hand-typist, so it is easy to imagine what joyous novelty all this was for us. But best of all was the lovely home life of Sul Monte. The long talks in the library or the sun-parlour, the discussions as we drove out to Perch Lake to see some builder about alterations to the house. Tea and cinnamon toast on the way back. Taking Fagin for walks and suddenly realizing we were in the country of *Queechy* and *The Wide, Wide World,* and finding to our amazement that the extraordinary types still persisted. It was wonderful.

Alas, this too had to come to an end. But this time, when we said goodbye, we were cheered by the fact that they were both coming to England on a concert tour the following year. To our lasting regret, Lita had already retired from the operatic stage. But at least we could always congratulate ourselves for our persistence in managing to hear some of her operatic performances.

When we returned to England, I was fired afresh at the prospect of writing a profitable article or two about our experiences. And as *Mabs Fashions* was now running a series of holiday articles, I wrote and submitted an article on my holiday in the Catskill Mountains.

Once again I was lucky. The article was accepted. More important, the editor wrote, saying that she liked my style, and asking if I had any other interesting holiday experiences I could write up.

Apart from the American journeys, a very short trip to Brussels was the full extent of our foreign travels. But I said,

"Yes, certainly," bought a series of guidebooks and set to work. Over a period of some months, I wrote various articles for her.

Meanwhile, operatically speaking, the wheel had turned full circle again. The preliminary notices for the opera season were out; this time, the most interesting newcomer to Covent Garden was Ezio Pinza.

From our vantage point in the gallery queue, it did not take any of us long to discover that, behind all that face fungus, which is the hallmark of so many operatic bass roles, there was a fascinating person with a charming, lively small daughter—Claudia. I suppose Claudia was about five when we first knew her. She used to smile shyly at the queue and made childish dabs at the chairs as she went along the street, clutching her father's hand.

To Claudia, we owe the beginning of our collection of star snapshots, a hobby that was to acquire considerable significance later. Many in the queue were, of course, ardent autograph hunters, but I thought it would be more fun to have snaps of the stars instead. Nowadays, dozens of people do this, but it was something of a novelty when I first produced my ten-shilling Brownie box camera, which was about my mental level, photographically speaking.

I never photographed an artist without asking permission first, so I started by asking Pinza if I might photograph Claudia one morning as he came from rehearsal. Not only was permission given, but Pinza insisted on being in the photograph as well, and made me take two pictures to make sure.

The result was one of the best snaps I ever took, and I sent an enlargement of it to Claudia's parents. A few days later, the little girl was brought along the queue during lunch time, and she thanked me in carefully rehearsed English. She was a charming child!

During that first season, the snap collection grew rapidly, though it was not until the following year that I plucked up enough courage to ask Ponselle herself. As I told her long afterwards, I used to follow her through Embankment Gardens, near the Savoy Hotel where she stayed, trying to summon enough courage to ask if I might photograph her. She was very much amused, but a good deal mystified as to why anyone should ever have been in awe of her. But in those days, our stars were gods and goddesses to us, and I must say that their remoteness and mystique added greatly to their charm and glamour.

On the night of what was to be Ponselle's final appearance, she was unwell and Pacetti sang instead. I remember when Louise and I arrived at the queue that evening, Ray announced with a sort of malicious relish for the drama of the moment, "Ponselle has sung her last performance."

Thinking she must have walked under a bus or something, we gave gratifying shrieks of horror. Then Ray saw fit to explain. He was referring only to that season and that there had been a cancellation. But he spoke more truly than he knew. She never returned to Covent Garden to sing again. The following season was an entirely German one, and in later years, the management changed, and of course Ponselle made other connections. She had indeed sung her last performance at Covent Garden. Fortunately, we were unaware of it then and went on hoping for some years longer.

The next day, Louise and I received some compensation for that final cancellation: one of the very few personal letters written by Ponselle at that period. She was never a great letter-writer and, in the busiest days of her career, she scarcely ever put pen to paper. But, in return for the snap I had sent her, she sent a wonderful photograph of herself in the third act of *Traviata* with a note saying that if we came to New

York again—which we had mentioned as a possibility one day—we were to come around backstage at the Met to see her.

Something else occurred about this time that tended to take my mind off any disappointment. I had continued to write the occasional article for *Mabs Fashions,* and I received a letter from the editor saying that she would like to meet me. Would I come to see her one afternoon?

I obtained permission to leave my Law Courts' office early one afternoon and went to Fleetway House to see Miss Taft—the woman to whom I owe all my training and all my early chances. I had never entered a publishing office before, much less been interviewed by an editor. But she soon put me at my ease and made that most flattering of all requests: to talk about myself.

I did so. At great length, I am sure.

"But did you never think of becoming a journalist?" Miss Taft asked.

"Oh, no!" I assured her, rather shocked. I was a permanent civil servant with a pension at sixty. Safe until I was nailed down in my coffin, in fact.

She was unimpressed and merely said, "Well, think about it now. I am going to start a new weekly in the autumn, and I should like you for my fiction sub."

I didn't really know what a fiction sub was, but I was flattered that anyone wanted me as anything. However, it still sounded terribly unsafe in comparison with my civil service job. This all sounds quite extraordinary now, I have no doubt, but in those days there were three people waiting for every job. So I continued to shake my head doubtfully.

"Well, go away," said Miss Taft, smiling, "and think it over. If you do want the job, it is yours."

I went away and not only thought about it, but being very

loquacious by nature, I talked about it too. Several people said, "But it's a great chance! Don't just throw it away. People are walking about ready to give their eye-teeth for that sort of chance."

When I thought about it again, the pension at sixty didn't seem quite so attractive, after all. In the end, I gave up my lovely safe job and the pension and went into Fleet Street as a fiction sub-editor at four pounds four shillings a week—one pound and four shillings more than I was getting as a government shorthand-typist.

And there, for the first several months at any rate, I was a complete failure.

I suppose it was inevitable. Most girls who go into that world do so at a much earlier age and learn the general jargon and rudiments of the profession as juniors. I hardly knew what people were talking about, much less what I should be doing, and I must have been a phenomenally slow learner.

When they gave me short articles to write up, I was fairly happy, but in periodical make-up I was an infant in arms, and not a very intelligent one, at that.

As fiction sub, one of my most horrible tasks was to arrange the proportional size of illustrations and copy. The original illustrations that come in are perhaps twenty by thirty inches. By a system of simple mathematical calculation, which to this day I have never grasped, a measurement along one side must indicate what the general size of the finished "pull" should be. Mine was the wildest guesswork. The pulls either came up like postage stamps or like recruiting posters, and I suppose I must have wasted a good deal of the firm's money in useless "blocks."

Also, I was not at all good at estimating the space that the "copy," or printed matter, would take up. Consequently, on press day I was faced with hair-raising and expensive cutting or with the even more grisly task of adding perhaps five hundred words to a story, without altering its sense, and so that no one could detect the "joins." This was the only part of my work at which I became adept—presumably because I had so much practice. Again, dreadfully expensive to the firm.

In addition, I had made as a condition of my accepting the post that I be allowed four or five weeks' leave early in the new year. Louise and I had made all our preparations for another visit to the States. I was sufficiently honest to make it clear that if this proviso was unacceptable, I was prepared to forego the job.

This proviso was accepted. What I had not sufficient sense to see was that for one member of a small staff—and the least efficient one by far—to go junketing off to the States during the difficult first months of launching a new publication could hardly make me popular with all and sundry.

Even I knew that I took my departure in anything but a harmonious atmosphere. Nowadays, I would have enough sense to compromise and smooth things over. Then, I was crude, and silly enough to stand on my—undoubted—rights, and go off, feeling justified, if uneasy.

In those early weeks of 1932, America was still suffering badly from the depression, and the atmosphere was very different from the gorgeous prosperity of our first visit, five years previous. Even so, there were vigorous signs of recovery. And so far as our own future was concerned, Louise and I saw things in pretty bright colours.

I was hardly shining at my new job, but I expected things to improve. Meanwhile, I was earning a larger salary than in any job I had held previously. Though we had no definite plans, we certainly had vague expectations of returning to the States again and again. We had found our pattern and felt that our future depended solely on our efforts. In our naïve and rather ignorant minds, we could never have conceived of the rivers of blood and high tide of war that were to sweep between this visit and the next. I realize now that, even though we were in our late twenties, we were not entirely grown up.

This time, the whole of our visit was spent in New York City. But the opera season was on, and we asked for nothing better. However, perhaps Fate had smiled upon us a little too often. Several things went wrong with this third visit. First, we arrived some weeks later than originally planned. Because of the financial upheaval, sailings had been altered and postponed. Of course, in those days there was no air traffic to ease the situation.

Consequently, we arrived almost as Lita and Homer were due to depart on a South African tour, and that gave us only one day with them in New York. They arrived in town with everything packed and ready so that we could spend the whole day together. But it was cruelly short, and the very next day, we went down to the boat to see them off to South Africa.

Louise and I felt thoroughly tearful, and possibly looked it, because I remember Lita whispering, "Don't cry, girls, or I shall too, and it looks so bad for me to start out on a concert tour in tears!"

Thus adjured, we preserved British calm and waved them away on a separation that lasted another two years.

Secondly, we had arrived when the most glowing nights of the season were already waning, so there was only one Ponselle performance for us. However, this was *Gioconda,* one of her finest roles, and we had her permission to go around and see her "any time we were at the Met."

We arrived at the opera house, full of joyful anticipation— only to discover that she was ill. An inconsiderable substitute sang in her place. We sat stolidly and miserably through the performance, and at the end, because we simply had to tell someone, we told the woman sitting beside us how we had come all the way from England, that this was our one Ponselle performance, and we had had to put up with a substitute.

She was full of sympathy and cried, "Isn't that just too bad! Wasn't Ponselle singing then? I never noticed."

We went back to our hotel hating everyone.

However, the next day there appeared an announcement that Ponselle would be singing in a concert at the Metropolitan, well within the limits of our visit. Greatly cheered, we bought our tickets and went.

This was the last time that Louise heard her sing in public, although I heard her twice more in Florence in 1933. I remember everything about her performance that night. She was in black, the dramatic black so suitable for her exotic beauty. With an almost backless dress, she wore long black gloves, and over these, the most magnificent, matching diamond bracelets. If anyone had described that get-up to me without my seeing it, I could have told who wore it.

Afterwards, we went around backstage and were received very kindly. But we were shy, and depressed because she was leaving New York the next day; we could not possibly hear her again. Also, she told us that she thought it was unlikely she would be at Covent Garden that year. It seemed there was not to be an Italian Season. Everything was going wrong for the disillusioned Cooks!

However, there was one tremendously bright spot in that visit: the first American performance of *Simon Boccanegra*. It was one of the finest productions I ever saw. Tremendously lavish, but everything had a real meaning. No slowly closing doors, unnecessary staircases or the other irrelevant clutter that often passes for "significant" staging today.

The cast included Pinza, unbelievably magnificent in the comparatively secondary role of Fiesco.

I had brought with me to America a specially dressed doll for Claudia Pinza. We had left it for her at the Metropolitan. Toward the end of our visit, we not only received a letter of thanks from her, but on the very last evening of our visit—after a superb *Simon Boccanegra*—we were taken home by the Pinzas to the Ansonia Hotel, where they then lived, and entertained at supper.

In those days, Pinza knew very little English, and Louise and I, even less Italian. But we all managed somehow, and our last night in New York was very gay and charming.

The next day, or rather late that night, we left New York for home once more. We stayed up on deck for a long while, watching the lights of Manhattan, as we slowly drew away into the darkness. Louise and I talked of returning soon, making tentative plans that were never to materialize. We did, I recollect, feel more than usually sad over our departure, but I am glad we had no inkling of what lay ahead in the years before we were to see New York again.

CHAPTER FIVE

By the time we returned to England, it was still only mid-March and I found myself up against a situation as bleak as the weather. No one could pretend that I was good at my journalistic job. I was not. In addition, I had to live down what was considered my underserved luck for having had a wonderful trip to the States while everyone else had been working hard.

At one point, I told one of my former colleagues at the Law Courts I had made a terrible mistake, and oh, why had I left my safe civil service job with its inevitable pension at sixty?

However, dear Wynne never allowed defeats to depress her.—It was she who said to me on the day France fell, "Isn't it a relief? Now there's no one left to let us down."—On this occasion she said, "Give it one week longer and see if things don't improve a little."

So I tried once more. Perhaps that week I made just a few less silly mistakes, and the illustrations were measured up just a little more successfully. Anyway, I stayed.

Then I had a stroke of real luck. At that time we were run-

ning a series of articles on, "Are you the So-and-so Girl?"
"Are you the Little Sister type?" and that sort of thing. Miss
Taft, who must have been wondering by now just what sort
of dud she had brought in as her fiction sub, detailed me to
do one of the series.

"And try," she said rather wearily, "to make it sound like
C—S—" a very successful woman journalist of the period.

I was really on my mettle and also pretty sure this might be
my last chance. I went home, wrote my article and brought
it back to Miss Taft next day.

She read it without comment—which is always very dis-
turbing—and then sent it up to the fiction editor. I heard her
say on the phone, "I'm sending you up an article. Would you
let me know how you like it and who you think wrote it?"

It was my lucky day! Twenty minutes later, he phoned
down and said, "I like it immensely. And there's no question
about who wrote it. It was C—S— wasn't it?"

That copying of styles to fill in those ghastly spaces had
paid off at last. It was the turning point for me. Now I had
clearly proved that it would be better to let me write more
and calculate less.

I was very lucky indeed to have Miss Taft for my editor.
Not only had she been monumentally patient with me, but
she had a great talent for getting the best out of people, giving just the right amount of encouragement at the right time.
One day she said, "Did you never think of writing a short
story yourself, dear? You are always subbing other people's.
What about trying something yourself?"

I was hard up, as usual, and I thought, "Well, why not?"
Louise was away at the Three Choirs Festival, and I was
slightly bored that weekend. So I wrote a not very good
story, which seemed to me a near-masterpiece, and took it
into the office on Monday morning.

Miss Taft looked it over critically and said, "It isn't very good, is it? But not bad, either. Just good enough to use when we haven't got anything better. I'll buy it."

This was the first signed piece of fiction I had ever had accepted. I was paid eight guineas for it, and I am not sure now which was the more acceptable, the honour or the money. Anyway, after that story, I occasionally wrote short stories under my office name, Ida North. One of these stories, in May, 1933, helped me to achieve yet another opera thrill to add to the other unforgettable memories.

Since we had said goodbye to Ponselle backstage at the Met that night in February, 1932, we had neither seen nor heard her. One Covent Garden season, as we had feared, passed without any Italian opera at all, and a second one was being launched without any sign of our favourite dramatic soprano. Then I learned, quite by chance, that she was singing in two performances of *La Vestale* at the Florence Musical in May.

Determined to go, I rushed up to the attic, where I did most of my writing and, over the weekend, turned out what was really not at all a bad story. Miss Taft approved it and also put up my fee. Best of all, she agreed to let me take one week of my annual leave right away and go to Florence. Louise, to our lasting regret, was unable to come, so off I went abroad, on my own for the first time. To mark the occasion, and feeling utterly dashing, I flew as far as Paris and took the night train on to Italy. I saved no time, really, but it made me feel especially excited and important.

I spoke no Italian and such inadequate schoolgirl French that I dared not address anyone on the way. By the time I arrived in Florence, my usually active tongue felt stiff with disuse. And I had a raging headache. However, as soon as I arrived, I went to sleep for an hour in hopes of feeling better by the time the first performance began that evening.

I shall never forget awakening in the late afternoon, roused by the sound of incredibly sweet bells. Completely restored, I rushed to the window and looked out over the flat roofs of Florence. Everywhere, the mellow sunlight was reflected from pink-and-white-washed walls whose green shutters were turned out from the windows. And, close at hand, before my astonished and enchanted gaze, Giotto's *Campanile* poured from the sound of those bells.

All my life, I shall remember Florence in the sunlight. In actual fact, it rained several times during my week there, but I recall very little of that. I see only the sunlight, hear only the Arno rushing under the arches of the Ponte Vecchio, and recapture the wonderful realization that I was to hear Rosa once more that night.

The Politeama—now the Communale—had only recently opened, and I was not the only one to go there with lively curiosity and pleasure. Except for Rosa's secretary, I did not know a soul in the audience. But looking round, I was thrilled to recognize Richard Strauss sitting in a box— the first time I ever saw him—and felt sorrier than ever that Louise was not with me to share my curiosity and interest.

I knew Ponselle had been ill since last I had heard her, and I was acutely anxious lest she should not have recovered her full vocal powers. But from the first moment she opened her mouth, I knew I could sit back and enjoy myself. As everyone who has ever heard her will remember, she had the most extraordinary power of projecting a ravishing pianissimo that sounded exactly the same in the front row of the stalls as in the back row of the gallery. Quite early in the performance, she had occasion to do this, and I learned for all time what is really meant by the expression "you could have heard a pin drop."

The vast audience—most of them were hearing her for the first time—seemed literally to hold its breath, and except for that silken thread of perfectly supported sound, there was the deadest silence I have ever experienced. The place might have been empty—until the end of her first aria when, with the suddenness of a clap of thunder, the most extraordinary storm of applause broke out. I was so personally proud of her, I could have stood up and cheered. I probably did not yell, now that I come to think of it. The performance was held up for minutes on end. According to an austere note in the programme, encores were strictly forbidden, but the clapping and cheering went on and on. So did the opera, but no one could hear a thing.

Finally, Ponselle came forward to the footlights and made a rather helpless gesture to Vittorio Gui, the conductor. And, overborne by events, he allowed a repeat of the aria.

Not so many years ago, when I came face to face with Maestro Gui in the grounds of Glyndebourne, I told him that the first time I ever heard him conduct was for Ponselle in *La Vestale,* Florence, 1933.

He smiled musingly and said, "You were there on that great occasion? Do you remember the applause after her singing of the prayer, how they demanded an encore, and I wouldn't let them have it, and that finally I gave way? And do you know," went on Maestro Gui, "*why* I gave way?"

I admitted that, of course, I did not.

"Because I heard a pathetic voice behind me in the audience say, 'Who knows if we shall ever hear anything like that again?' And I thought, 'Who knows, indeed?' and I let them have it."

After that great performance, I went around backstage to

see Rosa and was received, literally, with open arms. I told her that most of her London adorers had stayed home from Covent Garden that night to listen to her broadcast—on a crystal set with a "whisker" in those days, of course—and she said in that "dark," rather melodramatic speaking voice of hers, "To think they were listening to me in London!"

She always loved London and the London audience, insisting that they were the most faithful and the most warmhearted of all audiences.

I spent an enchanting few days in Florence and, on my last evening, had a repeat performance of *Vestale*—my last Ponselle performance and the last time I was to see her or hear her voice for thirteen years. But I was not the only one to remember those two *Vestale*s as landmarks. Years after the war, when he had retired, the great de Sabata visited the United States and went to Baltimore to see Rosa, who by then lived some miles outside that city.

He told her that during that Florentine Musical May, he had been conducting orchestral concerts and unfortunately had engagements on both evenings of her performances. "However," he added, "I managed to attend the rehearsals for your performances, and I have come to tell you that I still regard them as among the greatest artistic experiences of my life."

Later in 1933, Louise and I went to Verona. But we had not been able to have our holidays when we wanted them, and we had to leave Verona just before the open-air festival of opera began. It was a bitter disappointment of course, the more so since *Les Huguenots* with the magnificent Rosa Raisa—the creator of the role of Turandot—and Lauri-Volpi, then in his prime, was to be performed.

However, our luck did not completely desert us on this occasion. On the very last day, we ran into Pinza, who had

just arrived for rehearsals of the opera—I think *Lohengrin*—
in which he was to appear. We were delighted to see each
other, and he asked very kindly if there were anything he
could do for us to make our holiday end well.

I said, "Yes, please! Could you possibly get us into the
dress rehearsal of *Les Huguenots* tonight?"

Pinza made no bones about it at all. He merely remarked
that all visitors had been strictly forbidden and added that he
would collect us from our hotel at a quarter to nine.

For the pleasure of Pinza's many admirers, let me record
that, at that time, he was just at the height of his stunningly
good looks. Very tanned and dressed in white flannels—with
more of what used to be called SA in our youth than I ever
saw in anyone else—he certainly made a gratifying escort in
the streets of Verona, and needless to say, Louise and I were
enchanted to have his company.

As our informal guide, he frequently paused in the street
to address us as he would a public meeting, while pointing
out some showplace or other. Invariably, he was recognized
by the enthralled Veronese, and a small crowd would gather
to share the lecture. Whereupon he would smile, push his
way good-humouredly through the admiring throng, and
we would continue our stroll, Louise and I scarcely able to
conceal our amusement and pleasure.

I once read an article about Pinza that claimed he had no
sense of humour. That simply was not so. He had a most
lively, rather individual sense of humour, and he was, without
exception, the finest mimic I ever knew. He had a wonderful
repertoire: Sir Thomas Beecham; himself and a London po-
liceman—taking the parts alternately—when he had parked
in the wrong place; a rather affected salesgirl who tried to
sell him some cultured pearls; many of his colleagues—who

all enjoyed his performances—and I understand he did me very well, but he would never do that one for me.

One of the nicest stories about his mimicry and fun was told to me by Elisabeth Rethberg. She was giving a concert in some American city one evening, under a manager who was also very anxious to represent Pinza. Pinza, who could dress like a tramp at times—I remember a shocking windjammer jacket in which he fancied himself very much.—drove Rethberg to the concert hall. The manager who so desired to have the famous basso on his list of artists obviously mistook Pinza for the chauffeur and proceeded to give him orders in a rather cavalier manner.

Without a moment's hesitation, Pinza immediately assumed the identity of a respectful chauffeur, touching his cap, calling the manager "sir" and generally enjoying himself very much in the role. Later explanations were, I understand, highly diverting. At any rate, diverting for Pinza.

To return to Verona—Pinza collected us punctually at a quarter to nine and triumphantly escorted us down to the great open-air arena where opera is performed in Verona for three or four intoxicating weeks of the summer. At the back entrance, however, we received the firmest check. The man on duty there insisted that it was quite, quite impossible to admit any member of the public. The rule was unbreakable.

Louise and I, like good, law-abiding Britishers, were about to retreat in reasonably good order when we received a peremptory sign from Pinza to remain where we were. He then took the objecting official by the shoulders in a friendly manner, shook him good-humouredly to and fro, poured a stream of talk upon him, pushed him dexterously a little farther inside the gateway and finally signalled to us to slip in.

This we did with all speed. And, with a final joke or two from Pinza, and a final protest or two from the man at the gate, we were safely inside the darkened arena. Taking us across the half-built stage, Pinza triumphantly installed us in the best seats in the place; there we stayed until the early hours of the morning, enjoying the long dress rehearsal— our first, I suppose, now that I come to think of it—of *Les Huguenots*.

What fun it was! The purple night sky of Verona overhead, pierced by a thousand golden stars, the gorgeous voices of Raisa and Lauri-Volpi to enchant our ears, and the gratifi- cation of having that operatic charmer, Ezio Pinza, for com- pany. It was, indeed, another night to remember.

Next day, we had to return to real life and our respective offices, and I don't think we enjoyed the descent to earth any more than most people would. Nineteen thirty-four opened with another Cook trip to the States. This time it was our brother Bill who departed.

Bill, who last appeared in these pages as a rather stolid little boy, had grown up very much in character. He seldom made a fuss about anything, but what he wanted, he got. And, un- like his sisters, he was naturally a sensible and steady saver, even when he had no special plan in view. Even when he was a schoolboy and I was earning my own living, I used to say, "Lend me a pound, Bill," and he could nearly always produce one. Consequently, when he made up his mind to do anything, he did not have to save painfully for it. He was already prepared.

I remember when he suddenly decided that he wanted to learn to play the piano, although he was almost grown-up and too old to study it seriously. Mother was not especially anxious to have a beginner practise on her grand piano and said so. Bill amiably agreed. But when she came home from shopping a few days later, an upright piano was being hauled through the space where the front bedroom window should have been. On horrified inquiry, she learned that Bill had gone out and bought a piano, which was now being installed in the attic, where he studied. As there was an awkward bend in the upper staircase, the men, cursing audibly, had had to remove the window and haul in the piano that way.

They remarked, finally, that they had got it up there, and they hoped to God they would never have to get it down again. They never did. It is still there, though no one plays on it now.

When Bill wanted to know something about the United States, he just bought a ticket and prepared to go. He bade us all a good-natured, undemonstrative farewell and departed. Dad, a little perplexed, though I suppose he was growing used to his children flitting about by now, accompanied him to Waterloo Station to see him off on the boat train. Conversation, he afterward reported, remained at a minimum, but just as the whistle blew, Bill leaned eagerly from the window. Touched by Bill's unusual show of feeling and thinking that at least they were going to exchange a manly handshake, Dad immediately offered his hand.

"No, no," cried Bill, leaning out still farther, "You've got my umbrella!" And as the train began to move, he unhooked the umbrella neatly from Dad's extended arm and departed for America, secure against rain and, we felt, against anything else he might encounter.

In America, he also had a wonderful time, heard Ponselle in *L'Africaine*—for which Louise and I found it hard to forgive him—and was very kindly treated by our operatic friends, particularly the Pinzas. Lita and Homer literally passed him in mid-ocean, en route for the last tour of the British Isles they ever made.

Lita gave a dramatic description of the incident. "I actually *saw* his ship," she declared, "and rushed to the side and waved and cried, 'Jim!'"

"I got it right," Homer added, grinning. "I cried 'Bill!'"

But even if they got the brothers a little confused, they had left their agents with all sorts of kind instructions for Bill's entertainment, and these were interpreted in the most generous way possible. On our side, we enjoyed every moment of Lita and Homer's tour. Because of the slightly improved finances of this short-story writer, we were able to go to several of their provincial concerts and even as far afield as Edinburgh. When we finally bade them goodbye at Waterloo Station, on a depressingly foggy February morning, we talked quite gaily about meeting again soon. Possibly they would come back, or we would dash over to New York—at any rate, we would meet somewhere.

We had no idea—how could we?—that 1934, an epoch-making year for so many, would close a chapter for Louise and me too. And open another that would be written in much more dramatic language. When I look back, it seems to me that 1934 was the year the bright lines from the past and the dark lines of the future met.

Our depression over the departure of Lita and Homer was considerably lightened by the thought of the approaching Opera Season, always guaranteed to raise our spirits.

In the list of artists, there appeared some from Vienna who had never visited us before. Under Clemens Krauss, Viorica Ursuleac and Alfred Jerger were to play their original parts of Arabella and Mandryka. Many years later, when we knew her very well, Ursuleac used to describe for us those thrilling first rehearsals of *Arabella* in Dresden. Apparently, they closed the opera house for several weeks, and while Strauss sat in the stalls, Ursuleac and Jerger worked out those two complex and fascinating characters under the personal guidance of Strauss himself. No wonder every Arabella and Mandryka afterward always seemed rather pale in comparison.

We were naturally interested in the newcomers, though at that time, not passionately so, and I looked forward to adding snapshots to my now quite extensive collection. One lunchtime, when several of us were sitting on our camp stools, someone remarked, "The tall, good-looking man by the stage door is Clemens Krauss, I think."

Privately, I thought he looked almost too good to be true—so completely the great stage figure that I felt cynically sure he would turn out to be merely someone's husband, or chance friend of one of the singers. Reluctant to waste any of my precious film, I said to Dennis, "Go and ask him for his autograph and let's see who he really is."

Dennis obligingly approached, and I went and looked over the conductor's shoulder while he silently, and a little sardonically, inscribed "Clemens Krauss" with a variety of twirls and twists, calculated almost to obscure the actual signature.

"Oh, it *is* Clemens Krauss!" I exclaimed rather too audibly and asked whether I might take his picture.

I was unaware then that Krauss did not take very kindly to these frivolous trimmings of his job. Indeed, it is recorded that, on one occasion when he was pestered by autograph-hunters after a performance of *Carmen,* he gravely wrote "Georges Bizet!" on several programmes, and then passed on, leaving astounded speculation in his wake.

On this occasion, he did say I might snap him, but I was so overcome by his somewhat impatient manner that, for the first time in my snapping career, I fumbled and jerked the camera as I clicked the shutter. However, I dared not ask for time for another attempt. I simply had to hope for the best. And, as someone exclaimed at that moment, "Here comes

Ursuleac!" I promptly added an amused and intrigued Ursuleac to my "bag."

When the film came out, the photograph of Ursuleac was
excellent, but I had blurred Krauss badly, to my great chagrin.
One did not have the chance of snapping a famous conductor every day, but I was not sure that my courage was up to
risking Krauss's impatience a second time. However, once
more at lunchtime, I learned that all of what we now call
"the Vienna lot" were in the opera house rehearsing. And
I decided that if Krauss and Ursuleac came out together, I
would show her her snapshot—artists nearly always liked
that—explain about the failure of Krauss's and ask to be allowed another chance.

In theory, this was excellent. In practice, the end of the
rehearsal was delayed beyond all reckoning. I was due back
at my office; indeed, the extreme limit of any reasonable
extension had already passed, and still they did not come.
Even now, I can't imagine how I dared to hang on. But—I
lay claim to only one premonition in all this story—as I sat
there, fuming, on my camp stool, I *knew* suddenly that I
would be sorry all my life if I went away now.

And my one premonition proved correct.

Finally, at an impossibly late hour, they came out together
and I rushed up to Ursuleac to show her her picture. She was
charmed and made Krauss examine it too. He gave it what
we used to call afterward his "directorial approval," and so I
ventured to explain about the spoiled photograph and asked
if I might snap him again.

He puffed at one of his famous cigars, looked genuinely
amused and, apparently liking the unfamiliar word, said,
"All right. Snap me again, snap me again."

Thus encouraged, I even asked him to come and stand in

a better light, and as an amused Ursuleac came to watch the proceedings, I asked, "Shall I take you together?"

She hesitated. But Krauss said immediately, "Yes. Take us together!" And so I took what was to be the most important of all our snapshot collection—Krauss and Ursuleac outside Covent Garden in 1934.

It was a superb success. I had it enlarged, one copy for Louise and me, and one for Krauss. Or rather, as it turned out afterwards, for Ursuleac, because by the time the enlargements were ready, Krauss had already returned to Vienna.

When Ursuleac came past the queue one day, I gave her one enlargement and asked her to sign the other for us. This she did. When I asked about the possibility of obtaining Krauss's signature too, she shook her head regretfully and said, "He has gone to Vienna."

This was disappointing. But there was one more chance. We had been toying with the idea of spending our summer holiday in Salzburg. For one thing, the programme that year was to include the first performance of a new production of *Don Giovanni,* under Bruno Walter and with, as is now operatic history, Pinza in the role of the Don. In addition, we knew that Strauss's *Egyptian Helen—Die Aegyptische Helena—* was to be given and guessed that Ursuleac would have the title role. We were already enthralled by her special Strauss artistry, though it was not until later that we were to realize the full measure of its magnificence.

I asked if she were going to Salzburg that year. And when she said, "Oh, yes—" and looked enquiring, I said impulsively, "Then we will come too."

"You come to Salzburg?" She gave that her smiling approval. "Then you can bring the picture and Mr. Krauss shall—shall write."

She meant "sign," but her meaning was clear enough, so

I gave her a hug, which seemed to astonish but please her, and it was arranged.

The Italian part of our season that year was to include the much discussed *Cenerentola*. A tremendous amount of preparation had gone into this and there had been some inevitable delays. Consequently, it was not to make its appearance until the last week of the season. Two performances were to be given—on the Wednesday and on the last night, Friday.

Pinza was, of course, already in London, taking other roles and enjoying, as he always enjoyed, the amusements and absurdities of the queue. He never tired of our "system," which he used to explain to the other singers with great care and in some detail. As he had been so extremely kind, first to us in Verona and then to Bill in New York, we had, after some thought, asked him if he would like to come home and meet the rest of the family. I explained anxiously that we were a perfectly ordinary suburban family, but that if it would please him to come, everyone would be very happy to see him.

To our gratified surprise, his reply was unequivocal.

"I should simply love to come," declared Pinza, whose English had improved somewhat over the years. And so it was arranged that he should come on the Thursday evening, in between the two *Cenerentola* performances.

On the Wednesday before, we had all planted our camp stools early, and the only thing that disturbed us was the rumour that Borgioli was ill. Because the work was so seldom given in those days, the tenor role in *Cenerentola* was not one that could easily be handed over to anyone else. Literally no one else in London knew it. So if Borgioli's illness were serious, the performance itself was threatened.

Concurrently with this rumour ran another most interesting piece of operatic gossip. Elisabeth Rethberg—whose voice had been described by no less than Toscanini as the most beautiful in the world—was said to be in London on a private visit. She had not sung at Covent Garden since 1925, and her absence had long and often been lamented. Now, some of us hoped that she might at least be in the house for such an interesting occasion as the first *Cenerentola.*

In the early evening of that memorable Wednesday, when we all began to gather for the performance, the incredible report went around that the performance had been cancelled. Bergioli's cold had taken too serious a turn for him to be permitted to sing.

But, as I afterward heard the story, the management, at their wits' end for a substitute performance that would lessen the very natural disappointment, had learned that the famous Rethberg was in London. She was approached with a request to help them out of their difficulty and sing that night.

She asked what they could put on at a moment's notice, and they suggested *La Boheme,* as they had the cast and scenery for that immediately available.

It was two years since she has last sung Mimi, but she said, "Give me a couple of hours to run over the part and I'll do it." And so, as we returned to the queue that evening, we were met by the exciting announcement that though *Cenerentola* had had to be postponed and could be given only once, Elisabeth Rethberg was to be heard at Covent Garden once more.

As the time for opening the doors drew near, the queue seethed with excitement. The artists began to arrive, and presently the taxi drove past the queue—with both Rethberg and Pinza in it. Pinza beckoned to me peremptorily from the window, and puzzled but intrigued, I ran down to the stage door.

Rethberg went straight in, but Pinza paused to ask, with

devastating simplicity, "Will it be all right if I bring Miss Rethberg with me tomorrow night?"

Stifling the shriek of astonished delight to which I think most people will agree I was entitled, I managed to say calmly that it would be quite all right, but did he think she would care to come?

"Yes," Pinza asserted confidently. "She would like to come. Write her a note, inviting her."

I promised dazedly to do so and returned to my surprised and curious family. And—heaven forgive me for the bit of showing off—I said to Mother, in the clearest and most car-rying voice I could achieve, "Pinza wants to know if it will be all right if he brings Rethberg with him tomorrow eve-ning."

"Perfectly all right," replied Mother, acting up beautifully. And we became the centre of interested gossip and enquiry.

What fun that *Boheme* performance was!

Rethberg was in superb voice—that radiant, almost sil-very voice that also had a warmth one does not usually as-sociate with a silver tone. Everyone in the cast was in the sort of riotous mood of enjoyment that usually belongs more to an amateur performance than a professional one. That is to say, the whole thing had been thrown on, with everyone determined to save the day if possible. And I have seldom, if ever, seen the four Bohemians enjoy themselves with such genuine relish.

During one of the intervals, I rushed across the road to the sandwich shop in Floral Street and begged the loan of some writing paper. They supplied me with some in a fierce vio-let shade, and on this I wrote a note to Madame Rethberg, inviting her out to the suburbs to meet a family she could never have heard of before that evening.

It would be difficult to describe the sensations with which

Louise and I went to our local station the next evening to
meet Pinza, of whom we were still slightly in awe, and Rethberg, who was to us an unknown celebrity on a red-label
gramophone record. But so naïve were we still that we had
instructed them to come by train—in the homegoing rush
hour, now I come to think of it!—and we *walked* them the
short distance from the station to our house.

Feeling very nervous, we welcomed the star of the previous evening and made the immediate and reassuring discovery that she was at least as shy as we were. As we went
out of the station together, I said to her, "You do realize that
we're taking you to the most ordinary and homely household, don't you?"

To which she replied, "But that's exactly what I like best."
And it was.

From the moment she stepped over our threshold, Elisabeth became one of us. I think Mother really loved her best
of all our stars. For one thing, she came to know her best.
But Elisabeth was, in any case, as my mother used to say, "the
sort of person anyone would like for a daughter."

It is some years now since Louise and I have seen her, because she lives very quietly in retirement, looked after de-
votedly by her wonderful husband, George Cehanovsky. But
at the time, she was one of the leading figures of the international opera world, and yet one of the kindest, most ap-
proachable people it is possible to imagine.

She was unpretentious to the last degree, had a charming
sense of humour, the prettiest speaking voice I ever heard
and the most exquisite manners. These last were not put on.
They came straight from her heart and her special awareness of the other person's needs and feelings. Sometimes, I
think, she was almost too sensitively aware of others, so that

only her supreme gifts could have taken her to the top of the tough profession in which she lived her life.

How charming and amusing she and Pinza were that evening! We were simply enthralled with them both. At close quarters, the genuine stars give a curious impression of over-life-sized personalities. It is, of course, customary to pretend that operatic stars are unintelligent or objectionable or both. Some of them may be; I don't know. But those I have known intimately have all had considerable and varied charm, and without exception, one could see *why* they had become world figures.

Didn't someone once ask Noel Coward, "What must one do to be a star?" And he replied, "Shine."

That is the answer. They have star quality, that indefinable gift that, combined with great talent and hard work, will produce something that lifts them above the common run, in a way that fascinates all but the most ungenerous observer.

Of course, they have their weaknesses. Living on their nerves and at concert pitch, they are sometimes unreasonable and inexplicable. But, good heavens, who should grudge them a few foibles when they also have the gifts that set them apart in other ways? The really unbearable performers are the mediocrities who assume airs and peculiarities—and can, incidentally, always tell you what is wrong with the really great.

Anyway, if ever two people determined to make an evening memorable, they were Pinza and Rethberg on that never-to-be-forgotten occasion when the only people they had to gratify were an unimportant family who could give them little but affection and admiration.

The opera season of 1934 ended, so far as we were concerned, in a blaze of glory—the final glow being provided by the superb Conchita in the long-awaited *Cenerentola* on the last night.

We were not expecting any excitements before our projected trip to Salzburg at the end of July. But, early in the
month, I received a telegram from Rethberg—now somewhere on the Continent—saying that she was going to be in
London to sing at a private party and would I get in touch
with her at her hotel?

I did so more than willingly and found that she had been
asked to sing at an evening party given by Lady Ludlow at
Bath House—now, alas, taken down. Rethberg had never
before agreed to take an engagement of this kind, but for
once, she was breaking her rule.

The Bath House musical parties were one of the few affairs left of almost Edwardian magnificence, frequently, as on
this occasion, attended by royalty, and they still maintained a
degree of formality and grandeur that savoured of pre-1914
days. Elisabeth's proposal, arising from a disregard of cere-
mony learned in America, was that I should accompany her.

I explained, with the utmost regret, that it was quite impossible that I should turn up uninvited at such a gathering. But, not to be gainsaid, Elisabeth asked, "Well, will
you come as my secretary? Carry my music, and that sort
of thing?"

Naturally, I agreed with an eagerness equal to my previous degree of regret and undertook to play my role with becoming self-effacement and—I hoped—efficiency.

I presume mine are probably the only Woolworth beads
that ever attended a Bath House reception. But they looked
reasonably like jade—or so I thought—and they did match
my dress. Long black gloves completed what I felt was a toi-
lette adequate to the occasion. And thus attired—and clasping
an armful of music—I accompanied the gorgeously gowned
Elisabeth, in her wonderful "picture" dress of black tulle.

During the concert, I remained in Elisabeth's improvised

dressing room, but was able to hear everything from the wings, and later I had the opportunity to stroll through the rooms and examine some of the treasures of Bath House. In the intervals, Elisabeth and I had an opportunity for talk. Afterward, I accompanied her back to her hotel and stayed until the small hours of the morning. So we laid the foundation of what was to be a lifelong friendship.

By the time I left, we had arranged that she too should come to Salzburg—from Switzerland, where she had a summer home—and that we should therefore be meeting again in a few weeks' time.

Before then, however—on July 24, to be precise—there occurred the first international event whose repercussions deeply affected our private affairs. Dolfuss, the Austrian Chancellor, was murdered.

CHAPTER SIX

I blush now to think how ignorant we were of the significance of this event. Apart from being vaguely shocked by the way foreigners behaved toward each other, we were concerned with only one aspect of the murder: Would it put a stop to our holiday in Salzburg?

For a day or two, the decision hung in the balance. Then we learned that that frontier between Germany and Austria, which had been closed for an anxious few days, had been opened once more for tourists, and our holiday was safe.

We travelled through Germany by night—third class and sitting upright of course—and I remember the concern of the German family in our compartment when they heard we were going to Salzburg. The father, who was a bit of a *besserwisser*—a know-it-all—assured us that we could not possibly cross the border, that Austria was in a lamentable state, etcetera, etcetera. We were completely unmoved, merely reiterating that "the man at Cooks" had said it would be all right, so it *would* be all right. For this was how we thought in those days—all of us, I think. The British knew best and that was that.

When we arrived in Munich, everything seemed outwardly normal. And, too happy and too ignorant to hear the rumbles of the coming storm, we blithely took that well-known journey from Munich to Salzburg for the first time in our lives.

This was Salzburg before the ghastly red of the swastika flags threw a lurid reflection on the white walls, and we were fascinated by it. Already, of course, the shadows were falling, though people like ourselves were largely unaware of it. Already, the dreadful fungus that was to flower in the centre of Europe was beginning to swell and give out a faint, sickly, premonitory aroma of evil.

But for us that summer, Salzburg was the scene of a glorious feast of music. We were intoxicated by the beauty of the fortress city about the rushing Salzach, entranced to realize that one could gaze alternately at opera stars and mountain scenery and take rapturous pleasure in both. Above all, it was extraordinarily pleasant to have a bowing acquaintance with more than one of these same stars and, in the case of the sensational Don Giovanni himself, to know him well.

Claudia and her mother were also in the city and we met our little friend once more. She was a dear child, spoke astonishingly good English and was excellent company. She referred to my watch as my "little time" and openly expressed the hope that someone would give her a little time for her birthday, which was approaching.

No one who was present at the first *Don Giovanni* that year is ever like to forget it, but I should like to recall a few of its glories for those who were not.

The part of Giovanni is, of course, very often sung by a baritone and Pinza was essentially a basso. But, by the kind of dispensation of providence, he also possessed those vital few notes at the top of his range that are necessary; therefore the role was within his vocal compass and the colour of the voice was the same as that of the singer for whom Giovanni was written. As for his acting, I suppose no one before or since has ever been better qualified to play the part. Not only was he, by common knowledge, very much of a Don Giovanni in private life, he had the ineffable charm, good humour and vitality to carry it off.

The last scene in this masterly production was unforgettable. Giovanni was alone, except for Leporello, and when the statue of the dead Commandatore finally appeared, he did not stump in at ground level preceded by what usually looks like clouds of detergent. The door at the top of a double curving flight of stairs flew open and there was the ghastly, over-life-sized figure dominating the whole scene. At the moment when he bade Giovanni give him his hand, Pinza used to hesitate for a second, pressing back against one of the apparently massive pillars as though, in that moment of supernatural horror, even he felt the need of something solid at his back. Then, with a gesture of bravado, he sprang up the flight of steps and gave his hand.

In the horrifying moments that succeeded that handclasp, as Giovanni's years seemed to fall from him, in the extremity of danger beyond anything he had ever courted. Then, with a last despairing wrench, he tore his hand away and went springing down the steps, as though momentarily believing that the worst was over. But everywhere he set his foot, flames sprang up. In horror, he flung himself against one of the pillars, which swayed and collapsed. He seized the end of the table and the whole thing gave way, precipitating china and glass in one terrifying crash to the floor. Then, as he rushed behind the table, there was a final and fearful burst of flame, and Giovanni disappeared.

I have never seen that scene equalled for horror and drama in any other production. It was an instantaneous and tremendous success with a great personal triumph for Pinza. In addition to the performances he gave at the Metropolitan and Covent Garden, he repeated that role each year at Salzburg up to the outbreak of war.

After that great performance, we went with the Pinzas to have supper at their hotel. There is no use pretending that the domestic situation was a happy one, for the first Mrs. Pinza was, to put it mildly, a difficult person. But the situation did provoke a rather piquant scene in the hotel dining room.

Giannini was also having supper there, as were the Lazzaris—he had sung the Leporello. At a moment of gathering domestic storm, Giannini—in her beautiful rich soprano voice—suddenly began to sing "Who's Afraid of the Big Bad Wolf?" the catch-song that was sweeping the world at that moment. Pinza immediately took it up from our table, and Lazzari provided a sort of ground bass. Against their Anna, Giovanni, and Leporello earlier in the evening, it was startling, to say the least.

In contrast to all this, however, we had not forgotten that we had a foot—or, at least, a toehold—in the other operatic camp. We had boldly recalled ourselves to Ursuleac when she was strolling in the promenade at the Festspielhaus one evening. Krauss was conducting, but she was not singing that evening. She remembered us immediately, seized the photograph that we proffered, and cried, "I know! You want Mr. Krauss to write."

We agreed this was exactly what we wanted. She promised to obtain the signature and told us to collect the photograph from the box office in a few days' time.

This we did. On our last day, we met her again, this time walking along the bank of the Salzach in the direction of Stein Lechner. We ventured to stop and thank her and to ask when we were likely to hear her again.

She smiled and summoned up enough English to say, "You must come to Vienna." She evidently considered this an im-probable sort of journey for us—not knowing that even New York was not too far away when we really got going. And she looked both amused and taken aback when we replied airily, "All right. We'll come to Vienna."

At this she really scraped the bottom of her English bar-rel for a suitable reply and came up very charmingly with, "Eef you come to Vienna you must—you must *ring me up*."

We promised we would and finally went back to England feeling that new operatic horizons were opening.

Soon after our return home, I had a letter from Elisabeth Rethberg. She explained that she had not been able to come to Salzburg, partly because of private affairs and partly be-cause the possible dangers of such a visit had been somewhat exaggerated in her part of the world. She added, however, that she was singing for the radio in Amsterdam at the end of September and asked me to come over and meet her there.

As it was a weekend, I could, by flying both ways, just manage it without taking any more leave from the office. Louise and I still had one week's leave remaining, and we were already considering going to Vienna before the end of the year, if funds held out, so we were anxious to keep that week intact.

I flew to Amsterdam, where Elisabeth joined me. She came, I imagine, from Dresden where her family lived. She was obviously worried and angry at the events developing in Germany and told me she never intended to sing there again. At least, not until the Hitler regime ended. On the basis of my still rather vague concept of what was happening, I expressed a somewhat academic interest and sympathy. But I am afraid my principal concern was that she should sing where *we* could hear her.

We had a delightful weekend together, and for the first time, I went to a broadcasting studio and experienced the fun of being the only "audience" allowed in. She sang Marguerite's two airs from *Faust* and, without any stage props, reduced me unexpectedly to tears. I never actually heard her in the part, but Pinza used to say that he thought it was in some ways her finest role, that she was without peer in it.

While in Amsterdam, I discovered that there was to be a Strauss Festival Week there early in December, which would include two performances of *Arabella*. The composer was to conduct and Ursuleac was to sing the name-part. For the Sunday concert, Strauss would conduct the first half and Mengelberg the second, with Ursuleac as soloist.

This festival, I realized immediately, would be a venture more in keeping with the state of our finances than a lightning trip to Vienna, and I enlisted Elisabeth's help to find out all particulars about the Strauss week before returning to England.—One of the loveliest things about Elisabeth was that she never minded one being thrilled about other artists. In fact, when I first told her the story of our saving up to go to America to hear Galli-Curci, she exclaimed, "I could love you for that alone!"

On my return home, Louise agreed that a Strauss week in Amsterdam would be a delightful way of spending the remainder of our leave allowance, and after a careful count of our resources, we decided we could just do it. Happy chain of coincidences—or were they only coincidences?—that led to our making just that particular visit at that particular time.

It was the first time we had heard Strauss himself conduct,

and we were, like everyone else before us I suppose, indescribably impressed by the extraordinary economy of gesture
with which he secured his effects. Nowadays, of course, one
looks back on him as the last of a great line of composers,
but we should also remember that he was one of the great
conductors of his age.

Because of the good offices of Ursuleac's agent, we were
allowed to go to the dress rehearsal, so in the end, we really
had three *Arabellas* under the conductorship of the composer
and with his original Arabella and Mandryka.

Each time, we noticed a distinguished-looking, white-
haired lady in the audience whom we had seen once or twice
with Krauss and Ursuleac in Salzburg. But we took no notice of her than to be mildly annoyed that we were not the
only ones who had the distinction of turning up in different countries for different Ursuleac performances! However,
when we went around backstage to see Ursuleac, the white-
haired lady was introduced to us as Madame Mayer-Lismann,
the official lecturer of the Salzburg Festival.

Although from Frankfurt-am-Main, she spoke excellent
English, and we were all very polite to each other. But when
we got outside, Louise said, "You remember. We noticed the
advertisement of her lectures on the Salzburg programmes
and decided we didn't want *them*. These people with double-barrelled names are never any good. A lot of talk, when
what one really wants is the performance."

I'm sorry to say that I heartily agreed.

The concert—the last of the performances—was on Sunday afternoon, and I remember that Ursuleac sang the three
wonderful songs that Strauss had orchestrated especially for
her: "Frühlingsfeir," "Dein Auge" and "Cäcilie." In the second half of the programme, she sang the finale to *Salome*.

It was not a role she ever sang on the stage, but this concert performance was quite splendid.

She was leaving Amsterdam that night, and having obtained permission to see her off, we presented ourselves at the station. To our chagrin and annoyance, there was the woman with the double-barrelled name! Louise and I accepted the situation with reasonably good grace, but each knew the other was thinking the same thing—that we had wanted Ursuleac to ourselves this time.

And then a strange thing happened. Ursuleac took us by the arm and, with an earnestness and gravity that we could not quite understand, explained that this was a great personal friend of hers who was going to England for the first time to give a couple of music lectures. Would we please look after her?

We had no idea why she needed looking after. She looked much better able to do it than we did. But of course, we were immensely touched and gratified and—all minor annoyances forgotten—promised earnestly that we would certainly look after her.

In my mind's eye, I still see the scene on the platform of Amsterdam station as Ursuleac turned to her companion and said, in a tone of sombre satisfaction, "Now you will be all right."

We remembered that scene again and again in the years that followed. Ursuleac's confident, "Now you will be all right," was to extend our responsibility far beyond Mitia Mayer-Lismann and her family. For, though we did not know it then, our first refugee had been commended to our care.

As soon as Mitia arrived in England, we found that most of our preconceived notions about her were either inaccurate or absurd. To begin with, she was the most utterly charming person, and double-barrelled name or no, her lectures were enchanting. Indeed, much of our really deep appreciation of the German school of opera dates from the time when we knew Mitia and, later, her daughter Elsa.

On this first occasion, we took her on an informal sight-seeing tour to all the "right" places, and she asked—as she told us long afterward—what she believed to be the right and intelligent questions. In Westminster Abbey, she gravely enquired whether this was a Protestant or Catholic church, and when we reached St. Paul's, she asked the same question.

I thought, "Maybe we had better ask which *she* is before we get any farther." And so, under the dome of St. Paul's, I politely enquired whether she was Protestant or Catholic.

"I?" Mitia turned a surprised glance upon us. "I am Jewish. Didn't you know?"

I laughed and said no, we hadn't even thought about it, and that, for our part, we were not violently anything, but called ourselves Christian and tried to do our best.

We didn't know—imagine! In these days we didn't *know* that to be Jewish and to come from Frankfurt-am-Main in Germany already had the seeds of tragedy in it.

However, as our friendship developed during her short stay in England, we began to see things more clearly and to see them, to our lasting benefit, through the eyes of an ordinary devoted family like ourselves. This was one of the most heaven-sent things that ever happened to us. By the time the full horror of what was happening in Germany, and later in Austria, reached the newspapers, the whole thing had become almost too fantastic for the ordinary mind to take in. It took a war to make people understand what was happening in peacetime, and to tell the truth, very many never understood it.

But our understanding of the problem grew quite naturally. We were ignorant and well meaning when we first agreed to "look after" Mitia. The problem was not at first presented to us in the lurid colours of melodrama. It had not yet become melodrama for more than a comparative few.

To us, the case of the Mayer-Lismanns was curious and shocking, but not incredible. It seemed that, because they were of Jewish blood, it would be wise for them to start making plans to leave their country. According to Mitia's husband, who was more far-seeing than most, the time was rapidly approaching when Germany would be an impossible country for them to live in.

We were shocked, but we did what I suppose most people would have done. I asked: Where did they hope to go? What had they to offer in the work markets of the world? And, finally, what could we do to help? It was all what I can only describe as un-urgent to us in those early days. We did little more than discuss plans and suggestions during that first visit. But we had definitely set our hand to the plough of practical assistance, and we did not look back until the war stopped us.

After Mitia had returned to Germany, her affairs, though by no means forgotten by us, retreated somewhat into the backs of our minds. For one thing, the Opera Season was looming up on the horizon once more. That year at Covent Garden saw a very fine revival of *Prince Igor,* and Rethberg came over to play, among other roles, that of Yaroslavna. It was Silver Jubilee Year, and there was a very festive atmosphere everywhere. On Jubilee Day itself, after we had managed to see the procession, we went to the opera, and I remember so well how the old king's address to us was broadcast through the house.

It was said that no one was more surprised than George V himself at the overwhelming warmth and love with which he was greeted during the day. In consequence, he scrapped the formal speech he had been going to make and spoke al-

most extempore. I know as he began, "My very dear people," we all looked at each other and swallowed lumps in our
throats. It was an unforgettable moment, and I'm glad we
experienced it in Covent Garden.

That season saw our first "star-cum-gallery" party. I had
explained to Pinza and Elisabeth that their most ardent admirers and staunchest supporters were really to be found
in the gallery queue—an opinion with which they heartily concurred—and that, while Louise and I were the envy
of our gallery associates because we knew them personally,
we thought there was really no reason why the fun should
stop there. If I gave a party for certain members of the gallery, would they agree to come and be the guests of honour?

The idea amused, pleased and slightly intimidated them,
but in the end, their answer was yes. So Louise and I gave
the first of our gallery or "gramophone circle" parties. The
significance of the latter term is that, during the ten months
of opera-less starvation, some of us with gramophones and
good collections of records banded together to give parties periodically. In this way, we kept in touch, exchanged
opera views and gossip and bridged the long gap from one
Grand Season to another. Of course we saw each other with
reasonable frequency at the Old Vic—later Sadler's Wells.
English performances, which were often of a very high standard indeed.

The Pinza-Rethberg party was much the most ambitious
event we had undertaken, and our nervous anxiety beforehand was great.

But we need not have worried. Rethberg was a little shy,
but proved a marvellous hand with those who were more
so. And Pinza, who simply did not know the word shy and
was never able to understand any attempt to enlighten him,
took everything in hand. He told us operatic anecdotes, al-

lowed us to put on his records so that he "could tell us what was wrong with them," and was even persuaded to do a few of his famous imitations.

The party was an unqualified success, not only with us, but with our distinguished visitors too. The final proof was that, when I met Pinza at the airport on his return to London the following year, his first demand was, "Can we have another gramophone party?"

It is all nearly forty years ago now—I can hardly believe it—but the fact is that, even now, when we have the occasional "star" party, there are still several in attendance who came to that first occasion in 1935.

During 1935, we made two of our longest and closest friendships—with Nesta and Jane Guthrie. And since they play a considerable part in the later pages of this book, a word on them now will not be out of season. Like ourselves, they were sisters with only a few years dividing them, and like ourselves, they were born romantics with a passionate interest in all things operatic. Our introduction to them was by way of the gallery queue and had an element of pure comedy in it.

We knew them quite well by sight: during the 1934 season, I had seen one of them "snapping" a soprano rival of Ursuleac's. Drawing what I believed to be a very shrewd conclusion from this, I said to Louise, "We'll avoid those two. We don't want any unnecessary disputes, and they've obviously got all the wrong ideas." Louise agreed.

One evening during the following winter, however, we found them sitting very near us at a Queen's Hall concert. It was always almost a physical impossibility to ignore a known Covent Garden-ite during the long winter of our discontent, which stretched from one Grand Season to the next. So we exchanged rather remote smiles with each other and presently, in the interval, entered into wary conversation.

As it happened, I had some Ursuleac photographs with me, and feeling, I suppose, in an aggressive mood, I flourished them under the Guthrie noses and stated provocatively, "We thought Ursuleac simply magnificent."

Like magic, their reserved air melted, and they cried, "So did we! Oh, isn't it wonderful when you find someone who shares the same enthusiasm?"

Oh, *that,* they assured us, was just one photograph among many. It had no significance for them. And from that moment, we never looked back. Nesta and Jane were firmly swept into our orbit, becoming our closest friends and confidantes. Among other things, they were immensely interested in any modest literary successes I might achieve—and this brings me to the incident that made 1935 personally important to me.

Sometime during that year, Miss Taft called me into her office and said, "You know, dear, what we need is a really strong serial. And I believe you could write it. Why don't you try?"

A "strong" serial in my type of literature, in case anyone doesn't know, is where you have such an exciting or provocative scene before "To be continued" that everyone buys it next week to see what really happened to the girl.

Why didn't I try? As usual, I was hard up, for our appetite for foreign travel was beginning to grow alarmingly, and I knew how handsomely successful serial writers were rewarded. So I went home, and in penny Woolworth notebooks—they *were* a penny then!—I wrote the first three instalments of my first romantic serial, *Wife to Christopher.*

When I typed these and took them back to Miss Taft, her mood had changed slightly, and she was not quite sure that a "sweet" serial would not suit our purpose better. But she said the instalments were good so I had better finish the story. I went to work again.

It took me a long time to write that first one. But I had a wonderful time over it. I cried over all the best bits myself, and when it all came out right in the end, I could hardly believe it. And in the end, she bought it. I was never so excited in my life. For one thing, I had never seen so much money in my life.

The next great problem was—what was I going to call myself? When you first write my kind of book you are self-conscious about it, and you think, "I wouldn't like the people up the road to think I wrote that scene in chapter seven." So I decided I would change my name and never tell anyone about my writing. I chose Mother's first name, Mary, and the maiden name of Dad's mother, which was Burchell. Thus my writing name, Mary Burchell, was born.

I need hardly add that, when the story came out, I was so pleased with myself I told everybody. I might just as well have called myself Ida Cook. But it is quite a good trick to practise on yourself in the beginning. Later, you become completely hardened. You don't even mind when people come up to you—as they frequently do—and say, "Of course, I don't read *your* sort of stuff."

It used to wound me very much when I was young. But now I don't mind a bit. I just look them in the eye and say, "No? And you can't write it either, can you?" Then they fade away.

Wife to Christopher appeared as a new serial, either late in 1935 or early in 1936. And almost immediately after its appearance, the fiction editor of the firm sent for me and informed me that he thought the story would make a good romantic novel. There were at least three firms he thought might be interested, and he would give me the pros and cons so that I could decide which we should try first.

I chose Mills & Boon. And in nearly forty years, I have never had reason to be anything but thankful from the bottom of my heart for that decision.

Wife to Christopher was sent along to Charles Boon—the father of the men I now work for. And in a week's time— think of that in these days when publishers take nine months to tell you they don't want the thing—back came the answer: It was highly approved, and the firm would accept it, provided I would sign a contract giving them the first refusal of my next two.

Just as I had never meant to tell anyone I had written a book, so I had never visualized myself writing more than one. But I said, "Of course!" and went along to sign my first contract.

I was so bemused and excited that I would have signed anything. When Mr. Boon handed me the contract, I reached for a pen immediately.

"No, no!" he said firmly. "You must never sign anything like that. You take that contract home and show it to your father, and if he says you can sign it, you can."

How's that for the wicked old world of publishing? No wonder I knew from that moment that I was in safe hands.

While *Christopher* was going to press for book publication, I thought perhaps it was time to start on that problematical second book. My efforts resulted in *Call and I'll Come,* and this was chosen by one of our distinctly less highbrow daily papers as "the best romantic book of the month."

That, of course, gave me publicity, which resulted in requests for serials and a general broadening and brightening of my literary and financial horizons.

I remember now how Louise and I, in company with

Nesta and Jane, used to walk miles discussing the extraordinary phenomenon of my increasing income and deciding
on the purposes to which it should be put. Cars and fur coats
came under rapid review, as well as trips to America or to
Europe. We even discussed Louise's possible retirement from
the office. Indeed, we spent thousands in our imagination—
on the strength of two books and—I believe—an advance
of thirty pounds.

But our guardian angels must indeed have been looking
over our shoulders at that time. Before we had any chance
to alter our way of living or get into the habit of spending
what seemed to us then great sums, the full horror of what
was happening in Europe finally, and for all time, came
home to us.

CHAPTER SEVEN

We had kept in close touch with the Mayer-Lismanns, and it was at their home in Frankfurt that we really came to know Krauss and Ursuleac well. It was also through them that it became clearer and clearer to us that there were hundreds of thousands who were trying to escape from an ever-pursuing and ever-deepening horror of persecution.

It is perfectly true that the Nuremberg Laws—which, broadly speaking, deprived all Jews living in Germany of any rights as human beings at all—were not strictly applied in all areas during those earlier years. The situation differed very much from city to city and district to district. But these laws were on the books and *could* be applied at any time, depending on the outlook or mood of any official in power. It was from 1938 onward that the tempo quickened horribly and the Jewish population came to realize that death was encircling them, constantly tighter and tighter, that their one chance of life was to escape somewhere, anywhere, into the outside world. But that was possible only if help, usually financial help, were forthcoming from outside.

And so, at the very moment when I was making big money for the first time in my life, we were presented with this terrible need. It practically never happens that way. It was much the most romantic thing that ever happened to us. Usually one either has the money and doesn't see the need, or one sees the need and has not the money. If we had always had the money we might not have thought we had anything to spare. But I still had never handled more than five pounds a week in my life, and suddenly my income was rising to five hundred, eight hundred, a thousand a year: big money then.

I was intoxicated by the sight. And—terrible, moving and overwhelming thought—I could save life with it. Even now, I can hardly think of it without tears.

Gone were the days of light-hearted pleasure trips, the days when our greatest anxiety was whether office leave and strained finances would permit our going to hear opera when and where we liked. From now until the day war broke out, we lived with an ever-deepening sense of responsibility toward alleviating the growing horror and misery, which we had, by a strange combination of circumstances, come to understand almost as though it were our own problem.

In order to place the picture in its right perspective, it might be well to give a résumé of historical, as distinct from personal, events.

Early in 1936, Hitler remilitarised the Rhine Valley, administering the first shock, which even the most casual observer in other countries could not entirely ignore. But, as always after these unwelcome sensations, the degree of shock lessened and explanations and justifications were found that quietened some anxieties. Hitler offered a twenty-five years' peace pact—having torn up the previous one—and presently people resumed their normal lives. They bought hats, went to the films, took themselves off on foreign holidays.

"Nine Days in the Rhineland—Ten Guineas" as announced by Thomas Cook. Yes, that is what it was then!

All that the ordinary man in the street thought about this was that "that man" was at it again and that Germany seemed likely to be a perpetual pain in the neck to those who wanted a quiet life. The Nuremberg Laws was a vague term to most people, very imperfectly understood—except for the fact that they were something Hitler had thought up against the Jews. And, if the Jews were being put in their place in Germany, some people thought it was not a bad thing.

Early in 1938, Austria was invaded and absorbed, willy-nilly, into the German Reich. That was so much more difficult to explain away than the remilitarisation of the Rhine, even if no one could quite agree about how much had been "willy" and how much "nilly." The degree of shock and uneasiness this event occasioned was never entirely ignored again. But it must be remembered that there was no television in those days and, for good or ill, no way of forcing a picturized version of the whole thing right into one's home.

In September, 1938, there flared up the menace to Czecho-Slovakia. We trembled on the brink of war, and for the first time, many people saw things for what they were. With the sacrifice of vital parts of Czecho-Slovakia, Hitler was bought off again, although anyone with the smallest pretension to intelligence knew by now that all that had been bought was time.

In November, 1938, the first great concerted drive against the Jews began. This was sparked off by an event in Paris: a young German Jew shot an official at the German embassy. It was said that his parents had been ill-treated by the Gestapo, that his mind became unhinged and that he had shot the first German official he saw. Another story, told to us in Germany, was that the whole thing was a put-up job to inflame feelings against the Jews. I doubt if the real truth will ever be known now. But, for the purposes of history, it hardly matters. True or false, this incident signalled the launching of the greatest pogroms in history. From that day, and for years to come, wave after wave of murder washed in a ghastly tide across Europe, until something like six million unfortunates had perished.

On the terrible ninth and tenth of November, 1938, throughout Germany and Austria and the borders of Czecho-Slovakia—now under German domination—the order went forth that every male Jew between the ages of eighteen and sixty was to be rounded up and sent to a concentration camp. And with very few exceptions, this came to pass, in circumstances of the most horrible brutality.

After a while, a shocked world heard that some of them had been released. That was true. Certain age groups and certain people who had served in the First World War were released. What was not generally understood was that they were released on one condition: that they signed an undertaking to be out of the country within eight weeks. They might take with them something under a pound in actual cash and a varying proportion—according to the mood of the official who handled their case—of their goods.

Every one of the unfortunate souls signed. Not a quarter per cent had the slightest hope of ever going anywhere. There *was* nowhere for them in the whole wide world. Who could take them in, with a capital of sixteen shillings or so? What country had an economy that could stand that influx of hundreds of thousands of penniless people—some desirable and an asset to any country, others of very ordinary value in any community and of less than no value if torn from their natural moorings?

And so, from the centre of Europe began to pour hundreds

of thousands of the most desperate letters that have ever been written in the history of the world. Every one of them represented someone's last hope. Prompted by terror and despair, people would remember that Cousin Anna had emigrated to America fifteen years ago, and that, in her last letter written twelve years ago, she had said she had married well.

Then one must write to her—or to Uncle Ernst, or that friend who had been so kind on holiday in the Tyrol three years ago or the unknown relations of great-aunt Leni—anyone, who was fortunate enough to live in the Great Outside and who might understand and help.

I suppose a great many of those letters were never even answered. How could they be? How could one letter from an almost forgotten relative or one-time friend hope to convey the absolute necessity of assuming financial responsibility for anything from one individual to a whole family? How could any ordinary person, living in an ordinary country in peacetime in the twentieth century, understand that murder and terror were closely stalking someone they had known as a rather prosperous businessman in Hamburg, or as a faded aunt in Frankfurt, or as a rather pushy young cousin—not especially likeable, now that one came to think of it—in Munich? It just didn't make sense. These things didn't happen in the twentieth century. There was some hysterical exaggeration somewhere—the whole thing was a put-on. Or, if not, it was something too big to tackle.

To Louise and me, knowledge of the situation had come gradually but inexorably. I make no claim to clearer perceptions than other people. We just happened to be lucky enough to see the problem in terms we could understand. In terms of personal friends, in fact.

Terrified, agonized need can be ignored if it is attached only to a name on paper. Or, if not ignored, at least it can reasonably appear to be of no direct responsibility to oneself. Change that name into a photograph of a human creature, who stammers out a frantic story, weeps some difficult tears, asks for nothing but hopes for everything, and show me the ordinary person who can refuse to help.

We had bypassed the stages of the names on paper and even the photographs. We were faced by the people themselves.

Our visits to Germany and Austria began to mean cases, cases and yet more cases, where we knew we were the last— often the only—hope of people who were in deadly danger and hourly terror. And from what had been an amateur gesture of goodwill to friends of two of our operatic favourites, there began to grow a regular and serious pattern of work that absorbed every waking thought and sometimes even followed us into our sleep.

To make it even more harrowing, the whole thing was really a fight against suicide as well as murder. We had to give people enough hope to keep them from committing suicide and not so much hope that they committed suicide when these high hopes were suddenly dashed. Sometimes we failed, of course. We would go back to Germany, with a case half completed, to find that someone's nerves had given way and they had thrown themselves out of a train, or put their head in a gas oven or opened a vein. We cried, of course, and we started again with someone else. What else could we do?

Each country had by now settled down to something like a settled policy. In England, broadly speaking, the position was this:

A refugee child could be brought over, provided a British citizen would "adopt" the child until the age of eighteen. A woman could sometimes be brought over on a domestic permit, provided you could give evidence of a job for her and provided the job had been advertised but not filled by a Britisher.

I am not going to pretend there was not a good deal of wangling and extension of meaning given to the word "domestic." Every woman anxious to escape promptly became a perfect domestic on paper, and many were the misfits and recriminations. But I too would have claimed, quite inaccurately, to be a perfect domestic in like circumstances. I hope I would have tried hard to live up to the description. The worthwhile ones did, of course. The others did not.

In the case of a man between eighteen and sixty, the position was much more complicated. Only those who had documentary proof that they were going on to another country eventually could hope to have the coveted British visa. In most cases, this proof consisted of papers to show that they were in the "queue" for emigration to the United States. And by the number in the queue, you could tell if he would have to wait six months, a year, two years or three years—in the case of some poor souls, even longer.

If only they could be sheltered from the ferocity of Nazi persecution while they waited for their turn, these people could glimpse a chance of life and hope far away in the distance. They could spend the waiting time in Britain provided—and here was the snag—that a British citizen would assume full financial responsibility for each case from the moment he landed in Britain until he reached the final country of his adoption. Only in a very few cases would he have a work permit.

A guarantor was required, and as may be imagined, few people could afford to make such a gesture or take on such a responsibility. With the best will in the world and the most sympathetic understanding of the situation, most people simply could not do it, even for a close relation or a good friend.

In the case of both men and women over sixty, the financial guarantee had to be, quite simply, for life.

By now, Louise and I were heart and soul in the problem and were beginning to find that many people, having heard part or all of what was happening, were very anxious to help to the limit of their capacity. They would say, "Well, I could give a shilling a week towards a fund." Or, "I could manage a pound note at the moment, but I couldn't possibly promise anything regularly." Or, "I could put someone up for a month or two, but not indefinitely."

All these offers were made with good heart, but were of little use to the refugee committees themselves, because they were so inundated with appeals that they had time to deal only with completed cases, where papers, guarantees and undertakings were all in order. Louise and I felt that we could do something about these smaller offers, since we were now going back and forth to Europe regularly and dealing with cases personally.

Having exhausted our own capacity for giving guarantees, we began to coordinate the smaller offers of money or hospitality around individual cases, until we had enough money or hospitality to "cover" a case. Then we would persuade some trusting friend or relative to sign the official guarantee form, on the understanding that the guarantee would never be called on because we already had the wherewithal to meet the needs of the case.

You never know what you can do until you refuse to take no for an answer. In this very amateur way, we did manage to rescue twenty-nine people and set them on new lives. The same mentality that had made us reckon the expenses of our first American adventure to the final penny now enabled us to think in terms of adding shilling to shilling, week to week, and effort to effort. The same naïve technique by which we had got ourselves to the States for our pleasure was used when we stumbled into Europe and began to save lives.

Louise, as her part of the work, began to learn German so that she could interview in German if necessary. I financed the work from the romantic novels—and very strange it was, switching from romantic fiction to tragic fact. I also did most of the correspondence—except when it needed to be done in German. And every few months, sometimes oftener if the work demanded it, we went to Europe to attend to our cases personally.

These journeys became more and more frequent and were often of suspiciously short duration. Louise could, fortunately, divide up her annual holiday allowance pretty much as she liked, and I, of course, could give myself time off from my writing when it was necessary. Sometimes our excursions occupied no more than a weekend.

Louise would take Saturday morning off—no five-day week in those days, *and* Saturday morning counted as a whole day's leave. She would leave the office on Friday evening and we would dash to Croydon to catch the last airplane to Cologne. We would be in Cologne by nine-thirty in the evening, in time to catch the night train to Munich. Either going or coming, we would probably stop off at Frankfurt where most of our cases were. If we went straight through, we would be in Munich in time for breakfast on Saturday morning.

Our return journey would be made through Holland on Sunday; it was better to go in by one frontier and out by another, especially if we were smuggling out jewellery, which was usually the case. We would cross from Holland by the night boat on Sunday, arriving at Harwich early on Monday morning, then on to London by train, and Louise would walk into the office just in time. But somewhere en route to

Frankfurt, Munich or Cologne, we would have attended to one or more of our cases.

After a while, we began to be known at Cologne airport, and some awkward and unfriendly questions were asked. At this point, our operatic interests came to our rescue once more.

By now Clemens Krauss was head of the Munich Opera House, and he and Ursuleac, having started us on our refugee work, took a considerable personal interest in what we were doing, though of course, we had to keep this entirely to ourselves. It was he who hit on an admirable way of cloaking our activities. Before we left Germany each time, we would tell him which dates we needed to have "covered" next time. Often, it was a question of only one or two days in a couple of months' time. He would then tell us what he would put on at the Opera House that night—occasionally we were even allowed to choose our own opera—and he would give us full details of the cast, etcetera. Then off we would go to England.

When we returned to Germany on the appointed date, we were simply operatic enthusiasts, coming for a special performance—or performances—about which we knew all the details. We *were,* of course, sufficiently opera fans to play the role completely. And, though there were sometimes a few smiles for the opera-mad English couple, we never again had trouble about the frequency and shortness of our visits.

Krauss never let us down once, and we always got our opera performances, but we also dealt with our case or cases under cover of our hobby. Sometimes Krauss and Ursuleac would be in Berlin and then we dealt with Berlin cases. And each year when the summer opera festival came on in Munich, we used to bring out from England a party of people who wanted to go abroad, but did not want the bother of organizing the trip.

I used to constitute myself "manager," even to the point of dealing with all the financial arrangements. In this way, I could arrange to have enough *Reiseschecks* in each member's name to avert any questions, but in actual fact, few of these "travellers checks" were ever cashed. I paid the party's expenses from money given to me by people who hoped to escape to England one day. Then, when we returned home, we credited these people with the equivalent in English money, thus transferring some of their capital, without any cash ever passing the frontier. That established something for them to live on when we hauled them out, by way of a guarantee.

If we were not exactly breaking the law, I suppose one might say that we were bending it rather sharply. Some of our party knew what we were doing. Others probably did not—and never will, unless they read this.

Crazy days! Sometimes we thought they would go on forever. Sometimes we deliberately had to remind ourselves and each other that there *was* another world to which we would be able to return one day. Gradually, we came to regard those last bright days of what we called "the Rosa Ponselle years" at Covent Garden as the norm, to which one might possibly return. There was a play running in London about that time called *There's Always Juliet*. And, in the absurd way that one does these things, we coined the phrase, "There's always Rosa!"

In how many hotel bedrooms, in how many German towns, have Louise and I said those words to each other? Meaning that somewhere beyond the fogs of horror and misery in which we moved were the lovely bright things that we had once taken for granted. One day, we told ourselves, we would rediscover them. One day, we would even hear Rosa sing again, and perhaps recapture something of the carefree lightness of heart that had once been ours.

Sometimes, we thought we could not bear to go back yet again into that hateful, diseased German atmosphere. Sometimes we even put into words to each other: "This will have to be the last time." But it never was, of course, until war made it so.

And for that extra bit of courage and determination that took us back time after time, Clemens Krauss and his wife Viorica Ursuleac must take full credit. It was they who sugared that horrible pill—with both their matchless performances and their dear friendship and support.

I knew that to speak in praise of any artist who occupied a high position in Hitler's Germany is to tread on very delicate ground. At the first word, even now, tempers rise, private and professional axes are taken out and reground, and friendships tremble in the balance. But, in that homeliest of phrases, *one must speak as one finds.* Louise and I would never have started our refugee work without the encouragement of those two, and we could never have maintained it without their help. It would be ungenerous and untruthful to say anything else.

And, though this has nothing to do with the ethics of the case, and is merely a fortunate circumstance, I very much doubt if we should have been able to force ourselves to go on with this harrowing and arduous task if the whole experience had not been irradiated for us by Krauss and Ursuleac's superb operatic performances. Just as the pursuit of opera had originally brought us to the refugee work, so the pursuit of the refugee work was made possible only by the support—or, if you like, the bribe—of great operatic performances, which lured us back again and again.

It is strange now to look back on those performances,

probably the greatest all-around performances we ever experienced, set like jewels in the midst of that most horrible part of our lives. Not that some of the individual singers were not rather second rate. They were. But one of the few masterhands of operatic history directed the whole.

Clemens Krauss was that phenomenon which occurs very occasionally in the world of music: the truly great operatic conductor. It used to be said of Krauss that he could see if there were too much light directed on a vase on the stage at the same time as hearing what was wrong with a phrase from the second trombones. He had a tremendous romantic grasp of a stage work, but an intensely practical eye for commonsense detail.

I remember a rehearsal of *Tosca,* when the Scarpia was making great play with his lorgnette in the first act. First, he examined the portrait through it, and then later, he examined the fan. Krauss stopped the rehearsal immediately and said, with dry good-humour: "Herr So-and-so, you might decide if you are short-sighted or long-sighted. You cannot be both."

Three times in his life, he built up a great ensemble—in Frankfurt, in Vienna and in Munich—always by developing his singers, never exploiting them. Any singer who worked consistently under him always described him as a true singer's conductor.

"He sings with us," explained Adele Kern, the lovely coloratura of his ensemble—and, incidentally, another operatic friend who was a wonderful help in the refugee work. She did not, of course, mean that he hummed and stamped—as has been done by various conductors, great and small, to the misery of those in the front row of the stalls—but that he experienced and appreciated every problem and every opportunity the score presented to the singer. No wonder

he could make a third-rate artist into a second-class performance, urge a second-class artist to heights never attained
before and polish every facet of a first-class artist's genius,
so that each performer found that he or she was doing better than any previous best.

I doubt if anyone who experienced his *Ariadne auf Naxos*
or *Cosi fan Tutte* at the little Residenz Theatre in Munich
will ever forget it; nor will he forget *Die Frau ohne Schat-
ten,* or *Palestrina,* or a dozen others at the National Theatre.

No wonder Richard Strauss considered that in Krauss and
Ursuleac, he had found the perfect interpreters of his particular genius and dedicated his *Der Friedenstag* to them. *Capric-
cio*—of which Krauss wrote the libretto—was also composed
for them. In the case of *Der Liebe der Dane,* which Strauss
intended to leave as a posthumous opera, Krauss persuaded
him to have it performed once. Because of wartime condi-
tions—the war was more than half over by then—the work
never came to public performance during the composer's
lifetime. But one presentation was given before an invited
audience, in honour of the composer's birthday, with Krauss
conducting and Ursuleac in the title role.

At the end, Strauss opined that it was the most perfect
performance of any of his works, and that, having heard it
thus, he was now ready to die. But, he added, if there were
any attempt again to perform his work within his lifetime,
he would give his permission only if the same cast were assembled and Krauss conducted.

In view of some subsequent performances, one is bound
to say one sees his point.

Although Strauss roles were her speciality, Ursuleac was
also a splendid Mozart singer, the best Senta in *The Flying
Dutchman* we ever heard, and—though we regretted having
to hear them in German—we still consider her Tosca and

her Turandot among the finest in our experience. She was a first-class actress, and it is a pity that so few of her records give anything but a faint impression of her overall artistry.

Anyway, those performances of 1937, 1938 and 1939 served to counterbalance our unhappiness during those years of the refugee work.

In retrospect, I know that neither the war nor the raids compared with the horror of those feverish visits and the frantic attempts to save people who must die if our persistence and ingenuity were not equal to solving their particular problem.

Our parents understood us splendidly, and pretty dim creatures we would have been without them. All through the years of the refugee work, we lived under the same roof with them. They loved us dearly, they knew exactly what we were doing, and they never put upon us the burden of saying, "You make me nervous." That's character, if you like!

They were always there, representing normal existence, and this kept us fairly steady. I remember once coming back one Saturday morning, after we had had an especially harrowing time. I went straight through into the kitchen, where Mother was making pastry—which is, after all, one of the basic things of life. I can see her now, with the flour on her arms. I began to tell her what we had seen and I burst into tears.

If she had stopped and made a sentimental fuss of me, I would have cried for hours. *She just simply went on making pastry.* In three minutes I was all right. Then she stopped and said, "It's no good tearing yourself to pieces. You're doing the best you can. Now tell me all about it."

Oh, the glorious relief of it all, after the madness we had experienced!

In Frankfurt, good friends used to put a room at our disposal, and there we interviewed our cases in the later months. Sometimes, we interviewed ten, twelve, fifteen, one after another. We never refused to hear a story. Sometimes, one could keep someone from committing suicide just by listening attentively and sympathetically and promising to *try* to help. Sometimes, the most complicated and difficult case would resolve itself with curious simplicity. And sometimes, the apparently simple case proved insoluble.

To this day, even when I am very happy, I occasionally recall with fearful clarity the faces of those we failed to save. It is not nice to remember that if you had been a little more ingenious or a little more persistent, perhaps someone might not, after all, have been burnt to ashes in the ovens of Auschwitz.

It was harrowing enough just listening to the stories. Many of the people spoke English, but Louise gradually was able to interview those who spoke only German. They came, poor souls, all keyed up, ready to tell their tale. They had half an hour or, for all they knew, much less time to convince two utter strangers that their case was worth taking on. It must have seemed to them that their lives literally depended on the way they expressed themselves in the pitiful little fraction of time allowed to them.

We tried to rid them of this dread, to explain that they could take their time, speak German, produce their papers at leisure. Some of them didn't even hear the reassurances that we tried to press upon them. They stumbled on, in what English they had, searching frantically in their inevitable leather cases for papers, with hands that shook so that they could sort out nothing. Perspiration poured down their faces, and sometimes tears too. Not that they were not brave— many of them were incredibly so—but their nerves had been stretched to the breaking point for too long, and sometimes it was the touch of friendly sympathy that finished them.

Afterwards, we in our turn used to retire to our hotel bedroom and cry. In this dreadful, emotional atmosphere of urgency and despair, it was difficult not to. Then, as Louise put it, we would dry our eyes, emerge sniffing and start again.

Something rather curious happened in connection with that room in Frankfurt where we did so much of this interviewing. During the war, we heard by roundabout means through Switzerland that the brave woman of the house used it for other, even more tragic, gatherings. The night before some of the deportations started for Poland and certain death, a heroic Catholic priest was smuggled into the house; the room we had used was fitted up as a chapel, and he administered the last rites to those who, though Jewish by blood, were Catholic by religion and sought this last comfort. Both he and the woman of the house, of course, did this at the risk of their lives, but thought it worthwhile for the comfort they gave.

When the Allied bombers laid waste so much of Frankfurt, every house in that district was flattened, except the one where this work had been carried on. A later raid destroyed most of the house. Only that room remained intact.

As we continued our work, of course our names became known to a certain extent, both in refugee circles in England and among the unfortunate victims over there. And, since it was known that we journeyed regularly to and fro, we were often asked to take verbal messages, suggestions or instructions that could not be trusted to the censored post.

For example, a chemist in Frankfurt had succeeded in obtaining the offer of a special post in England, but the German authorities resisted his attempts to obtain his passport. He knew just the kind of letter that, written by the important British firm who required him, would probably scare the authorities into parting with his passport. But, of course, he dared not write informing them of this. All the firm knew, on their part, was that their German chemist seemed unable to come after all.

When we were next in Frankfurt, we were called in, learned off by heart the terms of the necessary letter, and undertook to visit the firm in England immediately on our return. We explained the only half-understood difficulties and primed one of his directors with the effective wording required. I am glad to say that the letter worked the miracle.

A good deal could sometimes be accomplished by sheer bluffing too. I remember an occasion when a case of ours had been imprisoned in a small country town, and his mother was in despair over the possibility of his being transferred elsewhere before we could do anything for him. I promptly typed out a pompous official letter stating that a very important man in the City of London was giving the guarantee in this case and was exceedingly interested in the extraordinary methods employed in a particular town. He was arranging to have a question asked in the British House of Commons on the subject, and a good deal of public interest was likely to be taken in the case.

I added that "in order to authenticate these statements," I was having the letter transformed into a legal document. I then took it to an astonished local solicitor in London, persuaded him to put a seal on it, and he witnessed my signature, with the added intimidating note that he was a solicitor of the Supreme Court of Adjudicature in Great Britain.

So far as any legal aspect was concerned, it was not worth the paper it was typed on. But it worked. The last thing a small-town German official wanted was to have awkward questions from his own higher-ups about his having attracted

unwelcome attention from an important foreign country.
Our man was released immediately, and presently we obtained a guarantee and dragged him out via Switzerland. It
was one of the lighter moments of our work.

Just as our name was known on this side, so, by some extraordinary passing to and fro of any scrap of hope, we were
also beginning to be known among some of the frantic thousands who were trying to escape. This was brought home to
us the first time we visited Vienna early in 1939.

We had to go to the Kultursgemeinde there in connection with one of our cases. This was the official building
where any business to do with emigration was transacted. I
shall never forget it. In every room, in every passage, almost
on every stair, crowded hundreds and hundreds of the most
desperate people I have ever seen. They were of all ages,
from children who could hardly walk to men and women
almost blind with old age. And not one of them had any
hope of justice.

All they could hope for in life was that by some extraordinary chance, someone in the outside world had been sufficiently moved by their appeals or relationship to stretch out a
helping hand. They were all there waiting—hopefully, hope-
lessly—thumbing over their papers, building up pitifully inadequate cases to show themselves and others that they were
surely among the lucky few who had the means of escape.

Finally, Louise and I reached the particular waiting room
adjacent to the office dealing with our case. We were speaking to each other in English, and to our stupefaction, a man
came up and said, "Are you by any chance Miss Cook?"

We said in unison that we were, and I added, "How on
earth did you know? We never set foot in Vienna before
today."

"No, I know," he replied. "But I have a friend in Frankfurt." Imagine! Almost a day and night's journey away. "She wrote to me and told me you were coming to Vienna and that you had been trying to help some of us to get out. I've been round every hotel in Vienna asking for you. Then I thought you might have come here. I've been waiting all day."

I find it hard to describe the terrible sensation it gave us to have this frightful and pathetic importance thrust upon us. Again and again we used to ask ourselves, "Who are we, that the mere fact of our having a little time and money and sympathy to spare transforms us into figures of overwhelming importance to our unhappy fellow creatures?"

Sometimes this realization oppressed us almost more than anything else. And I still think the most terrible thing ever said to me consisted of five words spoken by an elderly woman who had lived a good and useful life until the remorseless tide of unprovoked, undeserved hatred and wickedness tore her from her rightful anchorage. We rescued her and her husband and brought them to England a week before war broke out. He died here during the war, but he died a free man and from what one calls natural causes. Then, not long before the end of the war, she went to America to join her beloved daughter. I saw her off from Euston Station and fumbled for the few conventional phrases that one finds on these rather trying occasions. I had almost forgotten the events that had brought us together originally and was thinking only of the future, when she leaned from the carriage window and said, with terrible simplicity, "Goodbye. I owe you my life."

I had long ago got over the sudden fits of crying that had punctuated the harrowing, emotional refugee days, but her words made me cry dreadfully. From her point of view, she probably spoke the truth, I suppose. But what had that dear, good, useful life cost us? Some trouble, some eloquence and some money. Nothing more. The lack of proportion between the two things is frightening.

It is difficult now to follow the story of those immediately pre-war years in anything like chronological order, as each individual story naturally runs on over the period to its conclusion during or after the war. However, there are one or two general points about our work, which remained consistent throughout.

For instance, as I have said, we made it a rule never to refuse to hear a story. In addition, we had no feeling one way or the other about Jew or Gentile, political refugee or what you will. As it happened, the cases with which we dealt were largely Jews, firstly because more of them were being persecuted than any other section of the community, and secondly because, since we had started with a Jewish family we were, rather naturally, recommended from one case or another. Some of them were Jewish by race only, being Catholic, Protestant or Quaker by religion. Some were practising Jews, and some of our cases, to use Hitler's own ridiculous phrase, were pure Aryan. To us, there was genuinely no distinction. There were just fellow creatures who needed help. If a man is drowning you don't ask him what his religious and political views are before you pull him out.

We happen to have very definite political views ourselves, but we never allowed these to influence us in our choice of people to help. We were simply moved by a sense of furious revolt against the brutality and injustice of it all and were willing to help any deserving case brought to our notice, to the limit of our small capacity. We tried as best as we could to apportion the pitifully small amount of aid at our disposal to what seemed to us, on brief investigation, to be the most worthwhile cases. But this choice was dictated solely by the feeling that what little help we could give should be used to the best advantage.

To those who had to make the hard and big decisions, I knew there *had* to be something of the policy that the young should be saved first. Only a small proportion of the whole could be saved, and the old had had their lives. I do not imagine there was ever a strict enforcement of this general principle. But, of course, there is a sort of ruthless justice and common sense about such a view, if one has to make a final and objective selection.

Louise and I did not feel bound by this, or any other, rule. What we did try to do was to concentrate on whole families. Part of a richly happy family life ourselves, we knew that it would be poor comfort to be rescued oneself if a beloved mother or father, brother or sister still lingered in danger and the shadow of death. Whenever possible, we worked right through a family, hoping one day to reunite them somewhere in the world.

Our twenty-nine successful cases, therefore, were largely made up of family groups, although of course we did have cases of single individuals too. When I speak of twenty-nine successful cases, I mean that we had twenty-nine completed cases and raised twenty-nine guarantees. There were, naturally, innumerable occasions when we were able to give a little help or advice, but they did not count among our actual cases.

Sometimes people like to know about what might be called the sidelines of our work—how we brought out jewellery and fur coats, to represent money for people once they were rescued. It was fairly simple at first, but then came the time when the Hitler guard used to come on the train at the frontier and check everything you had, and when you came out you were checked again. This made things a bit awkward, but we solved it by going in by one frontier—and probably by air—wearing no jewellery at all. We hadn't got very much anyway, but we dispensed with even wristwatches. Then, after a very short stay, we would come out by quite a different route and probably by train. So we simply could not get the same official twice, and there was no one to notice that we had become rather overdressed English girls with a taste for slightly too much jewellery.

We were careful on detail. We never took earrings for pierced ears, because neither of us has pierced ears, and that was the kind of thing they caught you on. They would suddenly say, "Which of you wears these?" and if you had earrings for pierced ears, but neither of you had pierced ears, they knew what you were doing.

In the case of fur coats, we had rather a good technique. We used to take one or two dress labels with us from England, begged from our few friends who patronised the really good English shops. When we arrived at the town where the fur coat was, we would go straight to the owner before presenting ourselves at our hotel. We would try on the coat ourselves while with the owner, and one of us arrived at the hotel wearing it, thus avoiding the suspicious circumstances of going out without an expensive coat and coming back with one.

We both had rather ingenuous faces in those days—perhaps we still have!—and we were never questioned. Certainly we could not rival the experience of a young half-Viennese, half-English friend of ours who undertook to come out of Austria wearing someone's very valuable pearl necklace.

The currency official who came on the train at the frontier gave her a dirty look and said, "Those are very good pearls you're wearing, aren't they?"

With great presence of mind and no sign of panic, she

turned on him haughtily. "And why not? Do I look so shabby that I might not wear good pearls?" She rose and inspected herself in the mirror, and then turned on him again, demanding, "What is wrong with my appearance?"

"Nothing, nothing," he hastened to assure her, very much taken aback by her grande dame air.

"But there must be," she insisted, following him as he retreated to the door of the compartment, "or you would not have said such a thing. What were you trying to imply?"

She pressed her role of insulted passenger so far that the man finally fled, covered with confusion, still protesting that he had not meant any criticism of the lady's appearance.

Soon after we started our refugee work, it became apparent to Louise and me that, apart from our own home, we must have some sort of clearing house or at least temporary accommodation for the people whom we brought to England. And at this time, I acquired what I had always hoped to have since I started writing: a small flat of my own. We continued to live at home, but used the flat as the central point of our work. Occasionally, we tried to reckon how many people lived in the flat or, at any rate, passed through on the way to a new life elsewhere. But we have long ago lost count. Only—if one may be permitted to feel a little fanciful—it sometimes seems that they have each left behind a faint trace of the relief and happiness that they must have experienced in their first haven after the storm. To this day, there is an atmosphere of brightness and happiness that most people remark upon. It may be only because it is a light, pleasant place with many windows. But it certainly has been a place of great happiness to us, as well as others.

The first person to live there was Mitia's daughter, Elsa Mayer-Lismann—now for many years a musical lecturer of great distinction in her own right, and the director of an opera workshop of a standard that would have delighted her mother's heart. Even now, when she returns to the flat, which she often does, she says it is a little like returning home.

They were a very interesting family, the Mayer-Lismanns. Mitia herself was half-Russian and half-German, with a charm and humour and vivacity quite impossible to convey to anyone who never met her. She was wonderful company, and we sometimes used to say we wondered just how late we would keep on talking if natural bedtime did not intervene. Then one evening, she and I were caught out in an air raid and had to take refuge in a public shelter. We talked quite happily until just after four in the morning—so we found out our limit at last.

I am thankful to say that all of the family escaped in time: Mitia and her husband and daughter, two of her brothers— one was already in France—her sister-in-law and her niece. Her nephew and his family escaped too, but we never met them until after the war, when we went to America.

We often told the family that the fate of our later charges depended on the fact that they themselves were such a fine and worthwhile family. I don't mean by that, of course, that if they had turned out to be disappointing and unsatisfactory we should necessarily have classed all refugees together and dismissed them from our sympathies. But, human nature being what it is, one naturally finds it easier to continue an arduous task with good heart if the first results are gratifying.

Such is the responsibility of each one of us! The good and lasting impression made upon us by the Mayer-Lismann family bound us irrevocably to the task of helping others, whom we expected to be something like them.

CHAPTER EIGHT

When I think of how we lived in a state of high drama part
of the time and continued our normal lives during the rest of
the time, I marvel now. I wrote novels, and Louise worked
at the office. We had holidays. We had our recurring opera
seasons. We had our family interests and our hobbies, particularly our gramophone records, which were a great consolation to us between opera seasons.

Our own collection was quite a handsome one now, but
paled before the splendours of Douglas's collection. Our
friend of the amphitheatre, who had spoken to us on the
night of Ponselle's debut, had accumulated a collection of
gramophone records—almost entirely vocal—that must have
ranked among the first half-dozen in the country. And how
we enjoyed listening to some of his treasures!

So far as I was concerned, my collection of operatic snapshots was almost as dear to me as our collection of records,
and many are the incidents I remember with pleasure.

Martinelli, to become in later years a very dear and valued
friend, was particularly charming about being photographed

and was rewarded by having his snap come out as among the finest in the collection. I gave him an enlargement for his own enjoyment, which he accepted with obvious pleasure and the smiling statement, "I make you the official photographer to the House of Martinelli."

Gigli was more solemn about the actual taking of his photograph. But later, when we met him at some Italian reception and I produced the snap for his inspection, recalling the occasion to him, he was charmed and insisted on autographing it for me.

The Italian stars usually entered thoroughly into the fun of being photographed and were extremely interested in the result. This was long before every fan sported a camera, of course, and long, long before people took coloured photographs by flashbulb on any and every occasion. Some of the German stars were less inclined to relax in this particular way, but usually yielded to a little tact and persuasion. Lauritz Melchior was especially cooperative, I remember.

One of the most amusing incidents occurred when I asked Lawrence Tibbett if I could take him. At that time, he was winning golden praise for his Iago to Martinelli's unforgettable Otello, but was also, poor fellow, greatly pestered by film fans, who cared little or nothing for his real artistic worth. The very sight of a camera and a beaming smile turned him sick. He replied to me, politely but firmly, "No. I'm afraid you may not."

I was a good deal taken aback but prepared to retreat in reasonably good order when out of the stage door came Mr. Evans, of Evans & Salter, who were Tibbett's agents and had been Galli-Curci's agents all those years ago when we had come to ask for her telephone number.

Louise, waited at a tactful distance, then came forward and I said, "You don't remember us, do you, Mr. Evans?"

"No, I can't say I do," was the discouraging reply from Mr. Evans, who had also had his fill of the wrong kind of fan.

"Oh, dear!" I exclaimed, feeling that our stock was sinking impossibly low. "Do you remember the two girls who crossed the Atlantic to hear Galli—"

"For heaven's sake!" cried Mr. Evans, wringing our hands. "Ida and Louise Cook—of course! Come here, Larry," he called after the retreating Tibbett, "and meet two opera enthusiasts. They're the *real* thing."

When Tibbett promptly returned, he was introduced and told something of the Galli-Curci story. We also told him how we had heard his first *Simon Boccanegra* and how immensely we admired him in the past.

"I'm awfully sorry," he said, in the nicest manner possible. "Of course, I wouldn't have refused to let you photograph me if I'd known all this. You can take me now, if you want to."

In an atmosphere of general goodwill, I took my snap, a copy of which I afterwards exchanged with Tibbett for an excellent photograph of him as Iago.

But nowadays, there was always the dark reverse side of the coin. There were plans to make, letters to write, appeals to draw up, and money to be laid out as carefully as in our less prosperous days, because every pound well spent might save a life.

We still travelled third class on the Continent. We still sat in the gallery at Covent Garden during the season. And, except for the glorious extravagance of my flat, we continued our old style of living. Why not? It was no hardship to arrange our life as we had always known and enjoyed it. And one day, all the horror would be over, and then there would be time to make other plans.

Some of our friends made much more trying sacrifices than we. I remember a period when Nesta walked halfway to the office each day and gave us the saved fares for postage on our work. Another friend cut her cigarette consumption by half and contributed towards the maintenance of one of our cases. Several subscribed small weekly sums to help individual cases.

I know, from experience, that this is much more difficult than is spending lavishly from a superfluity of money, which has suddenly appeared more or less from nowhere. Nothing is easier to give than money, if you have it—or more difficult if you have not!

Gradually, of course, we began to exhaust our own resources and those of our immediate circle. And then I had a tremendous stroke of luck. I was asked to go—as a sort of especially interested spectator—to a lecture on the refugee problem that was being given just outside London. I went, but I was disappointed to discover that, though interesting, it was on quite academic lines. More on the problem of settling refugees in general, with special mention of occasions in the past when this had been satisfactorily done. It was all rather far from the hideous, urgent problem I had left behind in Germany less than a fortnight previously.

At the end, questions were invited, and someone asked if the speaker would explain the guarantee system under which refugees could be brought to this country.

To my mingled embarrassment and relief, the lecturer replied, "I think perhaps Miss Cook has more personal experience of that than I have. Would she like to explain it?"

I had never before in my life spoken in public, but I thought, *This is my chance! And I'm not sitting down until I've said all I want to say.* I stumbled to my feet, and in a rather high, squeaky and nervous voice, I described the workings of the guarantee system. I went on to explain how two or three people could band together to assume the collective responsibility for a case, so long as one of them felt sufficiently confident of the others to give the guarantee.

It was nearly tea time, and people were getting a bit bored really, when in despair, I launched into a short account of what I had seen and I heard less than two weeks ago. I said, "I will give you an actual instance. There is a man of over sixty. His name is So-and-so, his circumstances are this and that. He has asked me to save his life. He is under sentence to go back to Buchenwald Concentration Camp—and almost certain death—unless he can be got out of the country in a matter of weeks. I have no guarantee. I have no means of saving him. He must die, unless I can find both—and find them quickly."

Then I sat down in the most profound and uncomfortable silence I have ever created. Once at least, I had nearly cried from mingled nervousness and the pathos of the facts with which I was dealing, a circumstance that was, of course, dreadfully embarrassing for the unfortunate audience. And I had probably committed every fault a public speaker should avoid. However, I had said what I felt I ought to say, and there was nothing more to be done about it.

During tea, two elderly ladies approached me, and one asked, "Would you have time to come and speak to our church circle? We think it would create great interest and perhaps do some good."

I explained that I had never spoken in public before, but I was prepared to try anything that might help, and they promised to arrange the matter.

Three days later, I received a telephone call from the initial organization's secretary. Without preamble, and to my extreme astonishment, she began, "My husband says it's no good—we can't go on like this. I've been crying about that poor old man, on and off, ever since you told us about him.

And now my husband says we'd better give the guarantee ourselves. We have some good friends who will help, and I'm sure it can be arranged."

It was like a miracle.

It was also the beginning of a different side of the work. I accepted the invitation to speak to the church circle mentioned by the two ladies. And, as a result they themselves—they were sisters and retired school teachers, I think—offered me a guarantee and a place in their home for a middle-aged or elderly woman, who might be expected to fit in with their style of life.

We found them one of the nicest people we'd ever dealt with. And she lived with them until the middle of the war, when she went to her son in America. By that time, there existed among the women a deep and warm friendship that gave nothing but pleasure to all three.

After this very amateur beginning, I did a good deal of speaking and lecturing. I learned to conquer my nerves and to pitch my voice reasonably well, but I never adopted the methods of a professional lecturer that befitted my subject. I merely expanded what I would have said to personal friends and kept the thing on an entirely informal basis.

About the same time, I was given my first chance to make appeals in one or two church newspapers. I knew that it was outside my province to make wide-scale appeals of a general nature. My line was to cite individual cases in such a way that someone, somewhere, would feel an urge to help. I shall never forget the result of the first article, which I called, simply, "Will Somebody Save Me?"

I explained once more the general position and, briefly, the guarantee system, and I outlined two cases. One was of an elderly man who—judging by his quota number for America—needed three years' hospitality and a guarantee, and the other was of a young man who needed six months' hospitality and again the inevitable guarantee.

The day the article appeared in print, we received a telegram from some people in Scotland stating clearly and coolly that they would guarantee the elderly man and keep him for three years. The next day a postcard arrived from an old farmer in Yorkshire, offering to do the same for the boy.

After further correspondence, we put both cases on a definite basis, and Louise and I went off to Germany once more, with the heart-warming knowledge that we could tell two people that they were as good as rescued.

When we arrived to interview the elderly man—who had been strongly recommended to us by a good friend, but whom we had not personally met before—we found, to our dismay, that there was also a very delightful wife in serious, though not quite equal, danger. The men were always in the greater danger, because they were outside concentration camp only by some special dispensation that could be withdrawn at any moment.

We explained apologetically that our present arrangements covered the rescue of the husband only. His wife was completely dignified and resigned—a woman whose beauty of character shone in her face. She told us that, as it happened, we had arrived on the anniversary of their wedding day.

"Forty years ago," she said slowly. "We promised never to part. But now the time has come to do so. All I ask is that you save my husband. I shall be all right."

Deeply moved, we told her that we would willingly put her case on our ever-lengthening list and see what we could do. We added that we would try to find a home for her somewhere in Scotland, so that she would at least be in the same part of the country as her husband. More than that we could not, of course, promise; but she seemed to find even this overwhelming.

As soon as we reached home, I wrote to our unknown Scottish couple, explaining the exact position and asking if they could, in their kindness, possibly extend the guarantee to cover the wife, too, provided I could find some sort of home for her. They knew nothing of me, of course, and would have to trust my word that I would fulfil the obligation that I was asking them to underwrite.

They replied by telegram—they were great people for telegrams—that they were coming to London on a day trip to discuss the case. I sometimes think of them now when people say disheartening things about the human race. They were a middle-aged couple, in very moderate financial circumstances, who travelled over three hundred miles to London and three hundred back again—all within twenty-four hours—just to discuss how they could best help two people they had never seen. It is breathtaking, when one thinks about it!

When we met—it was the only time we ever did meet, as a matter of fact—Mrs. G— explained their circumstances with commendable clarity and brevity.

"Of course," she said, "we shall give the guarantee for the wife, too. And of course, we couldn't think of having them separated. We will take them into our home. But, quite frankly, though we can afford the maintenance of one, we should have to have some assistance if we take both. If you can find someone who will pay a pound a week for the wife's keep, the matter is settled."

Oh, blessed light romance that kept the money rolling in! I said I could and would willingly pay that myself. And two more people could live. We brought them out on August 29, 1939.

Years and years afterwards, when I was speaking on the subject of the refugee work in New York, the daughter of this couple came out of the audience and said, "I want you to know that the couple Ida has spoken about were my parents. And I would like Louise and Ida to know that my mother prayed for them every day until the day she died. It was almost the last thing she said."

It is difficult to know which cases to pick out, for each had a complete and human story attached to it. I have kept all the letters from those terrible years. They are not neatly filed. That is another of the things I have always meant to do one day—if I had time. They are packed away now in a box, because, tragic though they are, I cannot bring myself to destroy those pages out of history.

It is inexpressibly sad now to look at them, and the photographs that accompanied them, and see face after face of the people for whom we could do nothing.

Here are two little boys, eight and ten, who insisted on writing out their own records in round, painstaking handwriting. They beam at me hopefully from their little, faded photographs. But we were not able to help them in time.

Here is one of the really dramatic messages. A telegram that is part of a much longer story I will tell later. It simply states, "Georg not at home. Helpless. Gerda."

That meant a husband had been taken away and his wife had exhausted all means of saving him. Could we do anything?

This was the kind of message that invested the very sound of the telegraph boy's motorbike with terror for us. It was years before I was able to hear that ordinary sound without a sense of alarm and startled apprehension.

Here is letter after letter, beginning with anything from "Dear Madam" to *Engelchen,* the term a few of them used

when they realized that our efforts on their behalf were suc-
ceeding. Some of them were forever to remain sad strangers,
with whom we had nothing but a passing connection. Some
of them now rank among our dearest and most valued friends.

Of these Friedl was one. Her story is interesting, and it
has the virtue of a supremely happy ending.

Friedl Bamberger was the great school-friend of Elsa
Mayer-Lismann, daughter of our beloved Mitia. As early as
1937, Elsa told us that her friend was desperately anxious to
get out of Frankfurt; that she had been some years in Italy,
but had had to return home for family and health reasons.
Now, her passport had been taken away and there would have
to be some definite action from outside in order to have it—
as well as any hope of escape—restored to her.

We were going to Frankfurt about that time, and as it was
long before we had extricated all the Mayer-Lismanns, it was
arranged that Friedl should come to lunch at their home and
discuss possibilities.

When I first saw her, I thought she was very positive and
self-possessed. In fact, when I enquired mildly over lunch
what plans she had for the future, I received the unequivocal reply, "We will talk of that later."

I was a bit taken aback at the implication that she would
run this particular show. But, as we were to find later, she
really had only a little, carefully studied English. She had
learned by rote what she needed to say to us and simply
had to say it in one piece. To discuss the matter chattily at
the lunch table was more than she could bear—or indeed,
achieve. And, calm though she appeared, she was really keyed
up to a high pitch of nerves. This might be her best—it might
be her only—chance. And she must not mishandle it.

After lunch, we retired to Mitia's music room, which was
put entirely at our disposal.

Poor little Friedl! I can see her now. She took up her stand in the curve of the grand piano and addressed us as though we were at a public meeting. Then, as her agitation got the better of her, she began to walk up and down the room, still pouring out what she wanted to say.

As we listened, one certain thing emerged. She wanted to lean on no one. She was prepared to do any work, live at any level, sacrifice anything, in order not to take more than the barest necessities needed to maintain herself until she could struggle to her own feet in a foreign country. Long before she was through, I had made my decision, and I knew Louise had, too. It was one of the quickest decisions we ever made about anyone, and one for which we have never ceased to be thankful.

At the end, I said, "It's all right. I have thought of something. We will get a student's permit in your case." This was still possible in those days. "You will come to England, live at our flat, and be enrolled in an English language course. When that is completed, we will find some way of extending your studies and your stay. Maybe you can do translations for me, or film scripts or something." She was already a journalist of some experience. "But, anyway, you will have an invitation to come to England and therefore a reason to demand, or have us demand, your passport. The question of final emigration need not be raised at this point."

The idea succeeded by its sheer simplicity. This was, I must emphasize, before the situation had taken on anything like its final degree of danger and difficulty. Friedl came to us and lived longest of all in our flat, keeping it beautifully for us, doing endless jobs of every kind for us, and causing us only one serious anxiety: we could not make her eat enough, because she wanted to cost us as little as possible.

After a while, we were allowed a new light on Friedl's affairs. It seemed she had a fiancé in Italy, an Italian journalist whose one goal in life, now that Friedl was in London, was to join her there.

This he presently achieved, but only by taking a position with the Italian Radio as their representative in England. This, of course, was an Italian government concern, and as an Italian official employee, he was, in those days, unable to marry a Jewish girl. But at least they were in the same city and could see each other daily. And we all hoped that, one day, things would be better.

As everyone knows, things unfortunately became worse. The war came, but still an uneasy peace hovered between Italy and Britain.

Then came the final disaster. Italy declared war.

I remembered that night. Louise and I were at home when Friedl telephoned us to come to the flat, and we went at once. Ruggero, her fiancé, was there and another Italian journalist whom we knew slightly. The two men had to decide whether to return to their own country, whose regime they detested, or to try to remain in Britain—rootless, jobless and technically an enemy.

The other man elected to go; I think he had a wife and family in Italy. Ruggero unhesitatingly elected to try to stay. But even with this decision made, the way was not very clear. He took counsel with an English colleague in a fairly responsible position, who explained that all journalists, diplomats, radio officials and so on were ordered to return by the last "diplomatic" boat, leaving almost immediately. If any were permitted to remain in Britain, some British opposite number would be detained in Italy.

"If, however," his adviser continued thoughtfully, "you make every arrangement to go, but are unfortunate enough to miss the boat, it is no concern of ours. Later, of course, you will have to give yourself up as an enemy alien and be interned. That's all I can tell you."

It was enough.

Ruggero made every arrangement to depart with the others. His luggage was sent down to the boat. But on the day the boat was due to set sail, he just was not there. As a matter of fact, he was at our flat a large part of the time. Then later, when he and Friedl judged it wiser not to remain in any fixed place, they went to one of the outer suburbs and walked about the streets until late that night, when they knew the boat must have gone.

Once this had been confirmed, he gave himself up to the police and was interned for a while. Presently, however, he was released, being among those chosen for radio propaganda purposes. He was told that he would have to work in one of those semi-secret and rather remote propaganda centres dotted over the countryside. Also, he was asked if he happened to know of a reliable shorthand-typist, perfect in both Italian and English.

"Yes," Ruggero replied promptly. "My fiancée."

"Well, could you marry her right away and take her down there with you?" he was asked.

To which he replied, "I am marrying her in a few days, anyway."

So, one busy, air-raidish morning, I dashed off to witness their marriage at Caxton Hall.—Louise was, dismally enough, evacuated with her office by then.—As they both came running up the steps, late as usual, with Friedl carrying her hat in her hand, and I thought, "Happy ending!"

Which, as a romance merchant, I consider I was entitled to think.

One of the most dramatic stories concerns the Maliniaks, and we came into this case, also, indirectly through Clemens

Krauss and Ursuleac. The Maliniaks were part of the magic circle of Viennese operatic life during the early 1930s. Jerzy Maliniak was assistant conductor and choir repetiteur at the State Opera and, according to Krauss, "probably the finest operatic coach in Europe."

We already knew them by name quite well when Mitia received a letter, early in 1939, from Gerda Maliniak, Jerzy's very lovely non-Jewish wife. She, her husband and little daughter were in the same desperate straits as all families where the man of the family was a Jew. His employment had been taken away, his contributions to the pension fund washed out. Starvation and despair were coming daily nearer. Could Mitia make any sort of connection for them in the outside world? There was a faint possibility of their getting away to America eventually.

The letter, only one of dozens poor Mitia used to receive at this time, immediately became the subject of earnest discussion among us.

As I said, the Maliniaks were part of the magic circle to Louise and me, definitely among those to whom Ursuleac's words, "Now you will be all right" must, in our view, be extended. Friends and colleagues of those who had started us on the work could not be left to perish. So Louise and I went to Vienna to see them personally.—As recorded earlier, this was the occasion we visited the Kultursgemeinde.—We found them the most enchanting family, even in their distress, and set to work at once to make what plans we could.

The first sad essential, as always, was to split up the family temporarily, as one could never, particularly at that late date, have obtained a guarantee for three people. We managed to get the little girl adopted temporarily and she arrived safely in one of the children's transports—those sad boatloads of children who came without their parents. But after that, everything went wrong.

First, I tried for a domestic permit for Gerda. That broke down. Then I managed to raise a well-meant but very shaky guarantee, on which I hoped to get them both out. At the last moment, it was judged insufficient. And the same post that brought us this information brought also a frantic letter from Vienna, telling us that Jerzy was threatened with arrest at any moment. Not only was he Jewish, he was also Polish, and the Polish Jews were daily threatened with a complete round-up.

It was one of the worst moments in all those years of work. There was not another soul in the whole of England to whom I could apply for a guarantee, and I literally walked London that day, trying every faint chance I could. I came home that night, unsuccessful and so completely dispirited that I cried. Whereupon Bill, our silent Bill who never said a thing unless he thought it was worth saying, suddenly looked up and spoke to some purpose.

"Well, I haven't got a bank account," he said. "But you can take my Post Office Savings Bank book, if you like, and a statement that I'm a permanent civil servant, and see if they will accept me as a guarantor for the two of them."

It was the most hopeful thing that had happened that day and well worth trying. But I knew that no pipsqueak official would accept it. I had to get to one of the big men who would take the responsibility for accepting an irregularity.

I telephoned Mitia to ask if she had any ideas.

She had. She gave me an introduction to someone who could smooth my way to Sir Benjamin Drage, the head of the Guarantee Department at Bloomsbury House.

By dint of pressure all round, I managed to get myself ushered into Sir Benjamin's presence the following afternoon, my story perfectly arranged in my mind in its most telling phrases. I was prepared to pull out every organ-stop in my voice to make the best effect, and no star actress had her role better prepared.

Imagine, then, my dismay when I discovered that the man I had to impress was stone deaf; I had to tell my story into what looked like a small radio set. As I have always been rather better at manner than matter when I am trying to persuade anyone, I felt as though, from the outset, I had been deprived of my best weapons.

However, I started off. I suppose it was just one story out of thousands that he had heard. And yet, appliance or no, he gave every detail the utmost perfect attention. He hardly said a word until I had finished. Then he sent for the file and completed all the stages of the case in front of me, while a horrified official stood by, saying at intervals, "But you can't do that, Sir Benjamin! You can't do that."

"But I've done it," replied Sir Benjamin, as he made the last entry. "Now—" turning to me "—that's four weeks saved in the case. From this point, it has to go to the Home Office where, in the ordinary way, it will take four weeks more. I can't do any more for you. But if you have any sort of Government string to pull, pull it now."

I did a bit of quick thinking.

There was a chance I had always kept in reserve and never used before. We had a friend in Downing Street, who just might be able to help. I asked for permission to use Sir Benjamin's phone and telephoned Downing Street. By the mercy of providence, our friend was available, and I rapidly explained the position to him.

"Well, of course, there is nothing I can do for you officially," he told me, "but can you get hold of the name of the Home Office official who would deal with this case in the ordinary way?"

On my anxious enquiry, Sir Benjamin was able to supply this information.

"Very well," our friend said. "I can ring him up and say that you're coming along, and ask him if he will please see you personally? After that, it's for you to do the best you can with the opportunity. I'm afraid I can only get you the interview."

It was enough.

Because it was already late in the afternoon, Sir Benjamin bundled me into a taxi and paid my fare for luck. Presently I arrived at the Home Office and was ushered into the presence of a very courteous, but completely hidebound, official. He was sorry, but he could see no reason why this case should be specially hurried. I patiently explained about the threat of arrest and about the expected round-up of all the Polish Jews in Vienna.

He looked thoughtful then and said, "You had better telegraph to the effect that White Form 227A"—or some such number—"is about to be authenticated. That should stop the Gestapo."

I stared at him helplessly and cried, "What are we talking about? Do you really suppose anything will save him but the telegraphed information that British visas are on the way? What do white forms mean to the Gestapo?"

He found me as trying as I found him. And he wanted to go home. That, of course, was my best card. I just sat on and on, refusing to go. We talked around and around the point, and presently he told me the real difficulty: when there had been the abortive attempt to get a domestic permit for Gerda, a Maliniak file had been opened, but unfortunately this file had been lost.

"And it's quite impossible to take action without the file, of course," he explained patiently.

"Well, then, open another one," I suggested.

He was horrified. This, it seemed, was even more impossible than taking action without a file.

"What is the good of your finding the file after my friends are dead?" I asked.

That moved him a bit, and he finally agreed to have a special search put on that night. "And once we've found the file, we'll take immediate action," he promised.

"Very well," I told him. "I'm going out now to telegraph to my friends in Vienna that British visas are on the way. They must have *something* in their hand."

"But suppose we don't find the file?" he cried anxiously.

"You've got to find it," I replied. "You've got all night, haven't you?"

"Well, it should be all right," he conceded doubtfully. And I staggered out.

I sent my cable, with some misgivings, and went home feeling like the proverbial piece of chewed string. However, I was pretty sure that file would turn up by morning, and then the visas should be forthcoming.

I was hardly dressed for the next morning before the telegram boy came roaring up to the door. And I received that dramatic telegram mentioned earlier.

"Georg not at home. Helpless. Gerda."

Georg, of course, was the German form of Jerzy, and the telegram meant he had been arrested.

I telephoned my official at the Home Office and asked grimly, "What about that file?"

"I'm afraid it hasn't been found yet," came the bright reply.

"Well, they've got the husband," I said. "What are you going to do before they get the wife?"

"Oh, lord! We'll telegraph the visas," came the reply.

There was nothing else we could do after that. Only wait for further news.

To follow the sequence of events, I shall have to change the scene over to Vienna, though it was many weeks before we heard this side of the story.

Having seen her husband as far as the prison, Gerda turned helplessly homewards. Her sister-in-law met her with the information that the Gestapo were waiting for her and she must not go home. Gerda dared not remain in any one place, and so, for two days and nights, she wandered about, not daring to go home.

Once or twice, she went to the British Consulate to ask if the visas had come, but an unsympathetic official simply replied that there were hundreds like her, and she would have to wait her turn. Finally, in despair and fear, she went to the Polish Consulate, since she was technically Polish by marriage, and asked if they could do anything for her there.

"We can send you to Poland," was the reply.

So frightened was she of the ever-nearing shadow of arrest that she agreed to go to Poland, and a Polish visa was issued. There was still no question of her returning home for her luggage. It is a fact that the poor girl set out for Poland with nothing but what she stood up in, her handbag in her hand. She has sometimes told us since that if it had been possible to die just from misery and despair, she would have done so on that journey. The train was practically empty, and she lay down and thought: *My husband is in prison. My child is in England. I shall never see either of them again. Here am I, on my way to Poland, knowing hardly a word of Polish. And there is a war coming.* She felt pretty sure that by now, her name was on the blacklist for arrest, and she knew that she could no longer stand up to the kind of questioning she would have to face at the frontier.

Presently, a kindly Polish train official found her. Seeing her terrible distress, he asked her why she had no luggage and what was wrong.

Fearing that he was perhaps an *agent provocateur*, she refused to answer. Then he showed her his Polish passport and said, "See, madam—I have the same passport as you. Won't you trust me now?"

She broke down then and, in tears, explained her predicament and that she could not, she simply *could not*, face the inevitable inquisition of the German officials at the frontier.

"Give me your passport and papers," the man said, "and go to sleep. I will look after things for you."

She could hardly believe this was possible. But he insisted he would manage. Then, since she said she could eat nothing, he went away and returned with an orange, which he peeled for her and fed to her in sections, as though she were a child.

Finally she fell asleep, or sank into some sort of stupor. And the next thing she knew, he was standing beside her once more, ready to return her papers to her, fully stamped. He had explained to the officials that he had a lady in one of the sleeping compartments so ill, she could not possibly be disturbed. By some merciful dispensation, they accepted this and stamped the papers with hardly a glance at him.

"Now you would like some breakfast?" he suggested, and Gerda nodded.

She said that, when he had gone, she staggered into the corridor and looked out on the most beautiful scene. It was early on a summer morning, and they were passing through lovely, peaceful countryside. It was like the morning of the world, before wickedness had come.

When the man brought her breakfast, she just put her

purse into his hand and said, "Please take whatever is necessary." But he returned it with the reply, "No, madam. The breakfast is my pleasure. You are going to need all your money."

All these years later, we still speak of him and wonder what happened to him when his unhappy country was overwhelmed. Here, at least, is a belated tribute to him, one of the kind unknowns who helped to irradiate the fog of misery with a shaft of pure charity.

Mitia used to call these unexpected manifestations of courage and kindness in people, "The Voice of the Lord, speaking in these terrible days."

Having arrived in Warsaw, Gerda went to her mother-in-law's house. A week later, to the astonishment of all, Jerzy joined her. Both the Polish Consul in Vienna and Clemens Krauss had made energetic representations on his behalf, and he had been released on condition that he proceed immediately to Poland, which he was not sorry to do.

About his sojourn in prison, he spoke with characteristic dryness and humour. "It was not so bad," he assured us. "The company at least was good. Probably the best in Vienna at that time."

From Poland, it was fairly simple for them to get in touch with us. We had new visas telegraphed to Warsaw and money for ship passages. They said goodbye to Jerzy's mother—later to be murdered in the Warsaw ghetto—and sailed for England. Early in July, they were reunited with their little girl.

This case was, I suppose, the supreme example of the apparently insoluble being solved.

"It shows that one should never despair," Gerda has said. "On that journey from Vienna to Warsaw, it seemed utterly impossible to me that things could ever come right again. And yet, you see, we were united safely in England. One should remember that miracles still happen. And one should not forget them or take them for granted when they do happen. Occasionally, even now, when I am alone, I sit down and think quietly over those terrible days, because I never want to forget—or get used to the fact—that we were saved by a miracle."

CHAPTER NINE

One morning early in December, 1938, I was called to the telephone to speak to one of the officials of an Austrian refugee organization. Did I, she asked, know any of the British consuls in Germany really well? Well enough to persuade him to reverse the earlier decision of another consul?

I said I knew the Frankfurt Consul and Vice-Consul, but only from interviews concerning various refugee cases. I added that I hardly thought one consul would have the power to reverse the decision of another, even if so inclined. But what was the trouble?

The case concerned a mother and daughter in Vienna. Mrs. Bauer and her daughter, Ilse, had both tried to obtain domestic permits to come to England. In the daughter's case, the papers had gone through all right. But at the last moment, the mother had been refused, on the grounds that she had rheumatism of the knee and would not, therefore, make a good domestic. Strictly true, no doubt, but a bit hard since she must die if she could not get out.

Now they were practically penniless, living on sufferance

in a friend's flat. If something could not be done soon, they must literally starve. Everyone's nerves had been screwed one peg tighter by the violent events of the previous month, when, after the Paris shooting of the German official, the reign of terror had begun in earnest.

They were just two of the countless thousands of human beings who had suddenly—in Austria—or gradually—in Germany—found themselves deprived of every elementary human right. They could not take any employment, draw benefit from any insurance or pension, live in any house or apartment that looked on a main street, stay in any hotel or boardinghouse, or enter any restaurant, café, theatre, church, synagogue or public place. The old people might not sit down on a public bench, nor do the children play in the public parks. And, if they wanted to sell anything to eke out a wretched existence, they were allowed to do so only at official valuation—which meant about a tenth or twentieth of any genuine value. They had only two rights left to them. They might starve or, if they had the money to pay for it, they might turn on the gas.

I knew the situation so well by now that I hardly needed to exert my imagination at all in order to visualize these two unfortunate women, and since they had been brought to my attention, I knew I must do something. Again, I considered the only consulate where I could expect even a personally interested hearing was in Frankfurt, and I had grave doubts of anyone being able to help there, whatever the inclination.

"However," I added, "if this mother and daughter are prepared to take a chance and come to Frankfurt—which would be on their way to England, anyway—I will undertake to go to Frankfurt, take them to the Consulate and tell the best story I can."

This rather doubtful offer was accepted with a fervour

that told me it was their only hope. I rang off and began to
add up the snags. To begin with, Louise had no more annual
leave, and I should have to go alone. She was the one who
spoke German, and—although I had occasionally got by in
a tiresome situation by playing the poor dumb Britisher who
determinedly knew no word of German—it gave me rather
a helpless feeling to go alone just at this time.

Even the British newspapers had been fairly explicit about
the carnage that had broken loose in Germany on the ninth
and tenth of November. Apart from the vile official policy,
the SS were almost completely out of hand, and all kinds of
violence had been perpetrated. The more I thought of the
trip, the less I liked it. However, I had said I would go, and
there was no drawing back now.

The parents were very good about it, saying, "If you feel
you must go, then you must go. But we shall be very thankful to see you back again."

The next problem to consider was where to put my poor
couple from Vienna, once they arrived in Frankfurt. As Jew-
esses, they were not allowed to stay in any hotel or boardinghouse, nor to take rooms anywhere.

Friedl solved this problem. On her suggestion, we sent
two telegrams: one to her mother, who was still in Frankfurt, stating, "Two women will arrive from Vienna on such-
and-such a date," the other to the Bauers, stating, "Go to
such-and-such an address."

Elsa lent me a thick winter coat, I remember, because I
didn't possess one and there was neither time nor money to
buy one just then. And Mitia—now safe in England—gave
me a list of names and addresses of people I was to try to see
and to whom I was to bring some words or reassurance and
hope. I have that list still—written out in Mitia's character-

istic violet ink. Across the top are the words, scribbled in a moment of deep emotion, "God bless you and help you."

This was a much darker and more uncertain journey than any we had made so far, and everyone came to see me off in a very sombre mood. I felt that everything was there except the wreath, and to tell the truth, I was unpleasantly scared. Though really I need not have worried, for the dark blue British passport still meant a great measure of protection.

At the last moment, I received a mysterious message. Would I bring out a valuable diamond brooch? It represented someone's entire capital; if I could get it over the frontier and safely into England, there would be no difficulty in obtaining a guarantee for the owner, as the brooch would represent support for the considerable period.

It was too late to say no. So I said yes. And off I went.

It was all very melodramatic. And I might say that when the brooch was brought to me in Frankfurt, I was appalled. It was a great oblong of blazing diamonds. The sort of thing I had hardly ever seen, much less worn. However, fortunately at that time, I was wearing a six-and-eleven penny Marks & Spencer jumper—of jacquard satin, with glass buttons down the front. And I thought: *If I plaster this on top and can make myself come out with my coat open, it wouldn't possibly be anything but Woolworth's.* Which is what I did—trembling a bit, but it worked.

But, to return to the main story. I arrived in Frankfurt feeling what I presume is meant by "low." I have always been especially thankful that I made the effort and went at that particular time, for I saw a demonstration of British justice and fairness that has stayed with me and warmed my heart ever since.

When I reached Frankfurt, my friends told me that, on the ninth and tenth of November, when the SS men were going through the streets, beating up old people, burning the synagogue and Jewish shops, and shooting whenever they felt the urge, the British Consul opened the Consulate day and night. Hundreds of those unfortunate people, most of whom could speak little or no English, poured into the Consulate and stood there—some of them all night in the garden in the rain—because there they could not be arrested. It was a piece of Britain.

Not only that. Those who came to the Consulate hungry and in need—no Jew was allowed to buy food for nine days—were fed. And I understand the Vice-Consul even went through the streets, with food in his car, to feed those in want.

One woman told me, "It was the only time I cried. My husband was in the concentration camp, and while I tried everything to get him out, it was too terrible for one even to cry. Then at last, I went to the British Consul to see if he could help me. And the first thing they asked me at the Consulate was, 'Have you had anything to eat today?' I hadn't of course—I was too worried to think of food. And, before they did anything else, they fed me with coffee and sandwiches, as though I had been a guest. And then I cried."

And don't let us ever forget that the only real strength and support those two men, the Consul and the Vice-Consul, had behind them was the strength of the British public opinion and the knowledge that, in the final showing, most of their countrymen would have supported them in their actions. To all who have always stood up for fairness, instead of prejudice or expediency, a little bit of the credit for that incident belongs.

The mother and daughter from Vienna had already arrived, and the next day I took them to the Consulate, prepared to tell the best story I could. I was a little doubtful of our chances of even getting in, when I considered how the consulates were besieged night and day by anxious applicants. But everyone assured me that I had only to show my passport.

Oh, the scenes in the Consulate! In any British or American Consulate at that time. Pale, drawn, anxious people turned over their papers time after time while they waited. They checked and rechecked every detail, telling themselves and each other that, this time, they thought everything would be all right. The idea that there might be yet another hitch was too horrible to contemplate. In the waiting room downstairs, the babble of talk and discussion and encouragement and despair was indescribable. And then, suddenly, a girl in her early twenties appeared and held up her hand.

Complete silence fell on the roomful of people, and all faces were turned to her with an eager, trusting expression that I have never seen equalled anywhere else. She smiled around in a friendly way, as though this were a perfectly normal occasion, and said, "All those with such-and-such papers go that way, please. All those with such-and-such papers go the other way, please. The rest, follow me."

And like children, they followed her. Men old enough to be her grandfather, businessmen, harassed wives—silent or loquacious, whichever way their anxiety had affected them. All did her bidding without question, with a piteous confidence in her kindness and efficiency that was the highest tribute possible to the reputation she had earned among them.

We were among the contingent instructed to follow her. We were conducted to another waiting room immediately adjoining the office of the two Consuls, and there we waited again. After about an hour, I managed to get near the door to the inner room. On one occasion when the Vice-Consul came to the door, I showed him my British passport and said,

"Mr. Dowden, might I speak to you for five minutes? I have come from England to do it."

He looked at me, and then around the room at all those waiting people. And he replied, "I'm sorry. But do you realize that some of these people have been waiting since seven o'clock in the morning to speak to me? I'm afraid you must go away and take your turn."

And I cannot possibly describe the effect that statement had on all the people in the room. Nowhere in the whole of their horrible country had they any rights left as human beings, except in that room. And there, they even had a right in the queue.

I said at once, "No, *I* am sorry. Of course you are right. I'll come another time."

Mr. Dowden asked then, quite sympathetically, if I had come on refugee work. When I said I had, he told me to come back after office hours, that their official hours belonged to these people.

As I and the Bauers withdrew, everyone smiled sympathetically, and I had the curious impression they had become human beings again. They *had* rights just like any other human being. It had just been demonstrated for them before their own eyes.

Later that day, we went back and were admitted to the private house of the Chief Consul, Mr. Smallbones.

First, a very pretty girl in her teens came to us and said, "Could you explain the case to me first? We're all in on this, and sometimes it saves Daddy a few minutes if I or Mother hear a case first."

When I explained the situation, she agreed that this was something her father must deal with personally. Presently, I was sent in to speak to Mr. Smallbones, while my poor Mrs. Bauer and her daughter waited outside. Once more, I told my tale, and by now it sounded pretty good to me. But, at the end, Mr. Smallbones said, without hesitation, "I'm sorry. It's quite outside my province to reverse the decision of another consul."

I gasped with horror. For somehow I had managed to convince myself that I was fairly sure of success.

"They're waiting outside now," I pleaded. "They've come all the way from Vienna, and they have no money left. It's their last hope. I *can't* go out and tell them there's no chance."

He made a face. But I knew that, in spite of his insistence on using the official channels, he was also one of the most resourceful and humane men in Frankfurt. After a few moments' thought, he said, "I could write to the Chief Consul in Berlin, telling him that I have before me a case from Vienna where the visa had previously been refused on health grounds, that I am now satisfied that the woman's health is restored, and would it be in order for me to grant the visa without referring the case back to Vienna?"

I said that sounded a marvellous idea, and asked how long would it take.

"I have no idea," Mr. Smallbones replied with devastating frankness. "I can only tell you that I will write the letter as soon as you are gone. But one Consul usually answers another fairly quickly. More than that, I can't say."

It is worth recording that many years afterwards, I was told it was Mr. Smallbones who thought of the famous "guarantee system" and persuaded the British Home Office to implement it. I believe that, to this day, it is known in the Home Office files as the Smallbones Plan. Under that plan 48,000 people were saved from death.

Well, I thanked him fervently and returned to my poor waiting couple, who by now, I suppose, had both reached the point of hoping I would come out complete with visa.

At any rate, optimistic though I tried to sound in my report of events, they both wept on the way back. And so did I, finally. It was a very damp homecoming.

I telephoned Louise in London that evening, which served to reassure them at home and cheer me a little. Then we settled down to wait.

Krauss and Ursuleac, who were always our chief support and comfort on prolonged visits of this kind, were miles away in Munich, and I had neither the excuse nor the money to go there to them. Frankfurt was where this business had to be worked out, and in Frankfurt I had to stay. Each day, we went to the Consulate. Each day, we learned that no reply had been received from Berlin.

I filled in my time visiting the various people Mitia had listed, as well as others I had heard of through other sources, saying what I could in the way of cheer and sympathy. Usually they were surprised that I was not elderly and responsible looking. I suppose a Miss Cook with an interest in "good works" does somehow sound like a grey-haired worthy. Again, it was humbling to the last degree to find how far a few kind words or, better still, a little sympathetic listening would go toward making people feel braver and more hopeful.

It was on this trip that I first met the dear Basches, old friends of Mitia, who lived in Offenbach. Mr. Basch had been released from Dachau only a few days previously. It was in their house, I remember, that I first received the overwhelming impression of the insanity that lay behind the ferocity of Nazi hatred.

The Basches' house had been a very pleasant, beautifully furnished home. They were reasonably, though not fantastically, wealthy people and had for many years collected beautiful things around them. In particular, they had some very lovely old glass, which was set in cabinets on the attractive divided stairway.

On entering the house, the first shock was the sight of a wonderful Venetian mirror, now splintered. One of the SS men had thrown a hammer at it. They had tipped over the cabinets of glass and thrown them down the stairs. The grand piano had been hammered, the notes torn out of the keyboard. Every possible destruction to the contents of the house had been accomplished. Even the pictures had not been overlooked. I remember Mr. Basch taking me over to a once beautiful Dutch painting and saying, "That is—that *was*—a museum piece. Any museum in Germany would have been glad to have it. If they had stolen it from me and given it a museum, I could understand. If they had taken it and sold it to make money for the poor, I could understand. But you see what they have done?"

It had been hammered all over and was damaged beyond repair or recognition.

Fortunately, their sons had already emigrated to the States, and one married daughter was in the process of doing so. Mr. Basch had plans for going to France, and the only two members of the family still remaining to be saved were Mrs. Basch and the second daughter Lisa.

I loved them on sight. Since means could be found, one way or another, to support them modestly once they were outside Germany, I undertook then and there to find guarantors for them both.

Through all the years and all the recent troubles, Mrs. Basch had still retained an unquenchable youthfulness of spirit and enthusiasm that endeared her to me and later to Louise. Sometimes her husband used to shake his head and say, "When will you cease being so youthful?" And she would reply, "When I close my eyes for the last time." I know no better way of describing my dear Mrs. Basch.

I might add that we did manage the guarantees for her and Lisa, that they were two of the most valued friends who ever found sanctuary in our famous flat, and that any reader who reads on to the later sections of this book will meet them again on our return to America after the War.

Uncle Carl was another good friend I saw much of during that strange week. He was the last of the Mayer-Lismann family to remain in Frankfurt. Brother of Mitia, he was literally Uncle Carl to Elsa, figuratively so to Louise and me and, later, to most of our friends.

Owing to his age, or some inexplicable oversight, he had been missed in the great round-up of Jews in November, and we were anxiously busy on his case now, trying to get him out before attention was drawn to him. Fortunately, the house where he still had a small apartment was undergoing extensive outside repairs, which necessitated a great deal of scaffolding and gave the place a completely uninhabited appearance. So long as no light showed at night, there was a chance that his presence there would be overlooked by any casual spy.

I used to have supper with him there. With a low light, carefully shielded, and thick curtains drawn, we would sit there, talking of the past and the future—although seldom of the problematical present.

Sometimes I used to think: *I am the same girl who saved money to go and hear Galli-Curci in the golden days of the 1920's. I am the same girl who spins light romances when she is at home. Now I am sitting here in the semi-darkness, hoping no one will guess that someone lives here, wondering if we shall be able to save this wonderful old man from concentration camp.* We did save him, I am thankful to say. He survived to a great age in England,

and although he eventually went blind, he remained a joy and a support to everyone who knew him.

A whole week passed, and still there was no answer from Berlin. I dared not stay longer, or allow the daughter to stay longer. Her visa would not last forever, and we had strained its effectiveness as far as we should. I broke it to the Bauers that Ilse and I must go, that Mrs. Bauer must wait on alone.

It was a hard decision for them to make: to separate after all they had been through together. But I was able to leave some money, and she had good friends; thus Mrs. Bauer was provided for during the foreseeable future until the visa came through. That it might never come at all was something we dared not contemplate.

In the early hours of a snowy winter morning, Ilse and I set off for England. We passed the frontier safely, and complete with one charge—and the diamond brooch!—I finally returned to the bosom of my much-relieved family.

A few weeks later, we heard that Mrs. Bauers's visa as a domestic worker had been finally refused.

We had to start all over again to try and get her out on a guarantee as an elderly person who would not be permitted to work. Making every effort and sacrifice, her son and daughter were sure they could support her, if only I could find a guarantee from somewhere. But where?

And then, one of those incredible coincidences happened that occur only in real life. I never dare to put them in any romances, because people then say contemptuously, "Things like that never happen." They do—all the time—if you do your best and look for them.

I was lunching with a friend in an Oxford Street restaurant, telling her some of the things I had seen and experienced in Germany. Presently, to my astonishment, another woman at the table exclaimed, "Excuse my speaking to you.

But I couldn't help hearing what you were saying, and I feel I *must* do something to help. What could I do?"

I must have gaped, quite literally. But, recovering myself, I said, "How very nice of you. Did you have anything special in mind yourself?"

She explained then that she and her sister-in-law had recently talked over the possibility of taking a refugee child, but had not known quite how to set about it. Did I know of a child in need of such an offer?

"I have everything, from five to seventy-five," I assured her. She and her sister-in-law might make their choice from a gallery of pitiful photographs.

She took my name, address and telephone number, promising to let me hear more. To tell the truth, when we parted, I hardly expected to hear from her again.

I was wrong. The next day, the sister-in-law phoned from Buckinghamshire and arranged for all three of us to meet in town. When we met, photographs were displayed, and one was chosen. At that point, she added, "Before we make the final arrangements, I think I had better tell my husband about it."

"Good heavens!" I exclaimed. "I should think you had. Doesn't he know yet?"

She smiled and shook her head, but promised to let me know the decision immediately.

Three days later, I received a deeply regretful letter from her, in which she wrote, "I didn't tell you before, but we lost our own little boy less than a year ago. My husband thinks that if we take another child and try—as we certainly must—to rescue the parents too, we shall simply allow ourselves to grow terribly fond of yet another child whom we shall ultimately have to lose. But is there anything else we could do to help?"

The husband was perfectly right, of course, and I am glad to say that the little girl was taken by other people. But I wrote at once to my lady in Buckinghamshire saying that, if their essential aim was to save a life, would they give me a guarantee for an elderly woman and accept my word— though knowing virtually nothing about me—that the guarantee would not be called upon?

They immediately gave the guarantee for Mrs. Bauer— they never even saw her—and we hauled her out, at the last minute, just before the war began.

Here now is the other half of the story, which Louise and I heard in detail only long afterwards.

Before we ever came into the Bauer case at all—in fact, even before the Germans invaded Austria—Ilse had been engaged. Her fiancé was an Aryan, but they had intended to marry just as soon as he could find a job. Unemployment was rife in Austria at that time, partly because it was subsidized by the Nazis from Germany. They used to pay enormous sums to corrupt officials in firms and public undertakings in order to keep the rate of unemployment high. Then, as a valuable weapon of propaganda, they could compare the large-scale unemployment in Austria with the "complete employment" in Nazi Germany.

Ilse's fiancé was one of these unemployed until the Germans came, when he was immediately offered employment under the Nazis. He knew, however, that once he accepted employment under them, his chances of marrying a Jewish girl were gone. Therefore he hedged, said his health was bad and that he would have to have his tonsils out. I am not quite sure whether his tonsils really needed attention or whether this was a bit of ingenious fiction. Anyway, he went into hospital and had his tonsils removed.

Then he applied for permission to go to his brother in

Switzerland in order to recuperate. Their immediate answer was that such an excursion was unnecessary—under National Socialism there was an admirable Health Service with everything provided free. He was offered a period of recuperation in one of the Bavarian convalescent homes.

However, he contrived to plead his need of Swiss air so convincingly that he was finally given a permit to go to Switzerland for two weeks. He went off immediately, intending never to return, and promptly arranged for Ilse to be rowed over Lake Constance by a boatman who was smuggling people out.

When the night of her departure came, bad news was brought to her. The boatman had acted once too often and had been caught. So there were Ilse and her mother stranded in Vienna, while Leo, her fiancé, was in Switzerland, under orders to return at any minute.

At this point, Louise and I came into the story and started our efforts to get Ilse and her mother to England. Meanwhile, of course, Leo had to do something to prevent his being sent back to Austria. He went around to every consulate, making endless enquiries, and found that the only place to which he could go with reasonable ease—so far as papers were concerned—was Brazil. And to Brazil he went.

By this time, we had Ilse and her mother safely in London, and the next thing was to engineer the final reunion. But, just as everything was ready, the war came, and there were no places available on the boat. Later, when it was possible to get places on a boat, all entry papers were out of date, and we had to start all over again to obtain fresh ones. This circular situation continued throughout the whole of the war and for a year afterwards.

Not long before they finally left by air in June, 1946, Ilse told us that, when she parted from her Leo in Vienna in their early engaged days, they had wondered how they were going to be able to bear a fortnight's separation. It was almost eight years before they were reunited.

On the night before the Bauers left England, we were all in the flat—whose walls have heard so many strange and sad and mad stories—and we talked of all that had happened in those eight years. Mrs. Bauer recounted details of their earlier adventures, which even Louise and I had not known until then. Throughout her trials, Mrs. Bauer's courage and optimism had served her well. Bless her heart, her optimism was justified. In the loving companionship of her daughter and her devoted son-in-law, she lived to a splendid old age—and long enough to see her granddaughter grow into a charming and beautiful girl.

CHAPTER TEN

Lulu Cossman belonged to a famous Frankfurt family. Her father, born the year Napoleon died, was a celebrated cellist and the first man to play the Schumann cello concerto. In addition to Schumann, he numbered among his friends Brahms, Berlioz, Tchaikovsky and most of the great musical figures of the middle and late nineteenth century.

Indeed, to the end of her long life, Lulu used to startle me delightfully from time to time with such phrases as, "When Tchaikovsky used to stay with us," or "I remember Berlioz once wrote to my father that…" And once, when I took her to a film in which Liszt—complete with glossy nylon hair and energetically banging a grand piano—was depicted, an angry voice beside me exclaimed, "Liszt wasn't a *bit* like that! I knew him very well."

Lulu was seventy-five when we first met her. She was not strictly one of our cases, since all we did was to straighten out a clerical error in the last stages, but the circumstances were extremely interesting.

It isn't any fun to have to find a new home in a strange

country when you are old. But then, there happened one of those heart-warming things that make drama out of the most everyday circumstances. From England, she received a letter, written by someone who had known her more than fifty years ago when they were girls together at the same finishing school. They had not seen each other, or even corresponded, for half a century, but her friend wrote to ask if she were all right or if she needed any assistance.

A rapid exchange of letters made the position clear, and the English friend and her husband offered a home and a full guarantee, which were joyfully accepted. Forms were filled up and references supplied; everything was in perfect order and the officials in London stated that the necessary permit for a British visa had been sent to the head office in Berlin. But when she applied for the visas to be transferred from Frankfurt to Berlin, they were met with the reply that no such visa permission had been received.

A great deal of futile exchange of correspondence had taken place, and nerves were growing thin, when Louise and I were asked if we would go personally to the head office in Berlin on our next trip and make enquiries. This we did, and after some discussion, we finally elucidated the mystery. The English woman, who had never known her girlhood friend as anything but Lulu, had applied in that name. Lulu, on the other hand, had made enquiries in her real name of Louisa.

We straightened out the muddle, and in the early months of 1939, the old lady flew over to England.

On our last journey into Germany in August, 1939, we undertook to visit her brother, Professor Cossman. The professor was enjoying a period of doubtful freedom after serving a long sentence in a Munich prison for opposition to Hitler. A man of extraordinary, one might say obstinate, courage, he refused to have any strenuous efforts made on his behalf, and we were unable to rescue him. He died in Theresienstadt concentration camp in the latter half of the war, an example of moral courage and great fortitude, from which many of his companions who survived him say they drew the utmost support.

A very remarkable man, and one we are glad to have known, even fleetingly.

Then there was dear Alice, soft-voiced and charming, but with her own brand of moral courage too. She was one of the most famous milliners in Berlin and, in happier days, used to make the Crown Princess's hats. As times changed and a new "aristocracy" grew up, Frau Ribbentrop and Frau Goebbels became customers. One day Frau Ribbentrop said abruptly, "You are only half-Jewish, aren't you?"

Alice said that she was.

"Well, you know," Frau Ribbentrop told her reflectively, "if you would divorce your husband"—who was a full Jew— "I could see to it that you kept your shop."

With courage, Alice replied, "Thank you very much. But I think perhaps it is better I keep my husband and lose my shop."

No more was said at the time. But the next day Frau Ribbentrop's manicurist came to the shop.

"Frau Ribbentrop likes your hats," she explained, "and wants to go on having them. But in future, she will not come to the shop herself. You'll deliver the hats to me."

To which Alice, to her lasting credit, replied, "Please tell Frau Ribbentrop that I may be a Jew, but I don't do business by the back door."

That, of course, was virtually the end of the hat shop. Her husband managed to escape to Holland, but at the point when Louise and I entered the story, Alice was still marooned in Berlin in such a state of despair over the prolonged separation that her relatives feared she might try to commit suicide. We were going to Berlin in any case—this was in March, 1939—and we undertook to see her, if only to have a talk and cheer her up a little.

With her white hair, hyacinth-blue eyes, and an enchanting complexion, she was one of the prettiest women I have ever seen in my life. When she came to our hotel, she was extremely calm and composed. But no sooner had we got her up in our bedroom where we could talk in comparative safety, than the tears began to flow.

We listened, dismayed, to yet another tragic story. She had, it seemed, finally made an attempt to join her husband in Holland, even though her papers were incomplete. She even got as far as the frontier and spoke to him—the last time she was ever to speak to him, as it turned out, for the Germans got him again when they invaded Holland in 1940—and then she was turned back. In her horror and despair, she fainted. And when she recovered consciousness, she was on the train, going back to Berlin.

We said what we could in the way of sympathy. And then she added, "But you haven't heard the worst. I had with me all my jewellery. It represents all my capital, in any country to which I can escape. And I was so upset that I forgot to give it to my husband at the frontier. Now the order has gone out that all Jews must give up their jewellery. It's all I have—my only means of living even if I escape."

Louise and I looked at each other. We were already loaded to the Plimsoll line with jewellery for other people and had firmly decided not to take any more. But at the moment, we would both have tried to take out the Crown Jewels, I do believe. Louise gave me a slight nod, and I said, "Don't cry any more. Will you trust it with us? And we'll try to get you a guarantee in England."

Oh, Lord! The terrible, heart-rending gratitude that the offer of these not-so-very-difficult services used to provoke. With more tears, and a few from us too I expect, it was arranged that we should visit her the next morning at the flat of a friend with whom she was living.

There were two friends there, I remember, when we arrived. At first, I thought one of them had a bad cold. Presently I realized it was just that she had been crying endlessly. She had "lost her husband in the camp," as the terrible phrase went, only a month or two before.

Presently, she insisted on showing us his photograph. It was of a nice, ordinary-looking middle-aged man, and while we looked at it, she kept assuring us that he was such a good man and had never harmed anyone, as though the only thing she could do for him was to make unprejudiced people realize he had not been killed for any real crime.

At last, the other friend said, in a faint attempt at consolation, "Don't grieve so. They'll be punished, these dreadful people who've done these things. They'll be punished. Their turn is coming."

But the widow said simply, in tones of lead, "You can't un-kill people."

I often thought of that afterwards, in the years of slaughter that followed. You can never un-kill people.

We took the jewellery and went back to England. There was a very bad half hour at the frontier when the Black Guard came on the train and stayed there for some unknown reason, parked in the corridor right outside our compartment. But we got away without an examination of our actual handbags, which was lucky, as we had all the really valuable stuff, quite brazenly, there.

We had decided that, if our amount of jewellery were discovered and queried, we were going to do the nervous British spinster act and insist, quite simply, that we always took our valuables with us, because we didn't trust anyone with whom we could leave them at home. I don't know whether the story would have "washed," but it is a good example of the sort of silly lie I mentioned before. It often succeeds by the sheer force of its simplicity and because it makes one look rather a fool.

Back in England, we were faced with the task of obtaining yet another guarantee. But luck was with us all the way in this case. One morning, a very old friend of ours phoned and said, "Could you come to tea this afternoon? I have a friend coming, and I *think* she might be good for a guarantee. She's awfully nice and understanding and has a very nice husband."

Our friend also had a very nice husband, I might say. It was he who had given the guarantee for Mrs. Basch and Lisa, and it was he who pulled a string in Downing Street that time I went after the Maliniaks' visas.

I accepted the invitation, of course, and over tea, I launched into the story of our recent visit to Berlin. It was a wonderful afternoon! I didn't even have to "fish" for that guarantee. The visitor looked at me kindly and thoughtfully and said, "I'm sure my husband would guarantee that poor woman if, as you say, she really has enough jewellery here to support herself."

With a secret sigh of relief that we had brought out the jewellery, I assured her that this was the case. In a very short time, the guarantee was forthcoming and Alice was dragged out of Berlin, with even a month or two to spare before war broke out.

As I said earlier, she never saw her husband again. But she did make a reasonably happy life for herself here in England. And for many, many years—until she finally retired altogether—

if I wanted to look especially nice, I used to go and see her, and she would make me a heavenly hat.

The most truly melodramatic case was Walter Stiefel's. He was the son of the elderly couple we had rescued from Frankfurt. When we were going to Berlin on that last visit, we were told about him and asked if we could help. Someone had already offered a home to his little girl. We were fortunate enough to get a home for him and his wife in the North West of England, and they got away at the very last moment. At the time, it seemed a fairly straightforward case to us. It was only about ten years ago that we heard the drama behind it all.

Walter had made one of his rather rare visits to London, and we were talking together of old times. And I said sincerely— I was not being coy or corny—"In a way, of course, it was not really very dangerous for us, except for the smuggling."

Walter looked amused and replied, "It was much more dangerous than you ever imagined. What was really dangerous was when you handled someone who was in the Anti-Hitler Underground. I'll tell you now—I never told you then—I was six years in the Anti-Hitler Underground. I was one of those who produced a secret news sheet. We printed it in the centre of a Berlin store at night, when the store was closed. No one had any idea we were there. I helped to produce and distribute it. And if, during those last weeks when you were helping me, I had been caught and made to talk—and don't let's pretend anything else, they could make anyone talk—not only would all my confederates have been arrested, but so would you."

We were stunned. And intrigued beyond measure. All those years ago, we'd been heroines, without the pain of knowing it!

Walter went on. "Don't you remember how careful I was about meeting you?"

"I do remember, we thought you were fussy," I recalled. "And you wouldn't give us an address, would you?"

"I couldn't give you an address," he assured us. "I changed it every few weeks. I changed my whole identity six times during those years. Don't you remember *how* we arranged to meet?"

With an effort, we did. We were to meet him in a crowded railway station in Berlin—I think it was the Anhalter—and we were to recognize him because he carried under his left arm an English newspaper. But what we did not know was that suddenly, that day, English newspapers were forbidden throughout Germany and he couldn't get one. So he bought a Dutch one and walked about with that under his left arm. But the Cooks didn't jump to that. We thought he hadn't come, and very worried, we went back to our hotel.

The awkward thing was that we had long ago discovered that if you were doing the sort of thing we were doing, much the best places to stay were the big luxury hotels where the Nazi chiefs stayed. Then if you stood and gazed at them admiringly as they went through the lobby, no one thought you were anything but another couple of admiring fools. That was why we knew them all by sight. We knew them all, Louise and I. Goering, Goebbels, Himmler, Streicher, Ribbentrop—who once gave Louise what we used to call "the glad eye" across the breakfast room at the Vierjahszeiten in Munich. We even knew Hitler from the back—because we all stayed in the same hotels. And there we were in the Adlon—where I suppose Hitler was probably having lunch.

We retired to our room in gloomy doubt. But finally Walter dared to telephone—though of course the phones were often tapped—and he said, "I'm going to get into a taxi and drive round a certain block"—he described the block—"until you stand on a certain corner. And I will pick you up."

It all seemed unnecessarily melodramatic to us at the time. After all, we're not a bit the James Bond type. We come from a very respectable civil-service family. But when Walter explained the background to us, we saw why it all had to be that way. Only, we were thankful we had not known at the time. It's amusing in retrospect—with everyone safe.

I suppose the narrowest margin of escape in any of our cases occurred with a young Polish boy, the last of these stories I will tell. In October, 1938—before the big November drive against the Jews—the order had suddenly gone forth that all Polish Jews were to be expelled from Germany. Some were given twenty-four hours, some were given two hours, and some a quarter of an hour, depending on the merciful, or otherwise, disposition of the local official concerned.

Curiously enough, I myself saw the departure of the Frankfurt contingent without knowing at the time what was happening. I saw a crowd of people being hustled like animals along the platform and, turning to my porter, managed to ask, in my inadequate German, "What on earth is happening over there?"

He glanced over his shoulder, explained indifferently, "Only Jews," and trotted on ahead with my luggage.

Much later, I remember mentioning that incident to a friend of ours, and she exclaimed, "Oh, but, my dear, you didn't see the end of their journey! I did. I was in a village near the Polish border, and the rumour went around that the Polish Jews were coming. For four days and nights, from all over Germany, trainloads of those unfortunate people were coming. Some were still in their nightclothes—they had simply been hauled from their beds—and some of the old people and children had been shot in the back because they hadn't moved fast enough."

From all over Germany, they had been coming in their helpless, horrible misery. It was peacetime. People were going to the theatre, to the shops, on holidays, pursuing their normal lives, and that terrible procession threaded its way through their midst.

I will not say that there was no protest, because I simply do not know. I will only say that I never heard of any protest being made on that occasion.

And there they were, gathered together on the border. The Germans tried to thrust them out, and the Poles would not let them in. In justice, one must say that there was something to be said for the Polish attitude. Every country was having to refuse hordes of unidentified and unidentifiable refugees. In addition, many of these people were only technically Polish and could hardly speak a word of the language. There was obviously a war coming, and there were no means of checking the bona fides of this hastily assembled multitude.

They were thrust into the improvised prison camp of Zbasyn. Great racing stables had once existed there, and where one horse had been, eight people were given space. And there they stayed all the winter.

Some of the older people died, of course, but an astonishing number survived. In the spring, we received a letter from a boy there. To this day I don't know how he got hold of our name and address, but news travelled quickly and by strange paths when there was any hope of safety involved.

He wrote that he hardly knew why he was addressing us; he had no more claim than thousands of other people around him, but had heard that we were trying to help. His quota number for the United States meant about a three-year wait.

It was foolish, he felt, even to ask—but could we do anything to save him and keep him alive during the intervening years?

I wrote back as sympathetically as I could, hoping to give him the courage to go on. I told him quite frankly that we had several cases already waiting for the next guarantee we could raise. But I promised to put him on our list and not let his case out of mind until time and opportunity served us better.

He replied that he could live for several months more on that alone.

Just about that time, I was asked to speak to a church congregation. The church members were proposing to adopt a refugee child among them. They needed both sympathy and a sense of urgency aroused in the congregation. I went very willingly, but was somewhat disconcerted to find that I had to address my audience from the pulpit. However, by now I was not easily put off. Money was running out fast, and my tongue—which had never served me badly!—was my best remaining asset. I said what had come to be known disrespectfully in the family as "Ida's little piece" and went away again, hoping that I had done some good.

Three weeks later, I received a telephone call from the clergyman of the church. Had I, he wanted to know, a case that required a guarantee and about three years' hospitality? Some other congregation had taken their refugee child; now they had lots of sympathy and no refugee. He left the choice to me, but suggested that, as they certainly had enough money and hospitality to cover three years, the chance should go to someone who needed the full amount.

It was such a chance—such an unexpected offer out of nowhere—that I felt it should go to our poor Polish boy, who did just exactly what was being offered. But first he had to get his papers in order. These were, as will be imagined, many and complicated. Indeed, some people died because they sent the wrong papers, and no one had time to straighten out the case and send them detailed instructions.

Back came all the completed papers, accompanied by one of the most heartfelt letters of incredulous joy I have ever received. And, nearly as pleased myself, I rushed off to Bloomsbury House where the next stage of proceedings would have to be undergone.

I interviewed the girl who usually dealt with my cases, and she congratulated me wholeheartedly on the sudden stroke of good fortune. Then she took one look at the papers and exclaimed, "Oh, my dear, how terrible! We have just had an order today that we must not accept anyone with a higher quota number than 16,000. He is 16,500 and—"

We stared at each other in dismay.

"I can't write back and tell him that," I pleaded. "I *can't*. He's nearly mad with joy at the thought of release. Think of something! You must think of something to get us out of this."

She was a most resourceful girl. After several moments' thought, she handed me back one of the papers and said, "Go home and take this with you. I will write an official letter, dated three days ago, asking for the missing paper, and the case will date from the time of the first letter in the file. That will qualify it before the new rule came into operation."

And on such details people's lives hung.

I did as she suggested, and the case began to take the accustomed course. There were the usual delays and hold-ups that one could not always foresee, and it was August before the coveted British visa was granted.

By that time, Louise and I were in Germany on the last visit we were to make there before war broke out. I received verbal information, via a network of mutual friends, that the

visa had been granted, but that the boy was in further difficulty because every boat out of Poland was fully booked
up to the end of the year. Most people knew that a war was
coming now, and every available escape route was jammed.
He could not, of course, travel by train through Germany.
But there was just one chance left. It might be possible for
him to get passage as one of the people in charge of a children's transport, if I could send him money for his fare.

From Germany, this was impossible, of course. But we
sent word that, if he could let us know in England what he
needed, we would send it.

Louise and I reached home less than a fortnight before
war broke out. By the time we knew what money was necessary, the few days left were cruelly short. I telegraphed the
amount. Almost at the same time, the Germans marched
over the Polish frontier.

I telephoned the shipping office concerned to ask if the
boat had left in time. They had no news then, but told me the
next day that the boat had got away, although no one knew
who was on board. They suggested I had better come down
to the London Docks when it came in, and see for myself.

On one of those cloudless, brilliant afternoons when all of
us knew at last that war was upon us, I waited anxiously at the
harbour. I shall never forget the arrival of that boat, the last
children's transport from Poland. There were 200 children
ranging from four-year-olds to youths of about fifteen and
sixteen. Every one of them had had to leave his or her parents behind. All the parents were later murdered, I suppose.

I see them now, in melancholy recollection, coming slowly
down the gangway, carrying their little bundles and gazing
around on a strange world. None of them spoke English.
None of them had a hope in the world, except to live, instead
of being killed. I had nothing but a passport photograph by

which to identify my Polish boy. But, when he finally came off, he was unmistakable.

He told me that, at the last minute, there was some final hitch in connection with his Polish papers, and he had had to wait, sweating with anxiety, while the matter was argued out afresh. Then, at the very last possible moment, he was allowed to go, and he rushed on board almost as they were removing the gangway. The last man to board the last boat that left Gydnia. Then civilian shipping had ceased, and the war had begun.

He was also the last of our successful cases. I remember very vividly all the people we interviewed on our own last journey to the continent. In every instance, we were too late to do anything. Perhaps that is why one remembers them so well.

For many heart-rending years, we both used to recall a particular family. The father was a Jew and the mother was an Aryan. He had been rounded up with all the others the previous November and sent to Dachau. Although he had gone in as a fine, strapping man in the prime of life, he was discharged to hospital six months later, half dead from heart trouble brought on by being forced to carry weights beyond any human capacity. In addition, he had lost a foot from frostbite.

Like all Aryan women married to Jewish husbands, the wife had been advised to divorce her husband. Her refusal to do so meant she could not officially be employed. She scraped along as best she could, doing cleaning for the few kindly or courageous people who dared to employ her. In this precarious way, she tried to support her three boys and one little girl.

Someone who had known the family well in better days told us that they had been the happiest family imaginable.

They never had a great deal of money, but enough. They had always said they would not part with any one of their children for a million marks.

When we came into the case, we were simply asked to see the woman, hear her story and find out what could be done, if anything. We asked her to come and meet us at the apartment of some Jewish friends of ours. She came in, clutching her little girl by the hand. She said no word of greeting. She simply broke into desperate, economical speech.

"I can't part with my little girl," she said almost fiercely. "She is too young. But my little boys you may take, for they are absolutely starving."

We spoke to her as gently as possible and asked her to sit down and tell us something of the circumstances. We really knew most of the sad story already, but she went over it again, while Louise and I considered what we could do.

At the end, I told her quite frankly it was unlikely that we should be able to get the children together in one home, but I promised to try to get all the boys in one village or town. I was already turning over in my mind the possibility of interesting one of the Northumbrian villages near our own old home.

"When your husband is better," I continued—though I'm afraid I really meant *when he is dead*—"we will try to get you over on a domestic permit, some place where you can bring the little girl, too. It isn't much to offer immediately, but we will try to reunite you somewhere, some day."

She was faintly comforted, poor soul. But it was all rather long-term planning. Most immediately important, we were able to leave her a fair amount of money, because a friend who was emigrating had a little left that he could not take with him. In the course of the conversation, we mentioned that we were going to the hospital in the Gagernstrasse that afternoon, and her face brightened at once.

"My husband is there," she said. "Would you go and see him?"

We said that, if she thought it would comfort him to hear that we were going to try to help, we would certainly go. And she arranged to meet us there.

It was a strange and terrible experience—unshared, I think, by any other, or by very few other British people. Every case in that hospital was a concentration-camp case; that is to say, every patient had been made ill deliberately. Only two surgeons had been allowed to remain to look after the unfortunates. Of these, one had a septic thumb at the time and could not operate.

The other was quite a young man who took us into his private office and said, "I want you to give me your advice about something."

We promised to do our best.

"I have a chance to escape," he explained quietly. "All my papers are in order for me to go to America. Have I the right to take this chance, or should I stay here with these people?"

Louise and I looked at each other in horrified silence. Then at last I replied, "I'm terribly sorry, but we couldn't possibly undertake to decide such a thing for anyone. It is for you to make your own decision."

We heard afterwards that he had stayed.

We were taken upstairs to the poor fellow we were to visit. At the top of the staircase, the wife and three thin, bright little boys were waiting. They beamed silently upon us and seemed unnaturally good. Presently, we and the woman went into the small ward her husband shared with two or three others.

It seemed to us that he was obviously dying, and though

fairly interested in our assurances that we would do what we could for his children, he appeared to have passed beyond any expression of deep emotion.

The friend who had brought us in—he had once been the chairman of the hospital—spoke to him kindly and asked if he had been in Dachau.

The patient nodded, and our friend remarked, "I was in Buchenwald. They said it was even worse there."

"Yes." The sick man nodded slightly again. "It was worse in Buchenwald. The man in the opposite bed was in Buchenwald. They took him out of the room while they brought you in."

There seemed to be little else one could say. We repeated our promises to do what we could, and then we left.

If anyone had told me when I was a girl at school that one day I should know what it was like to want to murder, I should, of course, have dismissed the idea as melodramatic and absurd. But as we stepped out once more into the August sunshine of the Gagernstrasse, I felt a fervent and personal desire to have a hand in killing those responsible for what we had left behind us. Naturally, the feeling fades gradually if one has no terrible and personal stake in the game. That is inevitable with civilized people. But I do know, though I cannot recapture the feeling now, that I did once think enthusiastically in terms of murder.

We returned to England the next day. The war came about a fortnight later. During the war, we often wondered what happened to the little boys and the sister who was too young even to try to escape. We asked ourselves—did they die on the way to Poland? Were they stifled in the gas chambers of Auschwitz? Or did they die of hunger when our money gave out?

It seemed quite beyond the realm of possibility that we

should ever know the answer. And yet, some time after the war, when I first began to write and lecture about our experiences, someone wrote to us, saying: "I think you might like to know what happened to the family you contacted on your last visit and whom you obviously mourned as dead. Contrary to all possible expectation, they survived. The war came so quickly that able-bodied workers were immediately in demand. So the woman was able to get work. To a certain extent, her husband grew somewhat better. And somehow, throughout the war, she managed to support them all."

Our correspondent did not say if the man went into hiding, but I imagine he must somehow have done so. Anyway, at the end of the war, they were among the first families who emigrated to South America, where they started a new life.

Characteristically, our last contact with Germany was strangely melodramatic. On August 24—I remember because it was my birthday—news was received that the German-Soviet Nonaggression Pact had been signed, and even the most naïve could not pretend to themselves any longer that war was avoidable.

It had been a curious and nerve-racking day. Just as we were going to bed, around midnight, the telephone rang. I answered it and was informed by an obviously harassed operator that there was a call coming through for me from Germany. Would I wait a few minutes?

As I waited, I realized that, in the hurry and muddle of the moment, my line had not been isolated. From every side, there rushed in upon me voices speaking in a variety of languages. They all sounded agitated, of course, and simply registered as a jumble of sound.

It was as though I were listening in to a mad and terrified Europe. In the silence of our hall, I seemed to be on an island, listening to the cries of those who were about to be engulfed. I was completely helpless. Soon, I too was to be swept into at least the outer currents of the swell. In just over a year, the very ceiling above my head was to crash down under the attack of the German bombers. But for the moment, I was simply "listening in" to what was coming. I have never forgotten those dramatic few minutes.

At last my line was cleared. The voice of a friend in Frankfurt came through, with a final request for help for someone, which she and I both knew must be too late. Then we said goodbye, and added, "for a long time."

I rang off. Our refugee work was over.

CHAPTER ELEVEN

It seemed odd to say that one's first impression of a war could be boredom and release from tension, but that was exactly the case with us. For years, Louise and I had been living amid melodrama and urgency. And, quite suddenly, there was nothing else that we could do. The horizons had shrunk to the limits of ordinary life, except insofar as "ordinary life" included those rearrangements and readjustments necessary in every family, now that war had actually come.

Jim, the youngest of the family, had been a Territorial Army soldier for several years, and he joined the army the day war broke out. And Dad, now seventy-five, informed the family that he intended to be a stretcher-bearer. This greatly annoyed Mother, who was severely practical. With the candour for which she was justly celebrated in the home circle, she said, "If you try to do anything like that, you're more likely to end up *on* the stretcher rather than at the end of it."

This statement was accepted in such complete silence that Louise and I wondered if Dad's feelings were hurt. We made it clear that we respected Dad's intentions, while agreeing with Mother's practical outlook. One of us said, "*We* think it is fine of you to want to be a stretcher-bearer, Dad, even if Mother thinks it's impractical."

Dad looked mildly and amiably astonished and replied, "I don't care in the least what any of you think, so long as I do what *I* think is right." Then he went off to the enlisting offices of the Home Defence Service and volunteered as a stretcher-bearer, in the event of air raids.

Instead, they finally accepted him as a full-time air-raid warden. He served throughout the war, though he was nearly eighty when hostilities ceased. And very marvellous he was, too. Several people from the same air-raid post told me that, during the Great Blitz, he was one of the best and most reliable wardens they had. Not even the worst raid ever seemed to rattle him.

To me, the significance of the war years is not so much what they contained for us as what they left out. Because virtually all connections with the outside world were broken, everything that was of overwhelming personal interest to us ceased. Those years represent a sort of gap in the essential line. Opera and adventure, intertwined so inextricably for years, both ceased. The cord had suddenly snapped.

One might have supposed that, in this sudden release from conflicting interests, I should have found it easier to devote myself to writing. On the contrary, never before had I found it so difficult to write. I had more time; I was undisturbed by hurried journeys to and from the Continent; my correspondence had dropped to one tenth of its previous bulk. And yet I found writing a genuine effort.

I think the sudden severing of those tremendously human ties had left me dry of inspiration. Not that I ever wrote of our experiences in my novels—far from it. But when you are very close to people and seeing life in terms of big, simple essentials, your top spins and your perceptions are immensely quickened.

During the first year of the war, Louise and I were separated. Her office was evacuated to some remote spot in Wales, and our contact was limited to the odd weekends I could spend with her or she could spend at home. We loathed it, both feeling that bombing was preferable to evacuation any day. When she finally managed to get a transfer back to a London office in September, 1941, we felt that the two worst years of the war were over.

The brightest spot in that first boring, horrid, frustrating year was Jim's marriage. Ena is the sort of sister-in-law for whom everyone longs and, I suppose, few deserve. We hope we are among the few deserving, for we do most certainly appreciate her. With our other sister-in-law, Bill's wife, Lydia, we have been equally fortunate. In fact, we always tell our brothers that if we had chosen the girls ourselves, we could not have done better.

On the occasion of the first great air raid on London in September, 1940, Louise had chosen to make one of her hurried weekend visits to us. Nesta and Jane, still our constant companions and good supporters in all our hopes and undertakings, came over to see us that evening. And, in the interval between two air-raid warnings, Louise arrived.

We all realized that the principal activity was in the east. Looking out of our top windows, we could see an occasional midge-like cloud of fighters go up to the attack.

Presently, we notice what seemed to be huge, slowly moving clouds massing in the eastern part of the sky. Then, as darkness fell, we noticed a curious red reflection thrown upon these clouds. And, with a sense of incredulous shock, we realized that the "clouds" were made up of thick, slowly billowing smoke rising from the burning docks.

It is an indescribably strange moment when you see *your own* city on fire. You can read of the same fate befalling other cities and be horrified. You can visualize the thing happening to places you have visited and known and possibly loved. But when your own place starts to burn, there comes a sensation that is entirely new and incredible.

Similarly, you may have seen house after house come down in raids, and you may have helped sweep up the remains of friends' belongings, thinking you share their feelings. But when you suddenly see your own dining-room ceiling lying about in jagged lumps, you know you've never quite understood disaster—in the material sense—until that moment.

Well, as everyone who was in London then will remember, it was a strange and oddly exciting night. We were frightened, of course, but the sheer sensationalism of the whole thing kept up one's spirits. It was much later, when night after night of the same thing turned into a sort of grisly boredom, that we found it much more trying.

Nesta and Jane stayed the night with us. When the "All Clear" sounded about six o'clock, they said they must start for home at once. Louise and I walked them part of the way. And as we came through Battersea we saw, for the first time, a collapsed and crumbling building that had been hit by a bomb.

It was one more strange "first impression" of what was to become commonplace in the following weeks.

Sunday was a beautiful day, but Louise had to go away again in the evening. Once more, as the light faded, we realized that the eastern sky was still red. The docks were still burning. Even the least experienced of us understood that they must make a perfect target for any planes returning that evening.

The planes did return—that night and for an incredible number of nights to come.

On September 13, we received our first hit.

That is to say, a smallish bomb exploded in the garden of a house opposite. Most of our windows blew in, part of our roof came off and our hall ceiling came down. But no one was hurt. And in the grey chilly dawn, we all went out and swept up the mess. It is strange to hear the clink of your own windows and the crackle of your own roof slates as you sweep them into the gutter. But oh, how soon you grow used to that, too!

A week later, a good deal of our local railway station was blown away, and we decided it was time Mother left London. Louise was still evacuated at this time; Jim was "somewhere in England," waiting for daily expected orders to go overseas; Bill, while waiting to be called up, had been evacuated with his office to Devonshire. He came to London that weekend and fetched Mother back with him to Devonshire, and there she stayed for nearly a year and a half.

That left Dad and me to hold the fort. There is no one companion I would sooner have had during those extraordinary days and nights. It was really quite difficult to be panic-stricken with Dad around.

A week later, we were hit again. This time, I heard the damned thing coming and had time to bolt under the kitchen table. While I was trying to decide if it was wiser to hold up the table and receive any impact of falling ceiling or just to crouch there and let everything cave in, I heard a tearing sound, and then something hit the ground like a giant mallet. All our front windows blew in and our back windows blew out once more.

But the moment was over, and I crawled out, feeling rather as one does after a bilious attack. Being bombed is quite a

bit like that. The long and half-hopeful, half-gloomy anticipation precedes that dreadful moment when you know it
is going to happen after all and there's nothing you can do
about it. Then comes the general upheaval—in every sense
of the phrase—and finally the lovely, weak, thankful feeling: *well, at least that's over!*

About this time, I decided that, with Mother away and
Dad often on night duty, there was no reason why I should
not volunteer for some night duty in one of the East End
shelters. Workers were badly needed, and I was freer than
most. So off I went to make enquiries. In next to no time, I
was sent to one of the big shelters in Bermondsey.

Here, I found again that tremendously close and simple
contact with people I had missed so much when the refugee
work ended. The story of our shelter differed little from the
stories of hundreds of similar London shelters during that
winter of 1940-41. But for that very reason, it is perhaps
worth the telling.

I had been asked if I would do "night-watching," and feeling that this was about my mental level in these days, I agreed
with alacrity. I was assigned to one of the really "swell" shelters that stood somewhere between Tower Bridge and the
Elephant and Castle, near that quarter endeared to us all by
a thousand music-hall jokes—the Old Kent Road.

In the hurricane of fire that had been battering London, this shelter had come to be—in the very real sense of
the hymn—"a shelter from the stormy blast." Sometimes it
seemed likely to become "our eternal home."

Remote though those times appear now, they seemed endless while we lived them. The days were little more than uneasy, work-paced intervals between the "All Clear" and the
siren's wail; the nights an ever-recurring test of endurance.

The Battle of the Blitz was fought out—in the air, on the ground and, with grim determination, beneath the ground.

The sirens had sounded and the guns were just starting up when I felt my way down the flight of stone steps to our shelter for the first time. A smell compounded of cement, disinfectant, Oxo, people and sawdust rose to meet me. And the sound of many voices made a cheerful and determined conquest over the rumble of distant gunfire.

People were already making up beds, exchanging greetings and sharing suppers. I stood about for a minute or two, feeling quite superfluous as a night-watcher, whatever that might be, in this busy and extraordinarily cheerful throng.

I decided to go to the sick bay to see if there were anyone with whom I could talk.

There was. Behind the heavy sheeting that curtained off the sick bay from the rest of the shelter, I found Alice, who was in charge there.

In answer to my rather bashful, "May I come in?" she cried, "Of course you can, ducks. There's nothing to be frightened of."

So in I went, and Alice took me under her wing from then on. First she gave me a tour of the shelter, which was composed of four very large sections, and explained that during the day, it served as an air-raid shelter for the workers in the factory overhead. At night, those workers who lived nearby brought their families down there. In addition, some people in the immediate vicinity, who had been bombed-out, stayed there.

Except on occasions when there was a big disaster near, and we would have some "temporaries" down for a night or two, our clientele was composed of "regulars."

Alice herself was the first-aid worker in the factory by day, and at night she continued the same work in the shelter, not even commenting on the fact that she was on duty twenty-four hours a day. She dispensed hot drinks, aspirin, bandages and good counsel with impartial good humour. I am sure she would have laughed or been embarrassed if anyone tried to class her as a heroine. But she was one, nevertheless. Just an everyday one, never to be named in any official citation. But in spite of the fact that she was just as much afraid of bombings as anyone else I know, she helped to win the war.

It was Alice who introduced me to one or two of the regulars, and they accepted me as one of them with an unforced hospitality that I was to find was an outstanding characteristic of Bermondsey. That—and their deep affection for their own bit of battered London. People often talk movingly of mountains or woods or moors. But these amazing women truly loved the familiar, and not very beautiful, streets falling about them in ruins. They shed no tears for them, but they spoke with cheerful determination of replacing them one day.

As one woman said, "Still, never mind. We'll build Bermondsey again after the war, even better than it's ever been." She found it hard to imagine any improvement on the Bermondsey she knew and loved. But it would go on as one of the constant factors of existence; that she did know. It was nothing to her that all the brazen hordes of Germany's might were pounding this island into what they fondly supposed was submission. When they found they were wrong and stopped, then we would "build Bermondsey again."

Someone who noticed how thrilled and moved I was, said, "There's nothing like the Bermondsey people, miss. They're nice, aren't they?"

I agreed that they were. And, even on that first evening, I meant by that a whole lot more than she knew. For the life of our shelter and its people was beginning to unroll before me—sketched in simple lines, but coloured in bewildering richness by unconscious courage, unselfishness and a blazing confidence that no bombing could dim.

That very first evening I was told, quite simply and unemotionally, stories of unflinching courage. No one thought very much of them, really. It was simply that one naturally accepted whatever trial was necessary for the ultimate bringing of victory.

"It doesn't matter as long as we beat *him,*" was the general verdict.

One of them had said that to the queen when she had come down to Bermondsey a few days before. And the queen had patted her on the shoulder, woman to woman, and said, "That's the right spirit!"

This same woman told me how, on the previous day, she had been helping her sister to sweep up what remained of their old father's home.

"And while we were sweeping up, Miss Cook," she explained, "my sister stopped and said to me, 'Well, Em,' she said, 'we must always remember we'd be much worse off under Hitler.' And it's true, you know. You have to think of that."

I doubt if a correct sense of values has ever been more tellingly expressed. Better destruction than dictatorship!

One of my most vivid memories of that first night was the five minutes before "Lights Out." There were prayers for those who cared to join in, but no compulsion on those who did not. Only a courteous request for quiet for a few minutes. In the crowded, rather dimly lit shelter, there was the murmur of a couple of hundred voices repeating the ageless words of the "Lord's Prayer." And the not very distant crash of a bomb lent a terrible point to the earnest petition "Deliver us from evil," breathed from the farthest, shadowy corner.

Then goodnights, and lights out. I was told to sleep until two o'clock, when I should be wakened to enter on my simple duty of remaining awake and seeing that all was well with the sleeping people.

"Call me if anyone has a fit or a heart attack or anything," were Alice's last encouraging words. "But you'll manage all right."

I lay awake for a long while, listening to unfamiliar sounds. Not the gunfire and the bomb blasts from the outer world; those had become familiar enough in the last few weeks, but the stirring and whispering of a great community settling to sleep in comparative safety while war raged overhead.

At last I fell asleep. And then it seemed only three minutes before someone was shaking me gently and whispering, "Time to get up."

I got off my improvised bed of blankets on wooden slats and put on my shoes, the removal of which was the only concession to undressing. And then I crept quietly out of the sick bay, where I had been sleeping, and made my way through the big shadowy rooms of the shelter to the one bright lamp under which a chair had been set for the night-watcher.

At first I read. Then I crocheted an interminable blanket, which lasted me through many a night of watching. And then, finally, because your eyes grow very tired about half-past three in the morning, I put down my work and just looked round.

On every side, lay sleeping people. People who were glad and thankful for a few square feet of concrete on which to make up some sort of bed. People who had no idea that there was any alternative to this, because they knew nothing about the technique of surrender and no one could teach it to them. It required no feat of fancy to imagine that, in time to that concerted, rhythmical breathing, beat the un-conquered heart of Britain.

There were young people and old people; men, women and children. Some wrapped in blankets, some were ambitiously tucked away in something approaching a bed, made up on an old mattress. Some were covered by the most exquisite patchwork quilts.

I had asked about those quilts earlier in the evening, for the sight of them had jerked my mind back to happy days spent long ago on that holiday in the Catskill Mountains. Strange days of changing values! We should have called the Catskills part of the New World in that faraway time. Now they seemed, in distant, happy retrospect, to be part of the Old World—that Old World of comfort and safety and brightness. The New World, the world to which we were fast becoming accustomed, was this strange, bomb-shattered, noise-torn existence, where we crept underground and pretended to each other that this was the normal state of living.

I admit my throat grew tight when I first looked on those quilts. I exclaimed, "Those must have come from America! They couldn't come from anywhere else in the world."

I was assured that, indeed, they had come from America.

"You wouldn't believe, miss, how good the Americans have been to us," I was told. "Bales and bales of stuff, and all of it good. Not a rubbishy thing among it. Good enough for anyone. I don't know what we'd have done without the Americans."

I hope some of the good ladies of those sewing parties in Maine and Connecticut, in Boston and Philadelphia, somehow sensed the gratitude with which their gifts were received. Night after night, under their patchwork quilts, slept people they were never to see or know, but to whom the word "American" now took on a personal and special meaning.

As the night wore on, I made some interesting discoveries. I discovered that more people than not talk in their sleep; that quite a number laugh, some of them chuckling away with a lively, private enjoyment that makes one long to share the joke; and that the snore of which the human throat and nose are capable ranges from basso profundo to coloratura soprano.

I could write quite a learned dissertation on snoring, after my shelter experiences. There is the staccato snore of the nervous person who has not quite cast off all cares in sleep. There is the gradual crescendo snore of the placid sleeper, who goes on with unhurried persistence up the scale, only to start at the bottom again when he has achieved the limit of his range. There is the *dolce fa niente* snore of the person who dreams pleasantly and with variety; the explosive snore, which makes others groan protestingly in their sleep; the slumbering volcano snore, with its steady, threatening rhythm that never quite achieves eruption; and there is the simple snore for snoring's sake.

By five o'clock, all sounds outside had died away, and presently, far away and then coming nearer, the unlovely but welcome sound of the "All Clear." The tide of war had receded for another 12 or 13 hours. It was time to start waking the early risers.

I had been given the times and had had my victims pointed out, and I went round shaking one sleeping figure after another, whispering the time and seeing that they did not drop off again. A cheerful, elderly baker. A big, quiet, kindly fellow who worked at the docks. An energetic little grandmother who cleaned offices in the City. I woke each in turn.

The little cleaner had her grandson with her, and he wept somewhat in protestation at being awakened so early. He was very cheerful in the evenings, specializing in an imitation of Hitler that was very popular; but at half-past five in the morning, his cheerfulness was at a low ebb. In subsequent weeks, I used to have a sweet ready for him as he went past me on his way out of the shelter, carrying his bundle of blankets. He would remove his fist from his eye as he passed me and accept the offer of consolation.

At six o'clock, up went the lights in the shelter. Everyone dragged themselves to the surface of another day, and then there was a general stir, an exchange of sleepy good-mornings, the folding of blankets and stowing away of bundles. One more night was over, and still we were alive. I rejoined Alice in the sick bay, and drank very hot, sweet tea from an enamel mug; and never did tea taste better.

It was hardly light when I stumbled out of the shelter and along Tower Bridge Road half-asleep, to wait for my early bus to "The Elephant." But the world of Bermondsey was awake and humming with activity. There was a lot to be crammed into the few short hours before the bombers came to us again.

We could count on the siren in the early hours of the evening, and it was not very healthy to go through the streets of East and South-East London after it sounded. So, as the hour of blackout grew earlier and earlier throughout the interminable weeks, so shelter life began at half-past seven, at seven, at half-past six. And, of necessity, it began to take on a much more settled and permanent character.

No longer was shelter life a temporary state of affairs in which one improvised as one went along. It became a natural state of being, and the evening had to be planned accordingly.

In our shelter, with a minimum of fuss, there grew up—I might almost say sprang up—a discussion group, a dressmaking class, a weekly class in Bible study, lectures, concerts, film shows, darts matches. And for those who knitted and sewed and crocheted, there were the endless talks and discussions from which emerged the true character of the nation to which I have the honour of belonging.

Profound truths were presented as natural conclusions; noble sentiments, clothed in very everyday speech, accepted as the ordinary standards; wise vision suddenly shown in simple conversation. I can hear them now!

Mrs. Gee—best and most valued of friends—saying, as the place shuddered under the infernal assault from above, "Whenever I feel I can't go on, I think of Mr. Churchill and the weight *he* carries. And then I feel much better. It's bad enough for us, but we know we've only got to hold on. *He's* got to make all the decisions."

Mrs. Coffee-shop—we always called her that, and I don't think I ever knew her real name—shaking her head and saying with a sigh, "I wish my husband would come down here."

"Why won't he?" I asked. "Does he dislike shelter life so much?"

"Oh, it's not that," she explained. "Only he won't leave the dog. He gets frightened, you know, but of course we can't bring him down here, so my husband stays with him."

The old hop-picker, telling us of the Battle of Britain, as seen from the Kentish hop-fields: "Anyone that's seen what I've seen wouldn't ever refuse to put their hand in their pocket for an air force all their lives. Falling out of the sky, they was—just falling out of the sky. And often enough, our boys coming down by parachute as their own planes caught on fire. They'd pick themselves up almost before you could ask 'em if they was all right, and off they'd go crying, 'Give me another machine, and let me get at 'em again.' Ah, what boys!"

And then, the same old woman telling how her own two

sons were killed at Dunkirk within three minutes of each other. One was shot through the mouth and his brother, hearing him cry out, went back for him and was killed beside him.

"They was such good boys," she told me. "Such good boys. Always brought their money home every Friday night, they did. Killed within three minutes of each other. Both of them gone. But, there, perhaps it was best that way. They were that fond of each other. My Bill wouldn't have wanted to come home without my Harry."

She sank into thought for a moment. And then she added, rather proudly, "The sergeant himself came and told me about it when he got back. Very nice, he was. 'Don't cry, Ma,' he said. 'We know what you're feeling. We'd been a long time together and we wasn't pals, we was brothers. We couldn't stay to bury them—there wasn't time. But we did the best we could,' he said. 'We left them side by side, with their hands touching.'"

In the welter of horror and haste that was Dunkirk, someone paused to put the hands of the two dead boys together, so that even in their death, they were not divided.

"Such good boys they was," the old woman repeated sorrowfully. "But, there, miss," she added more cheerfully, "we must all make sacrifices in these days, mustn't we?"

I said, I hope with some humility, that we must. And I have often wondered since if the brotherhood of man has ever been more movingly described than in those words, "We did the best we could. We left them side by side, with their hands touching."

One of the most striking things about this shelter life of ours was the way in which each thought for all, and a simple and general humanity created a natural community of interests and sympathy. Good humour, good sense and a kindly reasonableness triumphed over nearly all the limitations and shortcomings of a cramped, indeed a primitive, existence. Nerves must have been stretched to the snapping point, and yet I very seldom heard so much as a sharp personal argument in all the nights I spent down there. I think that constituted as big a victory over circumstances as the more obvious courage with which the bombardment was endured.

Perhaps, of course, the realization that minor differences meant nothing in the face of the terrible major emergency had something to do with it. After all, when death is prowling about overhead, life does seem rather too precious to fritter away on petty disputes. And certainly the reminder of what was waiting for every one of us was pretty constant.

It was not only the continuous sound of gunfire, nor even the dreadful increasing frequency of the bomb hits, which seemed to make the very earth beneath us shift strangely. It was the stories everyone knew and no one could resist telling.

Stories concerning the friends, neighbours, relatives of the people down there. Families wiped out, shelters—not so very unlike ours, when you came to think of it—that, in the telling phrase, "had not stood up to a direct hit." Disasters embracing whole streets, mass funerals where the victims were personally known to half the people in our shelter. It began to seem illogical that, when so many people were dying, we were left alive. Measured by nothing more than the simple law of averages, we felt we must be hit soon. Would *our* shelter "stand up to it"?

And then there was the evidence of our eyes when we left the shelter in the morning—or sometimes, when it was still too dark to see, just the testimony of tinkling broken glass underfoot or the unnatural crunch of slates that should have been on roofs far above our heads, but were now lying on the pavement along which we groped our way.

In spite of the dismal frequency of the experience, I never quite got used to the extraordinary sensation of passing a familiar building that had been solid last night and suddenly realizing that through ragged holes in its fabric, one could see the pale light of the morning sky.

No wonder we began to think increasingly often, "Next time it will surely be us."

Of course, we spent a lot of time telling each other that *our* shelter was especially safe. And the directors of the factory overhead most gallantly contributed their efforts to making us feel this was so. Instead of going home to the less bombed areas where they lived, they frequently took turns sleeping down in the shelter, because, as they casually mentioned, "they felt safe there as anywhere."

That made the word go around that there could hardly be any danger. "Shows they have confidence in the place, and *they* should know. It must be pretty safe. As safe as it can be, that is."

As safe as it *can* be. There was the rub. How safe could any shelter be if a bomb fell in just the right place?

We knew, and we knew everyone else knew, that nowhere was really safe in the increasing rain of fire and terror that was being poured on London. And when the bombers were overhead—*right* overhead, I mean—who really thought about how safe their shelter was, I should like to know? I suppose no one who has not actually experienced it can quite imagine the horrific sound of a bomber diving to attack. It combines in its screaming note all the melancholy of a banshee wail with the nerve-rasping warning of a danger-signal.

But who can avoid the danger it is signalling? There is not a thing you can do about it. You can only sit there, pretending it isn't happening, with an idiotically hopeful smile pinned on your frozen face—going on with your conversation by main force, even if you suspect that your sentences are tailing off into futile banalities. You must go on doing what is normal—*must* go on with it—because only that way can you hold off the fantastic and terrible just an instant longer.

Then there is a moment when you know that the sound of the descending bomber has merged into the sound of the descending bomb. In the few seconds remaining before the impact, you have time to think an astonishing number of thoughts. All the assurances you have ever heard about "not hearing the bomb that hits you," "if you can hear it, you know you're safe," and so on pass through your mind without leaving any impression. The reports about shelters that "didn't stand up to it" and "bombs that came right through and then exploded" also pass through your mind, and they do leave their impression.

With fatal certainty, you know that this time it is your bomb, your shelter, your death....

And then the fearful thud is not on top of your head after all, but some blessed distance away.

For a moment, you can't even recollect that it has probably meant death to someone else. You are literally sweating with the relief of finding you are alive. There is saliva again in your dry mouth, the salt taste of terror is going, your tensed muscles relax, and you hope you haven't looked more frightened than anyone else.

The danger is past; it never really existed, it was really quite far away, you only imagined...

And then it comes again. Whoooooooooeeeeeeee!

No wonder we used to organize sing-songs to drown the hideous sound as much as possible. There is something rather exhilarating in defiantly bawling, "Daisy, Daisy, give me your answer, do," in competition with German bombers. And "Roll Out the Barrel" has never seemed quite the same to me without a gunfire obbligato in the background.

Sometimes, as we sang the old favourites of 25 years earlier, it was hard to remember if we were in this war or the last one. "Pack Up Your Troubles," "There's a Long, Long Trail," "Keep the Home Fires Burning," "Tipperary"—they had all been sung thousands of times by the khaki columns marching across Belgium and France to stem that other German tide. Now, the children of those men, sometimes the men themselves, middle-aged but tough still, were singing them all over again. But this time, the Germans had reached London; they were right overhead.

And still we sang, "While there's a Lucifer to light your fag, smile boys, that's the style."

I had chanted those songs as a schoolgirl once. Now, with thousands of other women, I was wondering if we should live to sing those old songs many times more.

But we were not by any means always reduced to our own resources for a concert. Every night, in every part of East and South-East London, singers and pianists and stage artists of every description were going from shelter to shelter, bringing pleasure and cheer to the people marooned there.

Someone with a car, or a taxi driver, could nearly always be found to take them through the bombs and shrapnel. And if they had to walk part of the way—well, that was all part of the business of "serving the public," in the most selfless and exacting sense of the phrase.

There was no compulsion upon these people. Each one did it for no other reason than a desire to brighten the lot of those in the heavily bombed areas who were sticking to their jobs and winning the war by the grim process of "hanging on." Most of those artists could, no doubt, have spent their nights in comparative safety in very different areas. They deliberately chose to share the perils of the Blitz, because they knew that what they had to offer would help distract thoughts and toughen still further the iron morale that was pretty nearly our only weapon at that time.

More than one artist gave up a good contract in the States when the Blitz began, coming home to play or sing in the London shelters. For my part, I was never afterwards able to judge those artists on the cool impartial basis of artistic merit. Good, bad or indifferent, I always applauded them, for the sake of those shelter concerts.

The shelter concert I remember best was when a well-known contralto and her accompanist came down to entertain us. She had never been a favourite of mine, but I had heard her quite often before, in what now seemed the dim past.

Her personality, as such, had never appeared impressive to me. But, as she stood there now in our crowded shelter, singing popular songs, telling funny stories, leading the community singing, she was deliberately measuring sheer personality against the terror of the raid outside.

And she won. There was no question about that. She had us all singing and laughing in no time. We hardly thought about the raid outside. She sang and we sang and her accompanist played, indefatigably.

Then presently, she asked us to choose what we ourselves would like to sing, and someone suggested, "Drink To Me Only…"

"Why, yes, of course," she said. "Do you all know it?"

Incredibly, we all knew it. And suddenly, by one of those concerted impulses that do sometimes move a whole multitude in close sympathy with one another, we were all on our mettle.

The accompanist played the air over to us and then, from

the packed benches of our bare, stone-walled shelter, rose in admirable harmony and with quite exquisite restraint, the simple, beautiful strains of Ben Johnson's song.

> Drink to me only with thine eyes,
> And I will pledge with mine;
> Or leave a kiss within the cup
> And I'll not ask for wine.

How often had these very words sounded through the Mermaid Tavern, not so far away from where we were singing them now? Most of the generation who first sang that song must have been able to remember the defeat of the Spanish Armada. It was a different Armada now—and that last bomb was nearer than one liked—but we were the generation sharing its defeat.

> The thirst that from the soul doth rise
> Doth ask a drink divine;
> But might I of Jove's nectar sup,
> I would not change for thine.

At the end of the verse, the accompanist leaped to his feet, fairly blazing with enthusiasm and exclaimed, "I've seldom heard that better sung! You've simply got to sing the second verse now. It's not so often sung, but it contains some of the most beautiful words in the English language. Let's be sure and get them right."

He recited them to us. We repeated them after him. And then the battered old piano started again.

> I sent thee late a rosy wreath,
> Not so much honouring thee

As giving it a hope that there
It could not wither'd be;

What did it matter if Spaniard or German were trying to tear life from us? This was one of the great songs of great England, and we would sing it to the end, whether it were the sixteenth or the twentieth century.

But thou thereon didst only breathe,
And sent'st it back to me;
Since when it grows and smells, I swear,
Not of itself but thee!

Immortal words, immortal tune, immortal people. They were making history, and they sang as they did it.

To all of us who love music, and have been fortunate enough to indulge that love, there are half a dozen performances that stand out in the memories. An opera performance, with singers, orchestra, conductor and composer in the exact combination one has always hoped to hear it and seldom does. A Mozart serenade on a warm, starry night in Salzburg, when even the surrounding mountains seem to listen.

But, among my own list of great performances—every other one of which owed much to professional artistry and the exercise of trained and perfected art—I must place that strange and moving occasion when two hundred Cockneys sang "Drink To Me With Thine Eyes" in the cellar of a London factory and forgot that from overhead the bombs were falling.

CHAPTER TWELVE

Finally the event we had all been dreading occurred: the night when we really were hit. The factory overhead was not directly hit but a public house and block of flats next door to the factory and almost directly over one half of our shelter were.

We heard the sound of the descending bomber, the sound of the descending bomb—to which we were all quite accustomed—but the final thud seemed to hit us personally; it was succeeded by the new and terrifying sound of masonry crashing down over our heads for endless, horrible moments. We rose instinctively to our feet in a body, wondering, wondering if the roof above us would hold.

It held. But through the shelter came drifting clouds of dust from the rubble overhead, and there was an immediate call for volunteers to go out and help. Volunteers were particularly needed to enter the gradually collapsing public house and bring out those who were still alive.

A boy of nineteen, whom I had never before associated with anything but the rather tiresome playing of a piano-accordion, was the first one in. Afterwards, he described what had happened. After crawling in, he had switched his lamp around and the first thing he had seen was a woman, quite dead. "And me stomach came up and hit the roof of me mouth," was the expressive way he had described his feelings.

But he described the rescue work very matter-of-factly, while he drank hot Oxo and relaxed. And he finished by saying thoughtfully, "I don't think I'll tell my Mum and Dad I was in it."

"Won't you?" I exclaimed. For, unashamed sensationalist that I am, I was dying to get home and tell *my* Dad about it all. "But why not?"

"Oh, they'll only worry," he explained tolerantly. "But, coo!" he added reflectively, "I'll never be nearer to heaven than I was tonight. I heard them harps playing."

Curious though it may sound, there was a sort of relief about having been hit at last. It was the quite illogical feeling that we had had our turn and survived. I remember feeling indescribably cheerful as I went home the next morning.

During the day, I had occasion to go up West. As my bus went up Park Lane, I suddenly saw the wonderful, fantastic riot of purple, white and golden crocuses that, every year, burst forth at that side of Hyde Park in a glory of insolent colour. It was a perfect day, and I was alive. I should have been dead, but I was alive. The sky had never been more blue, the grass more green nor the crocuses more incredibly beautiful.

The memory of that tidal wave of thankfulness has never left me. Every year, when I first see the crocuses in Hyde Park, I feel the tears come into my eyes, and I remember again that wonderful, glorious sensation.

It was, I think, only two weeks later that we experienced our worst night of all. Most people in London at that time will recall the two fearful raids of April 16 and April 19. I was down in the shelter on that memorable Wednesday, and from the very beginning, we knew it was going to be what was euphemistically called "a lively night."

The lights were not turned out that night. Or, rather, I think we turned them out for half an hour and then, by common consent, turned them on again. The great tarpaulin over the doorway—for it was unsafe to have anything rigid like a door—was lifted almost to the ceiling again and again by the force of the bomb blasts, and a few of the women could not help crying a little.

I remember doggedly reading an evening newspaper over and over. By driving my elbows hard into my ribs and holding the paper in both hands, I could manage not to let its leaves tremble too obviously.

Once, dear Mrs. Gee came over and remarked, "It's a nasty night, isn't it?"

And, with false cheeriness, I managed to say, "Really, an awful lot of the noise is gunfire, you know."

Mrs. Gee laughed with real humour and replied, "But an awful lot isn't, Miss Cook." And we both smiled feebly.

I had been frightened before, of course. There had often been odd moments when I had thought, *This is it*. But that night, for the first and only time, the growing conviction came over me that we could not live until the morning.

I remember thinking, *I shall never see Mother again. I shall never hear Rosa sing again*. And those two acceptances seemed to make it absolutely final.

Every half hour or so our fire guards came through the shelter to see that we were all right and report on events above. They were wonderfully cheerful and chaffed us a good deal for having the lights on.

"What's the matter with some of you girls?" they wanted

to know. "If you can't get to sleep on a nice quiet night like this, what'll you do when it's really noisy?"

We laughed rather sheepishly, trying to look as though we didn't really mind what was happening.

But, as the night wore on, they took a different tone during their rounds of the shelter. They stressed how foolish people were who had stayed up above when they could have gone to shelter underground.

"You mean it's been a bad night for casualties?" someone asked.

Yes, it had been a bad night for casualties. Made you feel how glad you were just to be alive. Better to lose everything you possessed than risk your lives and the lives of your families by staying near your worldly possessions.

Yes, we all agreed fervently, the really important thing was just to be alive.

"You can buy fresh homes," one of the men said. "But you can't put back people who've been killed."

How true, we agreed again. None of us minded what was lost so long as we and our dear ones were safe.

At this point, one of them remarked casually that it was a good thing we felt that way, the only sensible way.

Then one of the women realized where the conversation was drifting. She said, rather hesitantly, "Is there a lot of damage up above?"

Yes, there was a lot of damage.

We looked at each other. "Some of our places gone?"

Yes, several people's places had gone.

Then one woman looked directly at her husband. "Is our place gone?"

"I'm afraid so, girl," he said. "There isn't much left up there. But we're alive. We're all lucky to be alive. We'd have been dead if we'd stayed up above."

"Oh, what a mercy we didn't!" she exclaimed. "How lucky we are!"

Incredible though it sounds, within a few moments, a whole lot of people were congratulating each other on their extraordinary good fortune in only having lost all their worldly possessions.

About four o'clock in the morning, things had grown a little quieter, so I asked one of the fire guards if I might go up to the top of the stairs and look out. He said I might; the worst was over. And up the long flight of stairs I went.

It is still difficult to visualize that scene. As I stepped out into the open air, I saw everything by a warm, almost cosy glow. It was not daylight. It was not moonlight. It was fire-light on a colossal scale. I was looking at the outside world by firelight. It is impossible to describe how monstrously in-congruous that can seem.

As I looked around, it appeared to me that ours was the only building that had not been hit. All around were burn-ing ruins. Since I had gone down to the shelter the night before, the whole skyline had changed. It was like finding myself in a totally unfamiliar part of the town.

When that incredible night passed into an incredible dawn, we all started picking our way homeward. The smell of burn-ing was everywhere and the air was thick with bits of charred paper: the last of the big book centres in the City had been hit that night, and in the tremendous draught created by the fires, the remains of millions of books had been drawn up and now were drifting down, sometimes miles away in the outer suburbs.

One charred sheet, which fell in our garden at home, came from a Bible. On it was something about the wicked being confounded. I found that oddly comforting, before the sheet fell to pieces in my hand.

On Saturday of that week, there followed an almost equally terrible raid, and then there was a pause until the famous May 10 raid, the last great raid of the Big Blitz. After these events, extreme terror retreated until the days of the flying bombs, or doodlebugs.

For the purposes of continuity, I have intentionally kept only to the history of the shelter throughout that winter of 1940-41, but I must go back now and deal with the one great personal tragedy that had hit us during that period.

One weekend in November, 1940, I had been up in Wales, staying with Louise. On my return, I telephoned Nesta's office, as usual, to arrange to meet her and Jane and give them all the news about our exile.

A rather subdued voice replied, "Oh, haven't you heard about Nesta? Then I think I'd better put you on to the man for whom she works."

After a short but agonizing delay, another voice spoke to me and, without any preamble said, "I'm terribly sorry to have to tell you. Their house was bombed on Friday night. Nesta and her mother are both very badly injured, but I understand Jane and her father are not so seriously hurt. Jane has been moved to a hospital outside London, but Nesta and her mother are too ill to be moved."

I stopped only to ask the name of their local hospital, put down the telephone, and set out, running. I remember running along the top of our road, unable to bear waiting for a bus. All the time I kept on thinking, *if only I'm in time*. I don't think I even allowed myself to realize what I hoped to be in time *for*.

Such a scene of devastation surrounded the hospital that I wondered how anyone had survived at all. And yet, somehow, I had never really accepted the idea of any of *us* being hurt. One doesn't. One hears about others, one is terribly sorry, one is often frightened. But one doesn't, I realized then, ever accept the complete idea that *one of one's own* may be a victim.

I was admitted at once to see Nesta, who was in a room by herself. She didn't know me. Poor child, I hardly knew her.

"Speak to her," the nurse said. "See if you can hold her attention for a moment and persuade her to rest. We can't."

I spoke to her. I repeated her name; I repeated my name. I tried to hold her attention for that one precious moment. But she only moaned and muttered and took no notice.

Then, out of the welter of shared recollections, I pulled the one I knew had always meant most to her. Of all the operatic loves we had shared together, no one had meant so much to Nesta as Krauss and Ursuleac.

"Nesta dear," I said, "try to go to sleep and dream of K and Vee." I was using our affectionate nicknames for them.

She stopped moving her bandaged head and said, "What?"

I repeated what I had said. After a moment, she replied thoughtfully, "Yes, I will." And for a little while, she was quiet and seemed to rest. Oh, blessed shared opera memories—they were almost all that were left to us then!

I went after to see her mother, who was conscious and spoke to me a little, quite coherently. To my inexperienced judgment, she seemed rather less seriously hurt than Nesta. But she died the next day.

And our brave, inextinguishable Nesta hung on to life day after day, though the nursing sister herself told me that by every known medical rule, she should be dead.

Every day, I went to see her. Every day, I hoped that she would know me and speak to me. And finally, the moment came when she recognized me. She looked very brightly at me out of the one eye left to her and said, "It's all right, Ida. Don't worry. We'll celebrate victory together."

She was the bravest thing I ever knew. In addition to the loss of an eye, she had terrible head injuries, which later necessitated months and months of plastic surgery. For a long time, we thought she would have to lose an arm. Yet I never heard her complain. And, more impressive still, she never altered her sense of values.

One evening, when she had been in hospital about a month, I was sitting by her bed and it was growing dark. We had not talked for a while, and then she said reflectively, "I'd like you to know, Ida, that all this hasn't made me feel any different about things."

"How do you mean, Nesta?" I asked.

"I still think," Nesta explained, "that we *had* to go to war to stop what was happening in Europe. I don't regret it. I give you my word that never once, not even when you told me Mother was dead, or when I knew I had lost my eye and thought I must lose my arm, never once did I feel so bad as the day we signed the Munich Pact. I *know* now which are the really terrible things in life."

There are so many crowded, yet clear-cut memories of those days. There was the afternoon of Christmas, 1940, when I had gone as usual to visit Nesta in hospital. As I came away, I was struck afresh by the scene of dreary ruin round me. The street leading from the hospital appeared to be an uninhabited shell.

No one had had time to clear the poor personal possessions that lay about in gardens or gutters. Pictures, broken ornaments, bits of furniture, books, papers, clothes; they were all there. Rain-soaked, forlorn, horribly familiar, because I passed them each day on the way to the hospital. Some of them I knew quite well. There was an engraving of Kitchener greeting someone after an engagement in the Boer War. Once it had hung on someone's sitting-room wall. Now it lay there in rain or snow, and I never could resist glancing at it as I passed.

That Christmas afternoon, the scene was drearier than ever. I felt a bit like crying from sheer depression. I heard the sound of a familiar voice speaking.

I stood still in the ruined street, in the grey chill of the December afternoon. From the basement of one of the apparently deserted houses came the voice. Someone *was* living in one of those ruined shells. Someone was listening to the radio. And over the radio, the king was speaking to his battered, but unbeaten, people.

I stood there all the while he was speaking, too far away to hear the words, but following only the sound of that unmistakable, faintly hesitant voice. Presently the strains of the national anthem signalled an end to the broadcast. But I felt a thousand times better.

The street was still in ruins. The afternoon was still grey and dismal. Kitchener was forever greeting someone in a rain-soaked picture. But the voice of Britain had spoken, literally, from beneath the ruins. It was strangely and heartwarmingly symbolic. For where there seemed to be only ruin and destruction, there was really life and hope.

I also found my spirits unexpectedly raised at a point when they were sagging badly the first time I went back into what remained of Nesta and Jane's home. It was impossible to enter some of the rooms, as the walls had shed most of their plaster. Only the inner framework remained, which gave the place a grisly likeness to the flimsy "slatted" walls in *Madama Butterfly*. I climbed what remained of the stairs, stepping over odd pieces of masonry and plaster, and found my way to Nesta's room.

All the ceiling had fallen here; the window had come in, frame and all; the floor was ankle-deep in rubble; and what remained of the furniture was in fragments. I don't know now why I idly pulled at a picture cord that protruded from a pile of rubble. But pull I did, and from this heap of ruins, with its glass still unbroken, emerged Nesta's enlargement of the snapshot taken of Krauss and Ursuleac outside Covent Garden on that sunny day in 1934.

It was dirty, of course, and the cardboard backing had been torn. But it was there, virtually intact, a symbol of the days that had been, but, I believed in that moment, would surely come again. I took the photograph away, and to this day it remains among us, treasured, in its battered condition.

Apart from the general fears and worries that everyone shared, I had hit a rather tough spot in my own affairs. I had gone into the war owing hundreds of pounds, which I had borrowed for the refugee work—literally everything I could raise. And I had undertaken to pay out something like half my income in maintenance for the various cases who were temporarily—or in some cases of old or sick people, permanently—unable to support themselves.

I know this sounds very improvident. But in the summer of 1939, the sands were running out with fearful speed. It was no good planning to give help in the future, when money might have been saved for the purpose. The only thing was to undertake the responsibilities *then,* and trust to heaven or luck or one's own gumption to be able to raise something to meet those responsibilities. Either one took the risk and people lived, or one played safe and they died.

If I had time—! But there was no time. And so I had borrowed recklessly and mortgaged as much future income as I dared. There were times where I literally wondered where to find the next penny.

I remember the most acute crisis, which had a flavour of real comedy about it. I simply *had* to lay my hands on eight pounds somehow. I had racked my brains, I had tried everything I could think of, and still the eight pounds remained elusive.

Then I went to visit Nesta in hospital, having decided I must produce a bright smile and put my financial worries behind me for the moment.

Almost her first words to me were, "Ida, there's something that's worrying me a bit."

I took a deep breath and asked what it was.

"Well, they keep on sending me my salary from the office," Nesta explained, "because this is the only address I have. But I don't like keeping it here. Would you take care of it for me?"

I laughed—much more heartily, even hysterically, than was fitting in a sick room.

"Nesta dear, with more pleasure than I can possibly tell you," I assured her. "May I borrow eight pounds of it? I'm in an awful jam."

"Borrow the lot, if you like," Nesta replied. "I shan't need it for a long time."

We often laughed about that afterwards. It was the nicest instance of "the Lord providing" quite unexpectedly.

It took me the first two or three years of the war to straighten things out, but I did it eventually. I have sometimes wondered since if I ought to have plunged even further than I did, in that mad summer of 1939. I thought I had stretched things to the limit of my capacity. But I don't know. I suppose if any of us could possibly have conceived of what was coming, we would all have done more than we did.

Every weekend, Jane, Louise and I used to visit Nesta in the hospital outside London where she had gone for long plastic surgery treatment. And presently, she was well enough at least to telephone us. We were expecting her call that first time, and the moment she spoke, one of us said, "Wait a moment. We think you would like to hear this." And we played her Ponselle's well-loved *La Vestale* on the gramophone, because we wanted her to feel there were still things of supreme beauty for her to enjoy.

She was thrilled beyond expression. After that, she would telephone us quite often. The telephone operator was very sympathetic and used to forget about time limits for toll calls, so we often played Nesta a favourite record or two, as well as exchanging the news.

I had always planned madly for the future and usually had one ridiculous project or another on hand; but at that time, I lived only for each day. One could not, *dared* not, plan for the future.

Louise and I occasionally permitted ourselves to say, "One day—" but we no longer used expressions like, "There's always Rosa." As the years went on, we almost accepted the fact that all links with the past had snapped. The bright hopes that had sustained us through years of refugee work seemed unreal now. With some shock, we realized that it was ten years and more since those days we had accepted as the golden norm of existence.

Were we really the same two who had saved our money, nearly twenty years ago, to go to America and hear Galli-Curci? Were we the same two who had basked in the beauties of every performance Ponselle ever gave in Europe? Were we the two who had sat in the opera queue in the sunshine and snapped the stars, until one day we took the snap that was to draw us into the dark melodrama that had enveloped Europe?

We dwelt very much in the past in those days. We now knew that the one thing that can never be taken from you is the memory of the great times that once were. But we no longer expected to repeat them in the future. Urgent work in Europe had claimed us, and while we did it, we had assured ourselves that one day we would have a radiant reward. We would go back to New York. We would hear the kind of operatic performances that had irradiated our youth. We would know the same carefree happiness again. Above all, we would hear our matchless Rosa in the many roles we still had never heard.

Now we knew that, at least, would never be. Ponselle had married and retired at a phenomenally early age. The bright, almost legendary figure of our happiest days was no longer before the public.

And let no one think this was a minor matter. I can say quite honestly that the money and energy and thought that we put into our refugee work never really entailed much sacrifice for us. But what we did give as the price for our refugee work was the chance to hear the performances we loved best in the world and that would never come again.

We do not regret our choice in the least and, of course, we would choose exactly the same way again. But when people say to us, "What it must have cost you to do that work!" I always think, *It cost us Rosa's Donna Anna and Carmen and Luisa Miller and L'Aficaine.* That was what mattered.

However there was to be one more phase that would jerk us out of any leisurely nostalgia, or indeed, out of anything but the defiant desire to live until the end of the war, whatever it brought.

In June, 1944, the first of the flying bombs came.

Personally, I was more frightened of them than anything

during the Big Blitz. Partly, I believe, because distant victory was in sight, and the thought of being killed now was unbearable. The horizon had been slowly expanding once more. We had begun to look cautiously into the future, any future. That it might be snatched away even now was unthinkable.

During a long night, when the infernal things seemed to be whirring over our heads almost without interruption, and as Louise and I crouched under the dining-room table side by side, I suddenly and boldly pronounced a plan for the future once more.

"If we ever live to see the end of this war," I shouted to her above the din, "you and I are going back to America. We'll fly there. We'll do ourselves well over everything. We'll go right over to California and see Lita and Homer again. And maybe, somehow, we will find Rosa. The Ponselle performances may be over, but I'm going to *see* her, if only to stand in front of her and look at her."

And much as she had replied to a similar plan twenty years ago, Louise said, "Of course. How soon after the end of the war, do you think?"

"The first minute we can," I vowed, as the ground shook under our knees, and our knees shook under us.

CHAPTER THIRTEEN

Our new American plan sustained us through the last ferocious months of the struggle.

Less than a week after our decision, a doodlebug came down and pushed in the back of our house. But, crowning mercy for us, no one was at home. Louise and I had finally persuaded the parents to go to Northumberland. I had written an old school friend of mine asking if she could find somewhere for them to stay in her small country town. And, with the letter in her hand, she went to her father and said, "What about it, Dad?"

To our lasting gratitude, he didn't say, "Well, now, let's see," or "If we think it over, perhaps...." He said, "Telegraph for them to come to us *now*."

We saw them off the next morning on the ten o'clock train. At one o'clock, the flying bomb came down. When Louise came home from the office at six o'clock, it was to find the whole house blasted. And when I arrived ten minutes later, she greeted me with a characteristic Cook-ish announcement: "Yes, we've been bombed. But never mind the house. Igor is missing."

I cannot imagine how I have written thus far and not dealt with Igor, prince of cats and probably the most important member of our family. He started as Prince Igor, because he came to us in all his black Persian beauty during the summer that Rethberg sang in *Prince Igor* at Covent Garden, 1935. His aristocratic name, I regret to say, rapidly degenerated into Iggie in all affectionate moments, but he retained his superb and kindly dignity under any name.

He had gone bravely through the war with us, running to his own personally selected air-raid shelter under the sideboard in the dining room whenever danger was near. And many were the nights we had gazed across at each other in sympathetic understanding—and strictly at ground level—as we crouched under the table and the sideboard. That he should now be missing was a tragedy transcending all mere material losses, and Louise and I went out to look for him immediately.

Eight houses had been reduced to rubble, and we were lucky, we realized, not to have had more damage than we had. Our luck had not ended there. We had the priceless assistance of our good friends, the Beers, who lived a few roads away. The moment Mrs. Beer saw the bomb flying down and realized that it must be near our house, she came running to our aid. She guessed that the house would be empty, and she was determined no looters should pick over our belongings before Louise and I returned.

She stayed in the house until we came, and when she finally left, she promised to bring back her husband the moment he returned from work. Mr. Beer, who was so like a craftsman out of Shakespeare that one could hug him, so utterly and absolutely a constant British type persisting in all ages—Mr. Beer, she assured us, would know how to re-hang doors and strengthen shaky locks, so that the house would be safe at night.

Louise and I, having returned from a fruitless search, were standing in the plaster-strewn hall discussing our next move when suddenly, through the doorway where the kitchen door used to be, came Igor—a very dusty Igor, extremely annoyed about the whole incident—for which he obviously held us personally responsible—but intensely pleased to see us.

We fell upon him with cries of joy. Then all three of us sat down on the stairs amid the ruins and congratulated ourselves on being alive and reunited.

Every clean-up had been accomplished before the kind Beers returned. And, sure enough, Mr. Beer knew exactly what to do next. We moved all movable objects from the ru-ined back rooms, and he nailed off the shattered part of the house, rehung the centre door, and boarded up the windows. By the time he had finished, Louise and I felt we could, with a clear conscience, leave the place.

With Igor in a large basket, we departed for the flat. When we were halfway there, it dawned upon us that *we* were the refugees now. Countless others had sought sanctuary in the famous flat. Now it was our turn.

We lived there nearly four months, with Nesta and Jane, until the house could be roughly repaired. There were still some bad moments, of course, but from then until the end of the war, our spirits slowly rose.

Will anyone ever forget that May day when it was sud-denly all over? Well, not quite over. For of course, in theory and, to many people, in hideous fact, it was not "all over" until August. But perhaps Londoners may be forgiven for feeling that their own special war was over on that wonderful sunny afternoon when the voice of Churchill—that voice that had sustained and inspired us through so many months and years of mortal struggle—told us that the war in Europe was over and we knew then that the bombing had ended too.

It was a superb day in every sense of the word. All London drifted happily through the streets and the parks, milling around the palace and calling for the Royal Family, who were so much part of us. So dear to us personally, so precious to us symbolically. For a few hours, it seemed that we must all live happily ever after. Grim realities were something in the past or in the future. On that day of days, I think we all recaptured something of the artless, carefree joy of childhood. We had come out, literally, into the sunlight once more, and we could only blink at each other, smiling incredulously.

Something of the glory and the relief lingered with us during the following weeks and months. The tension slowly relaxed, the walls of our tight little island were expanding once more, so that we could allow our thoughts and our hopes to reach out. It was like stretching after a long, nightmarish sleep. And, if we woke up gradually to some rather dismaying realities, at least we were among the lucky ones who did wake. Too many, in those terrible years, had fallen asleep, never to wake again.

Louise's and my determination to visit America no longer looked like a vague dream. There were going to be difficulties, of course, in getting abroad for some while after the end of the war. But when in August peace finally came, we began to plan in detail.

There was a certain nostalgic familiarity about calculating our finances, tackling official difficulties, working out a programme. And there was very real pleasure in writing to our many refugee friends in the States, telling them that we hoped to see them in something over a year's time.

We wrote also to the operatic stars whom we numbered among our friends, and as Christmas drew near, I decided I would not let the first peacetime Christmas go past without trying to make contact with the greatest figure of our happiest opera days, Rosa Ponselle.

I had no address to write to. But I knew that two or three years before the war, she had married the son of the mayor of Baltimore. So I simply addressed my letter, "Rosa Ponselle, Baltimore, USA," and sent it off.

In that letter, I tried to tell her something of what she had been to us all during those three great seasons at the Covent Garden, and how she had remained in the memories of so many of us when we had nothing *but* memories to sustain our courage and our hopes. I added that Louise and I intended to come to the States in about a year's time and that, if we got near Baltimore, we would perhaps pluck up courage and ask if we might see her.

I am not sure that we even expected a reply. It was simply the first attempt toward doing something practical when we did arrive on the other side of the Atlantic. I thought the letter would probably, though by no means certainly, be delivered. But prima donnas are notoriously bad correspondents—Geraldine Farrar being the only exception I have known personally—and while of course I hoped for a reply, I felt no more confident than the rawest fan sending a first artless request for an autograph.

But I need not have doubted. The reply came. And, with it, the first return of that sense of continuity the refugee years and the war had so cruelly torn away. Ponselle wrote as though we had parted yesterday.

No words, she said, could describe how happy and touched

she was to be remembered thus in London, where she had spent some of the happiest days of her whole career. It was true that much water had passed under the bridge since last we met, but we were moving on to the brighter future now, and at least we were alive and able to make the contact that meant so much. If Louise and I really came to the States, she and her husband absolutely insisted that we come to stay with them for a while, so that we could see her and hear her and feel that she was real once more. She ended by asking me to remember her to all the Covent Garden admirers who had remembered her so faithfully.

"There's always Rosa," Louise and I had told each other, half-laughing, half-crying, during those dreadful years. And there was! For years now, we had wondered if it had really become just a meaningless catchword. But we were to see her, know her, hear her sing again. It was a sort of private vindication of our belief in the ultimate rightness of things.

I lived on the telephone that day, ringing up all the old admirers I could reach. We nearly burnt up the telephone wires. All the conversations began carelessly with, "Who do you think wrote to me today?"

When I had answered Rosa's letter and settled down to a normal routine again, Louise and I decided that, on the anniversary of Ponselle's London debut—the never-to-be-forgotten May 28—we would give a party for as many of the old fans as we could cram into the flat, and we would have a ten-minute Atlantic call with her.

Everyone received the idea with enthusiasm, for Atlantic phone calls were pretty unusual things in those days. Our only difficulty was that the flat had not elastic walls.

I wrote explaining the idea to Ponselle and asked if she would like it. She simply wired back, "Will be waiting for your call—Rosa."

The flat had seen many sad, glad, crazy, serious—even tragic—gatherings since the day I first went into it. But it never saw a more excited, moved or strangely enough, nervous gathering than on that evening of May 28. I was the last to have spoken to her, but that was thirteen years ago in Florence. None of us had ever spoken on the Atlantic telephone before, and this attempt to bridge both time and distance was strangely unnerving.

Promptly at eight o'clock, the telephone rang, and dead silence fell upon the room. I don't mind admitting I was trembling a bit as I picked up the receiver and the operator stolidly checked over the details of names and time.

Then he said, "Go ahead." Out of the past, Ponselle's unmistakable "dark" Italian-American voice spoke, almost in my ear, "Hello, Ida! Is that you?"

Shades of all the great days of our youth. Of the times we crouched on an uncomfortable seat in the gallery to cheer her *Norma* and *Gioconda* and *Traviata!* Of those days I tracked her through London, not daring to ask if I might snap her.

"Hello, Ida!" said Ponselle, over three thousand miles and thirteen years. "Is that you?"

It was like raising the dead.

I forgot to call her Madame Ponselle. I called her Rosa, as we always had amongst ourselves. Incredibly enough, everyone who spoke to her over the telephone that evening called her Rosa.—Except Douglas, who then and ever afterwards, addressed her as "Casta diva."—She asked me how many were there. When I told her, adding that they were all as silent as they had been when they waited for her "Casta diva" years ago, she laughed and asked, almost diffidently, "Would you like me to sing for you now?"

"*Will* you?" I gasped.

"Yes," she said. "Call them all around and hold up the receiver. I'll see if I can get it over to you all."

I called them around. We sat, knelt or stood as near to the telephone as we could, and held up the receiver.

There was a moment's silence. And then—in miniature, but clear, matchless—her tremendous, characteristic entry in the "Pace, pace," from the fourth act of the *Forza del Destino* crossed the years and the ocean. The pianissimo, growing to an incredible fortissimo and back to the golden thread of her unrivalled pianissimo once more. We would have known it anywhere, any time, as Ponselle—at the North Pole or on the banks of the Styx. We nearly went crazy.

After that, she sang almost continuously for the remaining minutes, while we passed the receiver around so that each of us at least heard a few notes at full volume.

For many, many years afterwards, we repeated the party and the call, later attaching a loudspeaker to the telephone so that everyone could hear both ends of the conversation. Even today, Louise and I still phone her on the anniversary of her London debut, and it is always an enchanting experience. But nothing will ever surpass the drama of that first call.

If we had never loved her before, we should love her for that alone.

CHAPTER FOURTEEN

As will be imagined, the preparations for our American visit took on a very special urgency and significance after that first phone call. Not even in the days when we had saved strenuously for our first trip had we felt happier or more excited. Much of the old magic existed for us again, and with it, a new and, I suppose, more mature sense of enjoyment.

We have always retained something of the enthusiasm and the rather naïve enjoyment of the gallery girls we once were, and this new visit catered to those feelings as lavishly as ever. But in addition, there was the moving and heart-warming anticipation of meeting again so many of the friends we had known only in the shadow of great danger and tragedy. We had waved them away from the shores of Europe as refugees. Now they would be there to welcome us, in their new character of citizens of the country that had always enthralled us.

It was during these final months of preparation for our return to the States that we added our first post-war operatic friendship to our experiences. Marjorie Lawrence, that brave and splendid Wagnerian singer, with her husband, Dr.

King, visited England on a concert tour. It will be remembered that the height of her triumphant career—indeed, actually at a rehearsal of *Walküre*—she was stricken with polio and never walked again. But she had built another career for herself, singing in concert from a wheelchair.

It goes without saying that the radiance and brilliance of that heroic voice captivated us all from the outset. But what entranced us just as much was the beauty and courage of a very remarkable personality. We attended every concert she gave within reasonable—even slightly unreasonable—reach of London, and then it seemed to me that here was the ideal moment to try to revive the almost forgotten glories of the "star" parties, beloved of ourselves and our operatic associates before the war.

A little diffidently, we invited Marjorie Lawrence and her husband to the famous flat to meet about two dozen of her most earnest admirers. And, to the joy of us all, the invitation was accepted.

Practical difficulties existed, of course, for we were still on strict rations, and catering on even a modest scale was not yet easy. But everyone wanted to help, and never was a party prepared with more eagerness and goodwill. No restrictions, no difficulties were to stand in the way of showing how greatly we loved and admired Marjorie Lawrence, and how much we appreciated this little touch of glamour in a grey post-war world.

We scoured London for good things to eat. I even wrote to my old school friend in Northumberland—the one to whom we had sent Dad and Mother during the period of the flying bombs—explained the circumstances, and implored her to rustle up a chicken, or something of the sort.

Back came Rettie Douglas's reply by return post. "I'll do better than that! I'll bring you a Coquet salmon personally.

As the party is on Saturday, Elsie"—another Northumbrian enthusiast—"and I will catch the first train down in the morning. We should be in London by four in the afternoon. And we'll travel back on Sunday."

My anxieties ended there. But not so Rettie's!

On that Friday, of all days, the salmon turned coy. Or, in the local phrase, "the salmon wouldn't swim." And, according to Rettie's subsequent dramatic account, she spent most of Friday afternoon standing on the shore—rather like Sister Anne in *Bluebeard*—scanning the horizon in hopes of a salmon. Occasionally, a fisherman brought one in, but never one big enough for our purpose. Then, at the last possible moment, in came a fisherman with a perfect prince of a fish. Rettie was not the only one after that salmon, but surrounded by an interested group, she told the tale of the Marjorie Lawrence party, and everyone immediately waived their claims in her favour. The salmon was hers!

No wonder she arrived late in the day, more or less clasping the noble creature to her bosom. For, next to Marjorie Lawrence and Dr. King, it was undoubtedly the most important guest at the party. At this point, let me digress to say that if anyone who has never tasted Coquet salmon imagines that he knows what salmon can be, I must respectfully insist that he is wrong.

I don't know quite how to describe that party. It was cheerful and lovely and amusing beyond description. And yet, very deep feelings ran only just below the surface. Here was a glorious British star among fellow Britons. We could guess how much she had suffered in the past years. She guessed how much some of us suffered too, and there was an undercurrent of sympathy and tenderness that was very moving. I think the moment that remained with all of us was when, at the end of the party, Marjorie exchanged a glance with her husband and then addressed us all quite seriously.

"There is something we should like to tell you," she said rather gently. "You will understand that, in our position, we receive literally hundreds of invitations as we go about the world, and that, as things are, we have to refuse almost all of them. But when your invitation came, we talked it over together and decided it came from sincere and genuine people with a deep love of music and that is why we accepted. We know how difficult things are here. We know quite well how much trouble and thought you must all have taken to give us such an evening. And now, we want you to know that very seldom in our lives have we enjoyed a party so much."

We almost gulped with emotion and delight at this unexpected tribute, and only the hasty presentation of a bouquet—subscribed for by us all but somehow forgotten until this most auspicious moment—adequately expressed our feelings.

It was on a much later occasion that I ventured to ask her the question that must often have been in people's minds when they contemplated her wonderful victory over circumstances that would have crushed almost anyone else.

"What was it, Marjorie," I asked at last, "that keeps you so bright and courageous in spite of everything? You must have some very clear and remarkable philosophy to support you."

She smiled a little mischievously, but replied without hesitation, "Well, you see, many people believe in God and make themselves miserable. We believe in God and have lots of fun. That's all."

The charming and characteristic utterance of a woman who would have been great in her own right, even without the gift of a divine voice.

It was only a few months after this that Louise and I pre-

pared to say a temporary goodbye to England for the first
time in seven years.

Lisa Basch, whom we had last seen in England in 1940, just
before she and her family emigrated to the States, had made
all the New York arrangements for us. Her parents waited
to welcome us to Philadelphia. Mrs. Stiefel, to whom I had
said goodbye at Euston so many years ago could hardly wait
to introduce us to the daughter we had never seen. Half of
Mitia's family were looking forward to our coming. In Washington, in New York, in Virginia, we would be equally welcome. Friedl's mother, whom we had left in Frankfurt two
weeks before war broke out, and who had escaped finally,
via the Soviet Union and later China, was counting the days
until we should arrive with first-hand news of Friedl and her
husband and baby. Her uncle, whom we had last seen when
he came from the concentration camp in 1938, and his wife
and family were ready to welcome us in Los Angeles. Oh,
and countless others. There was not a city where we had to
set foot, but someone or someone's parents or children or
uncles or cousins wanted to see us.

It was like the old days, when we went to Europe with
messages to and from everyone. Only this time, we were to
meet for rejoicing. It was a happy ending on an enormous
scale.

But, if it was to be a tour of refugee friends, it was also
to be a tour of prima donnas. In New York, we were to see
Elisabeth Rethberg again; we had said goodbye to her in
Salzburg just before war broke out. We were to visit Marjorie Lawrence and her husband at their ranch in Arkansas. In
California, Lita and Homer awaited us with an affectionate
delight undimmed by twelve or thirteen years' separation.—
To them we would always be "The Girls" however many
years had rolled between.—In Connecticut, we were to meet

Geraldine Farrar, for all those years pen-friend with one of our oldest friends from the opera queue. And in Maryland, we were to find Rosa again.

No wonder the horrors of the last eleven years were beginning to seem unreal. What seemed increasingly near and real were the good old days, which linked up so perfectly with the joys that stretched in front of us. And, most strangely and satisfying and reassuring of all, was the realization that, at last, the two mainstreams of our lives were merging into one. If the refugee work had once taken us away from operatic joys, now it was returning us to them.

Those months in which we prepared for our return to the States were very happy ones. On January 4, 1947—twenty years to the day since Louise and I had first set foot in New York, had first walked along Fifth Avenue and turned along Thirty-Ninth Street to the Met—we left Europe once more, this time by air.

Bad weather delayed our journey a good deal, but nothing could dampen our spirits this time. The only trouble was that the hour of our arrival had become so uncertain that, in the end, no one was able to be at the airport. Indeed, we arrived at our hotel almost casually.

And there, sitting in the hotel lounge, waiting for us as she had once waited in a hotel in Frankfurt, was Lisa Basch.

We fell upon her with cries of joy that must have forever dissipated any idea of "the stolid Britisher" entertained by anyone around us. We hardly knew what questions to ask each other. We could only embrace, exclaim and laugh.

Three minutes later, Mrs. Stiefel arrived with her daughter. And, wafted on the wings of another joyous reunion, we all went up to our room.

I shall never forget how it looked. It was like a film star's room. There were flowers and telegrams and candy and cakes and letters and phone-call slips. Somehow, we had not expected anything like that. I took one look around and began to cry.

But dear Mrs. Stiefel said, no, I must not cry, that the time for crying was long past, and now was the time to rejoice that we were all happy and safe. So I cheered up and began eating candy, which had always had the power to raise my spirits in every phase of my existence, and soon felt much better.

Rosi Lismann came, her daughter called up from Washington, and every five minutes the phone rang to say there was either someone else to see us or to speak to us by telephone. Our particular section of the world seemed to have been hit by a hurricane—but a hurricane of affection and good wishes.

How sweet it is to be remembered. And to be remembered with love and gratitude. One doesn't do one's few good deeds with that thought in mind, but nothing is lovelier than to have it happen. It was a mad and wonderful day. And that night, though Louise and I had had about four hours' sleep per night for the last three nights, we rushed off to the Metropolitan where Pinza was singing *Boris Godunov*.

How the years and the miles fell away again. Last time, it had been *The Marriage of Figaro* in Salzburg and war was just over the horizon.

We went around afterward and just stood in the doorway of his dressing room and grinned.

"Good lord!" Pinza said. "Where did you two spring from?"

"We just arrived from England this morning," we explained airily, "and thought we'd come and hear the best basso in the world tonight."

Then we all laughed and were suddenly exchanging the news of the years in between. It was all like something one invents in a nostalgic daydream. But this was really happening.

Ten magical days in New York followed. Days of reunion and reminiscences and endless discussion. We ought to have been worn out, but one has wonderful staying power when one is so happy.

Backed by the letter of introduction from our old friend in the Covent Garden queue, we telephoned Geraldine Farrar and were immediately invited, in the kindest terms possible, to come out to Connecticut and visit her in her home there. And one cold day, when a light powdering of snow lay on the hills, we motored out to Ridgefield to meet one of the brightest stars of other years.

With characteristic and enchanting humour, Geraldine Farrar described herself as "a prima donna of ancient vintage," but if ever anyone had the secret of eternal youth, she had. I am, as everyone who knows me will confirm, a chatterer by nature, but I would willingly have sat silent for hours while Geraldine Farrar talked. She still retained a vitality, a charm, a wit that would have made her the centre of any stage, and we could not hear enough of her recollections of the great operatic years through which she had moved as a queen.

Her turn of phrase was superb. It was she who said of Caruso: "I sang with every great tenor of my time, but there was not one who was fit to polish a jewel in his crown."

Later in that unforgettable afternoon, our dear Elisabeth Rethberg came to collect us and drive us over to her country home nearby. But first, we all had tea together. And though, of course, the warm friendliness of the occasion was what really mattered to Louise and me, perhaps a certain measure of pride may be forgiven us. We smiled at each other across the table, as on either side of us sat an operatic star whom all the world had been delighted to honour. I think no operatic fan would hold it against us that our heads would probably not have fitted our hats at that moment.

A few days later, we took another airplane to California, where Lita and Homer waited.

We arrived early on a hot afternoon and called them before we had taken our coats off. Homer answered and promptly said, "Can you girls be ready in twenty minutes? We're taking you to a concert, and we'll be with you as soon as we can make the hotel."

It was wonderful how none of the previous reunions ever took the edge off the next one. It would have been worth coming the 6,000 miles only to embrace Homer and then rush out to Lita, waiting outside in the car, and overwhelm her with kisses in her turn. We were fulfilling all we had promised ourselves that night we had crouched under the dining-room table while the flying bombs whizzed past overhead.

For the four days we were able to spend in Los Angeles, Lita and Homer had cleared the decks of every other social engagement. All their time was ours. We drove around in their car and saw something of that then-beautiful garden city of the west, or sat in their enchanting bungalow or sometimes on the side of the beds in our hotel bedroom—or wherever it was most convenient and easy to park ourselves while we talked and talked and talked.

After all, we had thirteen years' news to exchange. There was so much we had done that had to be told and re-told and enjoyed. Our method of voice production must have been pretty nearly as good as Lita's own, we decided, for our vocal chords stood up to the strain splendidly.

Even when the all-too-short visit was over and we had to say goodbye, we were sustained by the thought that we could plan for a foreseeable future once more. We promised that we would not let more than two years go past before we came again. And this promise, I am glad to say, we were able to keep.

We went east once more to New York; then to Philadelphia, to Washington, even for one day to Virginia, just to take in everyone we had promised to see. And then, as we neared the end of this magical month, we took a train to Baltimore.

It was a beautiful sunny afternoon, I remember—what we used to call "Ponselle weather" in her years at Covent Garden because, somehow, we always seemed to queue for her performances in sunshine. Earlier in the visit, we had telephoned to make final arrangements, but Rosa had been away from home. However, we had spoken to her husband, Carle Jackson, who had made us unreservedly welcome and promised that he would himself meet us at Baltimore station.

We had no difficulty in recognizing each other—I suppose we looked very British—and we were soon in the car and heading for Villa Pace. At this point, and with a calmness we were afterwards to find characteristic of him, Carle dropped a bombshell.

"I didn't tell you on the telephone," he said, "because I knew you'd think it necessary to be polite and make all sorts of excuses about not coming after all, but Rosa isn't at home. She's in a nursing home and won't be back for a couple of days."

In answer to our chorus of anxious enquiries, he assured us that she was not seriously ill and that we should certainly see her during our visit. Meanwhile, he did everything a perfect host could do to make us feel at home, and several of their friends on the neighbouring estates were equally determined to see that we enjoyed our visit. It was impossible not to feel some disappointment, of course, but it was equally impossible not to have that disappointment yield before all the kindness and thoughtfulness that was lavished upon us. We might have been lifelong friends, rather than two unknown admirers out of the past. And to this day, Louise and I feel grateful to Carle.

There we were, installed at Villa Pace in a room that was so exactly like the last act of *Traviata* that every time I sat down before the mirror, I felt I ought to sing the "Addio." And although that room has become very much ours over the years, we still sometimes feel a little as if we have strayed onto the stage by mistake and may be called upon, most disastrously, to do some singing on our own account.

On the afternoon before he went to fetch Rosa home, Carle said unexpectedly, "You realize, I suppose, that Rosa's rather scared about meeting you?"

This was such a complete reversal of what we considered to be the natural order of things that we cried in chorus, "*Scared?* Of *us?* Why?"

"Oh, well, you knew her in the greatest days of her fame and glamour," Carle explained. "And she has some idea that you may be disappointed, may find her changed."

"But, good heavens, what about *our* sensitive feelings?" I asked. "If she remembers us at all, she remembers us as gallery girls, and we've come back as nearly middle-aged women, if you like to look at it that way. What about *our* feeling scared?"

Carle laughed at that, and said, "Oh, but you know what Rosa is."

We didn't, of course. But it was gratifying to have it implied that we did. And then he went to fetch her.

It was very strange, that last half hour before she came. Something like the nerve-racking wait for the phone call that first time we spoke to her again. We felt very keyed up until we heard the sound of the car returning, then all I could remember was Carle saying that she was scared at the thought of meeting us, and I said to Louise, "Don't let's leave her to walk in and have to make an entry. Let's go down to her."

So we ran down the stairs from our *Traviata* room lookout and flung open her own front door to her.

She stood there on the threshold, our Rosa, looking as we had always remembered her and had always hoped somehow to see her again. Her eyes were wide and dark, like a Verdi heroine, and there was that indescribable air of drama about her that was absolutely natural. She was as beautiful and glamourous as ever. And she was ours once more.

"Rosa!" we cried in chorus. "Darling Rosa!" And we threw our arms around her and embraced her.

It would be unrealistic to believe in a strict scheme of reward and punishment in this life, but I do know that was God's reward to us for the refugee work.

Really, there was very little we found to say to each other in the first few minutes. I think she was probably as moved as we were. But presently we began to talk very much of the past—it amused her to find that we remembered far more details of casts and dates and artists than she did—a good deal of the present and because we were already laying the foundations of a friendship that was to mean so much to us all, something of the future, too.

It was impossible to describe in detail the full joy and wonder of that visit. Then, and on subsequent visits that followed over the years, she sang to us, told us operatic stories, answered our endless questions about the details of her career, showed us the glorious stage costumes she had worn, allowed us to take our pick of the tremendous collection of photographs she had and in every way, did all that she could to recreate for us the things which we had feared lost.

Our greatest discovery on those early visits was that the voice, that dark, matchless voice that had set the standard for us for all time, was absolutely unimpaired. We also discovered that the fascinating, almost melodramatic personality that had enchanted us across the footlights was as endlessly intriguing offstage.

At first, we simply could not resign ourselves to the idea that she absolutely refused to sing in public any more, and we pestered her with, "Why?"

She finally came back with the indisputable reply: "For nineteen years, I was a slave to my art—and I mean a slave. I am not prepared to do that any more. But nor am I prepared to be less than perfect. That's all."

Anything after those days at Villa Pace would have been an anticlimax, and perhaps it was just as well that they came at the end of our trip. It was hard saying goodbye, but we knew now that we had forged links that would never be broken. *There was always Rosa,* and we need never fear anything else.

By the time we returned to England, we had not only done all the things we had vowed we would do, seen all the people we had determined to see and enjoyed every thrill that we had hoped to enjoy; we had also laid the foundations of a future in which we could expect something of the sort of crazy, delightful planning that had once been the breath of life to us.

Life would, naturally, never be quite the same as when we were very young. We did not even wish it to be. All we had asked was that it might be recast in something of the old pattern, and up to a point, this had been accomplished.

In the autumn of that year, we learned that the Vienna Opera Company was to pay London a visit. Krauss was to be among the conductors, and we knew that meant Ursuleac would come too. It was the first real news, as distinct from rumours and counter-rumours, we had had of them. All we had known for certain before then was that they were alive.

Louise and I had vague ideas that the time would come when we could revisit Europe at last and find them. We had somehow never thought that it would be the other way around, that they would come to us. We had visualized our meeting in Munich, in Vienna, in Salzburg, in any one of those ghost-filled cities. Instead, we met them in Victoria Station, amid the whistling of engines, the rumblings of trucks and the impatient cries of porters.

The train was full of Vienna Opera personnel. One figure after another from the old days presented themselves to our fascinated gaze, as Louise and I hurried from group to group, looking for the two who really mattered to us.

And then we saw them.

They had never expected us to be at the station. They had written several times, we learned afterwards, but none of the letters had arrived, and from us there had been only a deep and, I suppose, rather ominous silence. They had not even known that we were alive, until a very recent postcard from Mitia. Years of war had rolled in between, and who was to know how friends on opposite sides felt toward each other when so much blood had been spilt?

There was not much doubt about how we, or they, felt as we ran to greet them. The sheer discovery of each other again was all that counted. Once more, the rapture of re-union. Once more, the exclamations, the questions, the half-answers, more questions and the endless exchange of news. It seemed that we would never be able to say or hear enough of what had happened in the years in between.

And then, the next day, we took them for the first time

to the flat; the place where we had worked out in detail the task on which they had, almost unwittingly, started us. The visit was a curiously moving experience.

From the earliest days in the flat, we had amused ourselves by declaring that we would have them there one day. Now they were there, and amazingly at home they looked in that setting, too.

We asked after their own beautiful flat in Munich. When a phosphorous bomb hit the place, the apartment and practically everything they possessed had been destroyed. We started to say something sympathetic, but Krauss dismissed our exclamations with a gesture of his hand.

"Why complain?" he said. "We are alive, when many people are dead. We are lucky. Let's admit it."

It was true, of course. So we talked instead of the days before the war, when we had dashed back and forth to the Continent under cover of those operatic performances. We discovered for the first time just how clearly they had understood what we had been doing, and just how completely they had cooperated on some occasions when we had not even realized the fact.

We also learned, not from them, but from others, that the work had not completely ceased when war broke. Even after that, they had had a hand in some interesting escapes, notably that of Lothar Wallerstein, the well-known operatic producer who, having escaped before the war, was caught again when the Germans entered Holland. Krauss and two other good friends from the Vienna Opera exerted much pressure and finally succeeded in having him released with permission to go to America.

To Wallerstein's credit, let it be said, he returned years later to testify on Krauss's behalf at the deNazification proceedings. Although he had resisted all attempts to make him join the Party, these proceedings were necessary because Krauss had held a high position in the German musical world throughout the war years. This was, understandably, the fate of many fine artists who had done no more than pursue their profession during those troubled years. I don't think many of them resented the inevitable inquisition into their behaviour during those years. What was contemptible and damaging was the amount of intriguing and false witnessing among lesser artistic rivals who sought to oust those whose places they hoped to take.

In connection with these same deNazification proceedings, it is irresistible to tell one anecdote that shows the true Krauss-ian touch of humour.

He was asked—as he had to be asked—if he had ever visited Hitler at Berchtesgarten.

"Oh, yes," Krauss said frankly. "Certainly."

"How often?"

"Once," was the answer.

"And when?" he was asked.

"I cannot recall the exact date," Krauss explained courteously, "but it should not be difficult to check. It was exactly one week after Mr. Chamberlain visited him there."

During the weeks that the Vienna Opera Company remained in London, there were countless meetings among those who had not seen each other for years. For us, the most significant and charming was a supper party we organized at a quiet Soho restaurant.

There were nine of us. Krauss and Ursuleac, Louise and I, Mitia—representing the very beginning of our refugee work—and Elsa, and the three Maliniaks—almost the last people we had brought out of Europe, representing, in a sense, the completion of our work.

We were all in tremendous spirits, though inwardly deeply

moved to meet like this after so many years, and we were determined to drink a triumphant toast to "Reunion outside Vienna."

Our waitress, I noticed, was obviously interested in our group and beamed upon Krauss with such approval that I saw she must have recognized him. She so evidently wanted to say something that I whispered to her, "What is it?"

It appeared that she wanted Krauss's autograph.

Guessing that he was in a mood to refuse nothing that evening, I told her to go and ask for it, assuring her that he would give it. Sure enough, he smilingly complied, and Louise, in sympathy with a fellow star-gazer, said, "If you collect autographs, you should ask this lady too. She is a very famous singer, Viorica Ursuleac."

"Why," the girl cried, "of course! I hadn't realized for a moment that it was Frau Ursuleac."

We all gazed at her in surprise, and I said, "Do you know them, then?"

"Know them?" she exclaimed, flushing and laughing, and yet a little tearful too. "Know them? Of course I know them. I come from Vienna. Many, many times I heard Mr. Krauss conduct. I never thought I should wait on him in a London restaurant."

We were dumb for a moment. Somehow, she was a symbol, this unknown girl from Vienna, of all the thousands of grains of sand that had been stirred by the tide of history and now were settling down on the quieter shores. She was of the old days, and yet she was of the new. To her, Krauss and she were part of Vienna; to us, she and we were part of London.

So I said, "Go and fetch yourself something to drink with us. We have met together for the first time for many, many years. We are going to drink a toast to our reunion. Come and drink it with us, because you come from Vienna."

She brought her glass to our table and we all stood up. I suppose the other people in the restaurant thought we were a bit mad. But we clinked glasses with each other across the table and drank to the fact that we had all, in our different ways, survived the hurricane that had swept over Europe and lived to smile at each other again in a London restaurant.

It was a great moment. And if we laughed and made jokes about it, we were also near to tears. We might so nearly, any one of us, never have seen the others again.

It was during the last week of the Vienna Opera Company's visit that Louise and I made the final, and perhaps the happiest, decision in connection with the famous flat. We told Krauss and Viorica that we wanted them to regard it as their home whenever they came to England, to look on it as always ready and waiting for them when they were on their travels abroad. There was a certain unspoken poetic justice about their being able to regard as home the place that sheltered so many people we might never have known or helped, if they had not first committed Mitia to our care. On the day we accompanied them to Victoria Station to say goodbye, we gave them each a key, so that they would always know the place was theirs.

Smiling a little, Krauss returned his key and said, "Only one is necessary, because we are never apart and shall always come here together."

Viorica said nothing. She just turned the key over and over in her hand. And we guessed and he knew—because he knew every mood of hers—that she was trying not to cry. We hugged her and told her to put it away safely. Then, because it was nearly time for the train to go, we kissed them both and watched them get on the train.

They stood at the window together, smiling and looking very much as they had looked all those years and years ago, when I had photographed them outside Covent Garden. Then the whistle blew, and the train began to move.

CHAPTER FIFTEEN

Originally, this was intended to be just the story of two girls who followed their operatic stars through the comparatively carefree days of the 1920s into unexpected drama in the '30s and '40s; and when this book was first written, that was the full extent of the period it covered. But, looking back over a much longer period now, I realize that nothing is ever really over, and it seems to me unnecessarily arbitrary to break the narrative abruptly on that day in 1947 when we waved goodbye to Krauss and Viorica at Victoria Station. Consequently, in revising the book for present day publication, I have decided to take the story further.

To a very great extent, the pattern of life for Louise and me has remained the same. That is to say, we are still inveterate star-gazers and voice-lovers. And, although we had supposed that our refugee work had stopped at the outbreak of war, for many years after the war, we found ourselves involved in work for displaced persons when we joined the Adoption Committee for Aid to Displaced Persons—later Lifeline. Unlike the pre-war refugee work, there was no sense of danger or high drama connected with this, but it did bring us very close once more to tragedy and deep human need.

Our special interest covered the camps for non-German refugees in Germany, where there was a bewildering mixture of nationalities. Many of the unhappy inmates were Poles, who had been brought to Germany for slave labour during the war. They had been quite literally slaves for years, and when the end came, all that anyone could offer them was a return to Poland under the Russians. As this would mean either death or fresh slavery under different masters, they naturally refused. Temporarily, there was nothing to do but put them in camps.

Then there were Russians who had fled from their own form of national persecution, Czechs who had escaped from either the Germans or the Russians, depending on the date of their flight. There were people from the three Baltic States.— Who even bothers to remember the very names of Lithuania, Estonia, or Latvia now? But when the Russians flooded in, many people escaped to the West, penniless and rootless.— There were a few Hungarians, some Ukrainians, and individuals or groups from almost any country you could name in Middle or Eastern Europe.

Most of our work consisted of fund-raising for daily fresh milk provision for children under six, or helping to provide treatment and rehabilitation for the many tuberculosis cases. But we did sometimes go out to visit our camp, and so we came to know some of our cases personally, as well as the wonderful personnel who worked on the spot.

The first time we went, we were vaguely expecting a sort of collection of Nissen huts. But we found that our particular camp was housed in a huge barracks. Inevitably, the accommodation consisted of large rooms; and in each of these rooms lived four, six, sometimes eight families—most of them hating each other, naturally. If you wanted a bit of privacy, you put up a blanket or a piece of cardboard, but that often shut out the light. They went to the soup kitchen, then they came back and sat on their beds. No wonder they thought they were the forgotten people, until World Refugee Year came.

What does a human being crave when life has been stripped to the bone like that? The most strange and varied things. And in working with such people, you have to try to sympathize with what *they* want and not what your common sense seems to be telling you they *should* want.

I remember an elderly Hungarian, whose tragic story included the loss of his whole family as well as his way of life. What do you say to anyone like that? I put my arms around him and kissed him, and he broke down and wept. So did Louise and I, to tell the truth.

Afterwards, when I asked the compassionate camp worker what we could do, he said, "It may sound strange and trivial to you, but what that man needs is a suit of new clothes. He came of very good people, and the squalor of being a refugee and having to accept charity is killing him. Someone else's kindly donated second- and third-hand clothes are welcome to many people, but he needs something new. *And he needs to go into the town and buy it for himself.*"

Fortunately, our committee was also compassionate and understanding. He was sent enough money from England to refit himself modestly, and he was asked to go and buy the clothes himself, as sizes were always difficult if one were buying for a friend.

In some indefinable way, it helped him face life again.

Then there was dear Mrs. Rafalsky. She and her husband had been on the run either from the Russians or the Germans for a large part of their adult lives. We used to manage to talk to each other in a strange mixture of languages, and Louise and I found that Mr. Rafalsky was also an opera lover. He could hardly believe that we actually knew the names of Russian singers like Neshdanova and Sobinoff, though only from records. He had heard them both, he told us, in a performance of *Faust*, the cast being completed by Chaliapin. Some cast!

When Mr. Rafalsky died, his widow did not want food or warmth or comfort of any sort. She wanted a little head-stone for his grave. When you have been a displaced person for half your life and even in death you have no place, I suppose a headstone means a lot.

It was Rosa who paid for that headstone, I remember. When we told her the story she said, "That is something I completely understand." I think Mr. Rafalsky would have liked to know that a prima donna paid for his headstone.

One heartening thing about this particular aspect of refugee work was that, in the end, the problem was almost completely solved. Most of the displaced persons were either absorbed into the German community or they emigrated. It is one of the tragedies of this tragic century that as soon as one area is free of the refugee problem, another develops. But there is never a complete answer to anything that stems from man's inhumanity to man. So one always goes on to another facet; though of course, as one gets older, it has to be a slightly less active part that one plays.

On the lighter side of our lives, we remained star-gazers. Once a star-gazer, always a star-gazer. Though I must admit that the operatic firmament in the last two decades has not been thickly star-spangled. For good or ill, this is the age of the mediocre. It is also, as I have said, the most credulous age since the South Sea Bubble. Opinions and statements only have to be repeated often enough in certain publications or on certain radio or television programmes for most people to accept them as fact.

"Who is this new girl that everyone says is going to be the second Callas?" people ask us at regular intervals. And when we say we haven't the slightest idea, you can see they think the old girls are slipping.

Usually, we go to hear the current claimant to this, or any other, vocal throne. More often than not, there is a fine, bright top to the voice, a good deal of mixing of gears in the middle, unbounded self-confidence and the clearest evidence that the young woman had done about a third of her job.

At the back of the programme, there may be quite a list of recordings in which she appears, showing that the engineers have done a good job of turning the most useful knobs at the right moment. One can hardly blame enthusiastic, if unknowledgeable, members of the audience if they applaud heartily. They have come with the sound of those records in their ears, and if they are, unaccountably to them, a trifle disappointed, they soon cheer up. They love the good old tunes—who doesn't?—and they *know* they are hearing a great singer. Lots of people have said so, and the records sound splendid. So they clap a little harder. And the inexperienced performer feels more certain than ever that near-stardom had now been obtained without much further trouble being required.

Oh, for those knowledgeable old music directors mentioned in the early pages of this book, who knew how to develop a voice instead of exploiting it!

But it would be ungenerous and untrue to deny that we have had star-quality thrills over the last twenty years. Not very many of the real thing perhaps, but all the more welcome for that. Chief of those since the war was unquestionably the coming of Maria Callas. A star if ever there was one.

Whether or not you like her is quite immaterial. She is the stuff of which headlines are made. This has not always been to her advantage, and I suppose more nonsense has been written about her than about almost any other singer. Again, only in a credulous age could half of it have been believed.

Louise and I were present at the dress rehearsal of her first Covent Garden *Norma,* the opera in which she made her London debut. It is not fashionable to describe her at that time as fat, plain and ungainly. She was nothing of the kind. She was a handsome, well-upholstered young woman with, even then, a tremendous stage presence. The top of the voice was thrilling, the rest not completely in focus. And when, in later years, she pulled the whole thing together into a more even scale, there was inevitably a certain reduction in the actual size of the top.

Even at the rehearsal, we realized that she was the most dazzling star to enter the operatic firmament for a long, long time. When we heard later that she was to sing Cherubini's *Medea* in Florence in a few months' time, we decided to go. *Medea* was, at that time, virtually an unknown opera— certainly unknown to us—and I had never been back to Florence since the Ponselle *Vestale* in 1933. Louise had never been there at all. With something of the thrill of old days, we prepared to "follow our star" again.

It was an extraordinary occasion. I think we had both expected *Medea* to be something of a static period piece. Instead, as everyone who heard it later will know, it proved to be a tearing drama and a marvellous vehicle for a great singing actress.

Fascinated by this new experience, we went around afterwards to see the heroine of the evening, and she was intensely interested to hear that we knew Ponselle and her work intimately. Then she looked at us rather searchingly with those beautiful, short-sighted eyes and asked outright, "What did you really think of my *Medea*?"

At that time, of course, we were not at all used to the disconcertingly frank way Callas can ask for your honest opinion of her work if she has reason to think it may be worth having. I hesitated, wondering how to give a necessarily qualified approval and yet convey our very real admiration. And at that moment, Louise said, with sober truth, "You made a very good stab at it, didn't you?"

I think Callas always trusted us after that. Anything fulsome would not have satisfied her. She explained that she had had only a few weeks in which to prepare the work, and we all agreed—correctly as it turned out—that one day it would be one of her greatest creations.

Indeed, one of the best and most characteristic stories I know about her concerns her marvellous series of *Medea* in London some years ago. In one of the intervals, a self-confident young man was holding forth about "sour notes" and what she ought to have done here and there. A world-famous pianist was passing at the moment and simply stopped and said, "I will not have this woman spoken of like that in my presence. She could teach most conductors today more than they will ever know."

I told Maria the story later, and she considered it for a moment. Then she said, "Well, Eeda, in this particular case, I think he was right. I am probably the only person *in the world* who has studied this work intensively for six years. Why should some young man, hearing it for the first time, tell me how it should be done?"

Why, indeed?

Always fascinated to know just how great interpretative artists work, I asked her once what she did when she had a completely new role.

"I'll tell you exactly what I do," replied Callas smiling. "I go and sit alone in a small, uninteresting room, and I empty myself of myself as far as I can. Then I think about the woman I am to become, and I think of her in terms of basic gesture. I think of her age, her class—very important for the hands—her period and her fate. There are two or three gestures that are essential to that character and indissoluble from her, and until I have found them, I do not study her musically."

Intrigued, I said that now I realized why all her "mad scenes" were different. Something that can hardly be said of most people who attempt the early and middle nineteenth-century operas in which the unfortunate heroine so often goes mad.

She looked doubtful and said, "I don't think I know what you mean, Eeda."

So I explained that in *Puritani*, for instance, one was sorry for her, but felt she might recover, whereas in *Lucia di Lammermoor*, from the moment she appeared at the top of the stairs in the mad scene, everyone on the stage fell away from her instinctively, in terror as well as pity, knowing that she had become a homicidal lunatic.

Again she said doubtfully, "I don't know what you mean. I just come in. What do the other *Lucias* do?"

I giggled slightly, having heard many *Lucias* in my time, naturally, and I said, "*They* just come in, clutching the dagger. You're somehow there, you poor little thing."

And she leaned towards me and said in a chilling voice, "And without the dagger, Eeda. Do you realize?—*I don't need a dagger.*"

She was quite right, and I hadn't realized it until that moment. She just stands there, and you know that poor young creature has done a murder. Highest art, of course.

Another fascinating instance of her use of gesture came some years later, when she sang the heroine in Donizetti's *Poliuto*, revived for her at the Scala. In this work, which takes place at the time of the early Christians, the heroine is torn between two religions and two men. Again and again, Callas expressed her basic state of indecision by the extraordinarily touching little gesture of putting her hands bewilderedly to her face.

When we went backstage afterwards, I remarked, "I have never before seen you touch your face like that, Maria." To which she replied, "But I think *she* would. Don't you? I think she would."

I said that, of course, I thought she would, but I added, "Did you know that from the moment in the opera when you made up your mind which man and which religion you were going to follow, you never touched your face again?"

"*That* I didn't know!" she cried in frank delight. She had worked out that gesture and absorbed it into herself so completely that it became her natural expression of indecision. But the moment her basic emotion changed, she equally naturally dropped the gesture, without even realizing it.

When people hear that you know Callas, they tend to ask the favourite question, "Is she really temperamental?"

Well, of course she is! Or was during the tense days of her great career. You don't do those tremendous performances and then go home and cook the lamb chops with your own little hands. Of course she was temperamental. That is part of the makeup of a unique musical and theatrical genius. She is not bad-tempered, and as I have said before, most of the preposterous stories about her are complete invention.

What is entirely endearing about her is that she never forgets a friend. In our experience, *never*. The most retiring, undemanding person who has been good to her will always be remembered and greeted in any part of the world. I doubt if many of her self-appointed critics could have the same said of them. It is a rare and precious quality.

If I had to name the role in which I would most wish to see and hear her again, I think I would choose Anna Bolena. She was at the height of her vocal glory when we heard her in this, and the portrait was an almost uncanny amalgam of the Anne Boleyn of history and the somewhat idealised Anna Bolena of Donizetti's opera. Aided partly, I suppose, by the long full-sleeved dresses of the period and by her own quick, incredibly graceful movements, she gave the impression of some lovely, terrified bird ruthlessly pursued. And when, in the final scene, the guards closed around her to take her to execution, it was exactly as though the trap had been finally sprung. An ineffaceable memory, both musically and visually.

Apart from what one might call phenomenal operatic appearances—which one must not, I admit, ask for too greedily in any period—of course we have derived the utmost pleasure and satisfaction from fine performances, where gifted and hard-working artists have done honour to great works with everything they have at their disposal. These also are memories to cherish. For one cannot say more of any artist than that he or she did everything possible with what God had given. Always remembering that the greater the gift, the greater the responsibility.

CHAPTER SIXTEEN

Sometimes people rather resentfully suggest to us that we probably remember the stars of other days with the rosy glow of youth; that, as we look back, we tend to lose perspective. This view is, quite simply, nonsense—to be accepted only by those who have no faith in their own judgment. If one has a good aural memory and reasonable taste and judgment, it should not be very difficult to recreate a great experience. In any case, we have known some of those earlier "greats" in their days of retirement, and the old magic is still there.

It is there for the newcomers too. In witness, let me call to mind the return to London of Giovanni Martinelli in his eighties. Young and old rose as one to acclaim him, and rightly so. Not only did he electrify everyone by singing some fragmentary but unforgettable phrases at a master class; but just by talking he had, as the saying goes, everyone eating out of his hand.

Among our own cherished recollections of him in old age is the occasion when Lauder Greenway and Francis Robinson, of the Metropolitan, took him and us out to Connecticut to visit his old colleague Geraldine Farrar. He was in splendid spirits and, on the way out, told us he had recently become eighty. We did think he had been seventy-nine for some little time, but were charmed, when he added that he usually gave his age in French, *quatre-vingts* because, as he said, "I say the *quatre* very quickly and linger on the *vingts*."

When we arrived at Farrar's home, she was standing there ready to greet us, leaning slightly on a cane, her hair silver, her figure no longer slender. But one looked at that old lady and knew instantly why she had been the toast of two continents at the beginning of the century.

She also spoke of her age—even more frankly and a trifle boastfully—informing us that she was in her eighty-fourth year. This was a little awkward for Martinelli, who could not very well age within the hour. However, he firmly—perhaps not quite so firmly—repeated his bit about being eighty. Whereupon Farrar regarded him with those famous forget-me-not blue eyes twinkling and said, "Is it possible, Giovanni? Then *I* am older than *you*."

He blushed slightly at this and exclaimed gallantly, "I will run and catch you up."

She smiled at him them, with ineffable charm, and replied, "Giovanni, I cannot run so fast nowadays."

If that had happened on a stage and the curtain had then been rung down, the whole house would have risen and applauded to the echo. The wit and charm of those two old stars and, above all, their perfection of timing was little short of miraculous.

Something the same still happens with Ponselle. But with her, it is more a kind of dynamic projection of personality, with which neither age nor youth has any connection. Even now, if she enters a room, no one can look at anyone else. And to be with her while one of her own records is played is a fascinating experience. She will tip back her head, as though listening to something across the years, and then her whole appearance changes. Even the shape of her face seems to alter and become young, while her eyes widen. For a few brief, magical minutes, she is there again as one knew her in the old days—and unforgettable Norma, Violetta, Gioconda, and so on.

She also has the capacity to recall a great colleague with one or two telling phrases. Of Caruso, she once said, "His voice was not in any sense directional. Even if you were near enough to him to sing a love duet, the sound did not just come from his mouth, it came from his head. It was all around you—and at the back of your neck as well."

Once, when we were listening to a Chaliapin record and I rather expected her to say something about the phenomenal size of the voice, she exclaimed, "Listen—listen *now* for that pianissimo!" Then she added, almost humbly, "I always used to listen for that when I sang with him—and try to copy it."

Understandably, she is a wonderful judge of a voice—except that she tends to start with perfection as the norm and to be slightly irritated by anything that deviates from it. Among our treasured possessions, we have a tape-recording in which she describes how she got some of her own most famous effects. It contains the best throwaway line I have ever heard from a prima donna. At the end, she says almost plaintively, "It's so *simple*, really!"

Over the years, we have become very close indeed. We still telephone her across the Atlantic on May 28; and whenever we visit the States, we spend some days with her in her Maryland home. Our long association with Rosa constitutes one of our strongest and most valued links with the past. But those indestructible links are not always operatic ones. From time to time and over land and sea, some entirely unsuspected strand will tug us back in a startling and moving way to the days described in the earlier part of this book.

A year or two ago, when we were in New York, we went with our good friend Mary Ellis Peltz—the incomparable archivist of the Metropolitan—to a lecture she was giving at a Senior Citizens Club. It turned out to be a Jewish club, which made Louise and me feel particularly at home; and just before the talk began, a distinguished looking old lady came up to me and asked if I were the speaker.

I assured her I was not—that we were, in fact, just house guests of the speaker. Whereupon she looked at me more closely and said, "Are you one of the two sisters?"

Surprised, I replied, "We are Louise and Ida Cook, if that is what you mean."

"I met you once," she said. "In Frankfurt in 1938. You were not getting me out. You were getting out friends of mine. We all knew what you were doing, and we never forgot you."

I could have burst into tears. *Frankfurt in 1938 and New York in 1973!* If I had invented that in one of the Mary Burchell romances, someone would have been sure to say that such things don't happen in real life.

Here is a thought-provoking little story about the unbreakable links that exist between those who make great music and those who joyfully receive it.

Earlier in this book, when I listed some of those who shared our happy gallery days, I mentioned Jenny. I suppose we knew her surname at some time or other, but if so, I have forgotten it. Jenny, like Francis, could be very trenchant in her criticisms, but among the artists she truly loved was Elisabeth Rethberg. On one of our visits to the States after the war, I tried to recall her to Elisabeth. But though she thought she remembered the name, she said, "I can't actually visualize her. I wish I could!"

I said she could hardly be expected to remember more than a few of us. But when we met again some days later, Elisabeth said triumphantly, "Of course I remember Jenny! How could I have forgotten her? The strange thing is that I dreamed of her last night—so clearly that she almost stood there before me, and I remembered her instantly. Do give her my love when you get home."

We promised that we would. And on our return, I telephoned a mutual friend to ask for Jenny's address.

"My dear, I'm so sorry," came the reply. "Jenny died while you were away."

Inevitably, since I am now looking back over many years, there have been other gaps in the circle of our operatic friends on both sides of the curtain; the one that affected our lives most deeply was the death of Clemens Krauss. After our great reunion in 1947, Krauss and Viorica came quite often to London. They always stayed at the flat and came to be among our closest and most dearly loved friends. It was therefore a great personal blow to us—quite apart from the loss to our musical world—when Krauss died suddenly in May, 1954.

We had known him and Viorica for exactly twenty years, and one of the stories we never tired of hearing was how they had shared the world premiere of Strauss's *Arabella* together. I think many people knew that, in a whimsical, romantic way, Viorica was always Krauss's Arabella after that, as he was her Mandryka. But what is both touching and extraordinary is that the parallel ran to the last minute of his life.

Those who know the work will recall how Mandryka tells Arabella that, in his village, if a man woos a girl and she wishes to show she accepts him, she comes to him in the evening with a glass of water from the village spring. And naturally, Arabella makes great play with this in the final scene when she comes downstairs, bringing him a glass of water.

On the last day of his life, Krauss had conducted an enormously successful concert in Mexico. When they returned to their hotel, he said he felt unwell and asked Viorica to fetch him a glass of water.

In her own words, "I know I was not gone more than a minute or two, and when I came back he was dead. Do you realize that his last thought in this life was, 'She is coming— with the glass of water.'"

It was almost two years later, in March, 1956, that I was chosen as the subject of the famous television programme *This Is Your Life*. With the assistance of people who took part, the life story of a selected person is reconstructed. The whole point of the programme is that the central character should not know that he or she is going on television until the camera and the microphones are turned on. There are various ingenious ruses for getting the right person in the right place at the right time, and of course there has to be a great deal of backroom work beforehand, in which someone near the victim gives essential help. In my case, the "contact woman" was naturally Louise.

Everything worked perfectly that night, and I am bound to say that I loved every minute of it. There were old friends, refugees we had not seen for years, a worker from our displaced persons camp in Bavaria, Alice from my wartime shelter in Bermondsey, a recording of Rosa speaking to me across the Atlantic and so on. Most exciting of all was that they brought Viorica from the village of Ehrwald in the Tyrol, where she was living in retirement.

The programme was followed by a party in a hotel on the other side of town. The remarkable thing was that, although all the people came from different parts of our lives, they all got on like a house on fire, which shows that, throughout one's life, one chooses one's friends for the same reasons. Or perhaps one is chosen by them.

When it was all over and we had said goodbye to those who were not staying on in London, Louise and I called a taxi from the nearby rank and drove the whole way home. Just as I went to pay the driver he asked, "Am I right, madam, in thinking I saw you on TV tonight?"

I said, "You did."

"Well," he replied, "may I complete your evening? Will you have this drive on me?"

It could happen only in London!—where there are the best taxi-drivers in the world.

The whole evening was thrilling and memorable. But what followed must rank, I think, as the most remarkable of all our operatic-cum-refugee experiences.

Four months later, I went to speak at a Women's Institute in Surrey, and at the end, an old lady came up to me and told me how much she had enjoyed my *This Is Your Life* programme, adding, "What I can't get over is that couple."

I explained as tactfully as I could that there had not been a couple on my programme.

"Yes, you know who I mean," she insisted. "The *couple*— with the refugee work."

When I repeated that they had all been single people on my programme, she seemed quite annoyed with my stupidity, so I said something polite and got away. On the way home, I thought over what she had said. She had got the refugee part right. But for the rest, I decided she had just been mistaken. What else could I think?

A whole year later, I went to speak in Newcastle-on-Tyne, where I always stay with good friends of ours. The sister-in-law of my hostess telephoned and asked me to come to lunch with her and a friend of hers, Brenda, who very much wanted to meet me. Over lunch, the subject of *This Is Your Life* once more came up in the conversation. I discovered that my friend, Meg, had not seen the programme and was greatly disappointed about this, but Brenda, who was meeting me for the first time, had seen it. She knew nothing much about Louise and me, had never read any book of mine, was not interested in the operatic world—but she had remembered that her friend Meg knew someone called Ida Cook, and so she was interested.

"I had a wonderful time," she told me. "My husband was out and I sat and watched it all on my own. But there's something I want to ask you. Who was the tall, very good-looking foreigner who absolutely dominated the programme?"

"There wasn't one," I said. "What do you mean?"

"The tall, good-looking foreigner with the tremendous personality—and such charm," she insisted. "You *must* know who I mean. I remember him above everyone else."

Puzzled and intrigued, I asked at which point he had come in, and she replied unhesitatingly that he came in with the singer—Viorica—and remained during the whole of the refugee part of the programme.

I questioned her on other details, but I could not shake her story, and finally I said, "Well, of course, you are exactly describing Clemens Krauss, the husband of the singer. He started us on the refugee work and ever afterwards kept his hand upon us and hid our work for us. But he died two years before the programme."

"Oh, no! This man was there, like everyone else," Brenda insisted. "Only he didn't speak."

"Would you recognize a photograph of him?" I enquired.

Yes, she was sure she would recognize him anywhere—he had made such an impression upon her.

As will be imagined, when I revisited Newcastle in a few months' time, I took some photographs with me. When my hostess said we were going to have some friends in on a certain evening, I asked her to invite Brenda and send her up to my room beforehand, so that I could speak to her alone.

When Brenda came in and I had greeted her, I said, "Before we go downstairs, I want to ask you something. Do you remember saying you saw an extra person on my television programme?"

"Yes." She nodded. "I know what you mean."

"Can you still visualize that man?" I asked her.

"Give me a minute," she said, and she put her hands over her eyes. "Yes. I've got him—absolutely."

"Would you recognize a photograph of him?" I pressed her.

"Oh, I think I would, Ida," she assured me. "Yes, I think I would."

I spread some photographs on the bed. And she cried out immediately.

"Oh, beyond any shadow of doubt! There's no question about it—this is the man. It's almost funny that he's so like himself. That is how he stood—" She pointed to one of the photographs. Then she added wonderingly, "But how extraordinary. On the programme his hair was dark, not grey."

He was young again.

Eventually I wrote an account of the incident, which was published in *World Digest*. And even at that point of time, three complete strangers came forward from different parts of the country—including a tough East End businessman who to this day thinks we somehow "spoofed" him—and identified "the extra person" from photographs. Each said almost the same thing: "I just wondered why he didn't speak."

In some sense, I suppose, that would make a fitting end

to this book. But, in point of fact, it was not an ending but a beginning for Louise and me of what I might call a fresh series of discoveries and adventures, so fascinating and so rewarding that another whole book would be required to describe them.

Instead, since this is a book about star-gazing, in which the star-gazer has had full indulgence, let me give the last word to one of the stars on whom we gazed. It is true that these words were addressed to Louise and me from Marti-nelli, in 1967, but it is equally true that they may be taken to the hearts of all who have loved and appreciated great artists, humbly acknowledging that without them life would have been a much less glorious affair.

Dear Ida and Louise,

What could any singer do without friends such as you? Believe me, without the devotion so selflessly expressed by both of you, it would be almost impossible for a singer to have a career. Self-ego is that which sustains most of us—the childlike desire to believe we, gifted by God with voices to please, are creatures set apart from mere mortal men.

Yet doubt constantly assails us.... Are we as good as we think...? Do we have a right to the adoration cast upon us... and, most important, when our voices fade, and we are old, will we be forgotten? You two dear ladies have helped us, in your teen years and later mature life, to retain forever our dream of adoration, and in so doing have made so many veteran artists very happy, not the least of whom by far is Giovanni Martinelli. God bless and keep you both.

★ ★ ★ ★ ★

THE
BRAVEST
VOICES

IDA COOK

Reader's Guide

PARK
ROW
BOOKS

1. Early in *The Bravest Voices*, Ida recounts a conversation with her eighty-nine-year-old mother. "I've never seen you cry," Ida says, wonderingly. "What do you mean?" Mrs. Cook says. "I never had anything to cry about. I didn't ask very much, but I had everything that mattered." What does Mrs. Cook's comment say about the expectations of that time and place? What values were emphasized in Ida and Louise's childhoods? Do you share them?

2. Ida attends her first operatic performances at Covent Garden in London in 1924. She reflects back on their impact and describes how raw enthusiasm can lift one out of the ordinary world to the "golden heights" of loving admiration. Discuss the idea of "hero worship" as the Cook sisters experience it. Do you see a distinction between Ida's adoration of opera singers and the fascination with celebrities that pervades contemporary popular culture? How is fandom different today than it was in the 1920s and 1930s?

3. What was your familiarity with opera before reading *The Bravest Voices*? Does Ida's passion raise your own

level of interest? What is appealing about the world and experiences she describes as an opera fan?

4. After two years of scrimping and planning, Ida and Louise set sail for New York in 1926 to hear their favorite performer sing at the old Metropolitan Opera House. What does the story of their years of "skimpy lunches, cheese paring and saving" say about Ida's and Louise's characters and priorities? Have you had a similar experience in your life where you sacrificed day-to-day pleasures for some distant reward? Was the result as satisfying as Ida describes?

5. What qualities shine through Ida's narrative "voice"? To what do you credit her sense of humor and unfailing optimism even in the face of great tragedy? At what points in the memoir does Ida seem most shaken?

6. In 1934 Ida and Louise assist music lecturer Mitia Mayer-Lismann and her family in leaving Austria and finding refuge in England. Over the next five years, until England formally declared war on Germany on September 3, 1939, the Cook sisters raise consciousness and funds in England and make daring rescue missions throughout Central Europe. Discuss some of Ida and Louise's "cases." Do any of the images and stories in *The Bravest Voices* resonate with your own family history?

7. Ida's entry into refugee work coincides with her success as a romance novelist. "So at the very moment when I was making big money for the first time, we were presented with this terrible need…. It was much the most romantic thing that ever happened to us." Do you think Ida and Louise are unusual in viewing self-sacrifice as "romantic"? What did they gain by directing every spare resource toward saving lives?

8. Were you aware of the Nuremberg Laws and the Kindertransport before reading *The Bravest Voices*? Share your knowledge and thoughts about how the Cook sisters' story fills in or intersects with historical background you've learned through books, movies, or conversation with people who lived through those dark times.

9. Ida's account of her refugee work is not without glamorous elements and lighter moments. What manner of quick thinking and deception proved necessary on her trips to Germany and Austria? How did she use her passion for opera as a cover for her refugee work?

10. Discuss Ida's portrait of London during the Blitz. In what ways does she celebrate the courage and perseverance of the British people? What aspects of Ida's vivid account of "shelter life" were most terrifying to you? Which incidents or stories were the most uplifting?

11. In 1965 the Yad Vashem Holocaust Memorial Authority in Jerusalem bestowed on Ida and Louise Cook the honor of "Righteous Among Nations," listing the sisters alongside Oskar Schindler and others who saved Jews from Nazi persecution. Discuss the ways in which Ida and Louise's story is one of everyday individuals standing up to tyranny. Why is it important that such stories get told?

12. As a prolific romance novelist, Ida Cook writing as "Mary Burchell" created close to 150 heroines. Do you think Ida would describe herself as a heroine? Do you consider her one? If so, why?

When Ida and Louise Cook first began to haunt the gallery of Covent Garden, opera was in the midst of a golden age. Giacomo Puccini had only just died when the sisters attended their first performances, and major composers and conductors like Richard Strauss and Arturo Toscanini could be seen on the international concert circuit. While Ida's friend Maria Callas remains well-known, many of the singers most dear to Ida and Louise have all but passed out of memory. Here is some background on those great and colorful figures.

AMELITA GALLI-CURCI (Italian, 1882–1963)
Born to an upper-middle-class family in Milan, Amelita Galli was a gifted pianist. At age twenty-three she was offered a prestigious professorship at Milan's conservatory, but with the encouragement of a family friend, she began to pursue a singing career. Amelita made her operatic debut in 1906 at Trani, as Gilda in Rigoletto, and her fame quickly spread. In 1908 she married Marchese Luigi Curci, but the marriage did not last and Galli-Curci would eventually marry her accompanist, Homer Samuels, in 1921. That same year, she debuted at the Metropolitan Opera in New York as Violetta in

La Traviata. Galli-Curci remained at the Met until her retirement from the operatic stage in 1930. She continued to give concert performances, but throat surgery in 1935 is thought to have permanently damaged her voice. She retired to California, where she died at the age of eighty-two.

ROSA PONSELLE (American, 1897–1981)
Born Rose Melba Ponzillo to Italian immigrants in Meriden, Connecticut, Ponselle began performing in vaudeville at the age of seventeen. It was Enrico Caruso who recognized her great talent and arranged an audition for her at the Metropolitan Opera House. Ponselle made her Met debut in 1918 in Verdi's La forza del destino, opposite Caruso. Maria Callas called Ponselle "the greatest singer of us all," but the mental and physical exhaustion of constant performing and touring took its toll. Ponselle retired at the relatively young age of forty and lived out her days at Villa Pace, her home outside Baltimore, Maryland. She continued to sing, privately, and to teach. Among the singers Ponselle coached in later life are Beverly Sills, Sherrill Milnes, and Placido Domingo.

EZIO PINZA (Italian, 1892–1957)
Born Fortunato Pinza in Rome, this charismatic opera star showed promise as a professional cyclist, but ultimately chose a career in music instead. Pinza made his operatic debut in Bellini's Norma in Cremona, Italy, in 1914. He served in World War I and afterward returned to Italy to resume his operatic career, performing at La Scala in Milan under the direction of Arturo Toscanini. The dashing Pinza was so closely associated with his most famous role, Mozart's Don Giovanni, that music critic Virgil Thomson wrote: "It is doubtful whether without him the opera would be in the repertory at all." Pinza's daughter, Claudia, the little girl whose picture Ida took outside Covent Garden, would also become an acclaimed opera singer. After retiring from opera in 1948, Pinza had a successful second career on Broadway. In 1949 he appeared as Emile de Becque in the

Rodgers and Hammerstein musical South Pacific. Pinza would also make appearances in films and on television. He died at age sixty-four in Stamford, Connecticut.

ELISABETH RETHBERG (German, 1894-1976)
Born Lisbeth Sättler in Schwarzenberg, Germany, Rethberg was best known for her roles in operas by Mozart, Verdi and Wagner. She made her operatic debut in Dresden, Germany, in 1915, but moved to the United States in 1922 and was a fixture on the stage of the Metropolitan Opera for the next twenty years. Arturo Toscanini hailed Rethberg's voice as "the most beautiful in the world" and many believed her to be the greatest soprano of her day. Her chief rival for this title was Rosa Ponselle, who possessed a bigger, warmer voice. Rethberg retired from the stage in 1942 and died in Yorktown Heights, New York.

VIORICA URSULEAC (Romanian, 1894-1985)
Ursuleac was Richard Strauss's favorite soprano and she sang in world premieres of four of his operas. Strauss called her "the truest of the true." In 1924 Ursuleac heard that renowned conductor Clemens Krauss was assuming directorship of the Frankfurt Opera and needed a soprano. She asked for an audition, but was rejected by Krauss, who was contemptuous of Balkan singers. Ursuleac then submitted her request under a false name. When Krauss discovered her attempt to trick him, he hired her anyway, and thus began a legendary collaboration and a long, mutually devoted marriage. It is said that recordings of Ursuleac do not do justice to the magic of her performances. She was widely regarded as a great musician and actress; she died in Austria at the age of ninety-one.

CLEMENS KRAUSS (Austrian, 1893-1954)
Krauss was born in Vienna to Clementine Krauss, an actress and singer. As a boy, he attended the Vienna Conservatory and began conducting regional orchestras in 1913. He traveled to the United States in 1919, conducting the Philadelphia

Orchestra and the New York Philharmonic. Among numerous appointments, he was a regular conductor at the Salzburg Festival from 1926 to 1934. In 1935 Krauss became director of the Berlin State Opera. He continued to conduct throughout the Nazi era. After the war, Krauss came underscrutiny from colleagues and the Allied authorities for his close ties to Nazi officials. As a result, he was banned from public performance, but when officials discovered that Krauss had, in fact, aided numerous Jews in their escape from Nazi persecution, the ban was lifted and he resumed conducting the Vienna Philharmonic. He died while on vacation in Mexico in 1954.

To experience the artists and music beloved by Ida Cook, listen to the following recordings.

1. Amelita Galli-Curci, Lo, *Here the Gentle Lark* (Pearl, 1999)

2. *Galli-Curci: Prima Voce* (Nimbus, 1992)

3. *Bellini: The Supreme Operatic Recordings* (Pearl, 2001)
    Includes performances by Ezio Pinza, Rosa Ponselle, Maria Callas and Amelita Galli-Curci, among others.

4. Rosa Ponselle, *Casta Diva* (Pearl, 1996)

5. *Rosa Ponselle: The Columbia Acoustic Recordings* (Pearl, 1993)

6. *The Golden Years of Ezio Pinza* (Pearl, 1992)

7. *Le Nozze di Figaro*, Wolfgang Amadeus Mozart (Idi, 2002)
    The complete opera, featuring Ezio Pinza as Figaro. Recorded live in 1937 in Salzburg, Austria.

8. *Lebendige Vergangenheit: Elisabeth Rethberg*
   (Preiser Records, 1994)

9. *Der Rosenkavalier*, Richard Strauss (Guild, 2004)
   Selections from the Strauss opera, featuring soprano
   Viorica Ursuleac and conductor Clemens Krauss.

10. *Ariadne auf Naxos*, Richard Strauss
    (Preiser Records, 1996)
    The complete opera, featuring soprano Viorica Ursuleac
    and conductor Clemens Krauss, recorded in 1935 in
    Berlin, Germany.

11. *John McCormack: Great Voices of the Twentieth Century*
    (Castle Pulse, 2005)
    This compilation of recordings by the great Irish tenor
    includes "Drink to Me Only with Thine Eyes." Ida Cook
    writes, "Among my own list of great performances...
    I must place that strange and moving occasion when
    two hundred Cockneys sang "Drink to Me Only with
    Thine Eyes" in the cellar of a London factory and forgot
    that overhead bombs were falling."

12. *Anna Bolena*, Gaetano Donizetti (EMI Classics, 1998)
    The complete opera featuring soprano Maria Callas in
    the title role. Recorded live in 1957 at Teatro alla Scala
    in Milan, Italy.

13. *La Traviata*, Giuseppe Verdi (EMI Classics, 1997)
    The complete opera, featuring Maria Callas as Violetta.
    Recorded live in 1958 at the San Carlos Theater in
    Lisbon, Portugal.

14. *Norma*, Vincenzo Bellini (EMI Classics, 1998)
    The complete opera, featuring Maria Callas in the title
    role. Recorded in 1960 at Teatro alla Scala in Milan, Italy.

FOR FURTHER READING

FICTION
Bel Canto, Ann Patchett (2001)
Atonement, Ian McEwan (2001)
The Night Watch, Sarah Waters (2006)
The Heat of the Day, Elizabeth Bowen (1948)
The End of the Affair, Graham Greene (1951)
The Girls of Slender Means, Muriel Spark (1963)
Human Voices, Penelope Fitzgerald (1980)

NONFICTION
Opera 101: A Complete Guide to Learning and Loving Opera, Fred Plotkin (1994)
Opera Anecdotes, Ethan Mordden (1985)
The Righteous: The Unsung Heroes of the Holocaust, Martin Gilbert (2003)
Conscience & Courage: Rescuers of Jews During the Holocaust, Eva Fogelman (1994)